Advanced Oracle SQL Program.
The Expert Guide to Writing Complex Queries

Oracle In-Focus Series

Laurent Schneider

To my family who supported me in this quest.

Laurent Schneider

Advanced Oracle SQL Programming
The Expert Guide to Writing Complex Queries

By Laurent Schneider

Copyright © 2008 by Rampant TechPress. All rights reserved.

Printed in the United States of America.

Published in Kittrell, North Carolina, USA.

Oracle In-Focus Series: Book #28

Series Editor: Donald K. Burleson

Production Manager: Robin Rademacher

Editor: Valerre Aquitaine

Production Editor: Teri Wade

Cover Design: Janet Burleson

Printing History: December, 2008 & December 2009 for First Edition

Oracle, Oracle7, Oracle8, Oracle8i, Oracle9i, Oracle10g and Oracle 11g are trademarks of Oracle Corporation.

Many of the designations used by computer vendors to distinguish their products are claimed as Trademarks. All names known by Rampant TechPress to be trademark names appear in this text as initial caps.

The information provided by the authors of this work is believed to be accurate and reliable. However, because of the possibility of human error by our authors and staff, Rampant TechPress cannot guarantee the accuracy or completeness of any information included in this work and is not responsible for any errors, omissions, or inaccurate results obtained from the use of information or scripts in this work.

ISBN 10: 0-9776715-8-5

ISBN 13: 978-0-9776715-8-8

Library of Congress Control Number: 2008937201

Table of Contents

Using the Online Code Depot 1
Conventions Used in this Book 2
Acknowledgements 3
Chapter 1: Oracle SQL Query Overview **6**
Introduction 6
Syntax Review 6
   Subquery Inline view... 20
   Nested subquery 22
   Joins 28
   Sets... 37
   SQL expressions 45
Conclusion 59
Exercises 61
Solutions.. 63
Chapter 2: Oracle SQL Functions **67**
Oracle SQL functions.. 67
   Mathematic functions.. 67
   Binary functions.. 68
   Signs functions.. 68
   Rounding and truncating functions 69
   Modulo functions 73
   Functions to search and modify strings.. 74
   Regular expression functions 79
   Conversion functions 83
   NLS functions 94
   National character set.. 96
   Logical functions with true or false values 97
   Null functions... 99
Conclusion.. 101
Exercises 102
Solutions.. 104
Chapter 3: SQL Aggregate Functions **106**

Aggregate functions 106
   Standard Aggregate Functions *106*
   Distinct *109*
   Keep *110*
   Nested Aggregates *114*
   Subtotals *114*
   PIVOT and UNPIVOT *120*
Conclusion 125
Exercises 125
Solutions 127

Chapter 4: Oracle SQL Analytics **132**

Analytics 132
   OVER *132*
   PARTITION *133*
   Ranking functions *134*
   Window *137*
   Aggregation *142*
   FIRST_VALUE and LAST_VALUE *145*
Conclusion 150
Exercises 152
Solutions 156

Chapter 5: XML **159**

XML 159
   XML Instance *159*
   XMLTYPE *159*
   XMLELEMENT *161*
   XMLCONCAT and XMLFOREST *163*
   XPATH *164*
   XMLSEQUENCE *170*
   XQuery *172*
   Aggregation *176*
   XMLSERIALIZE *177*
   XMLCAST *178*
Conclusion 186
Exercises 187

Solutions...190
Chapter 6: Oracle Hierarchies...**196**

Hierarchies...196
   Hierarchical Queries..196
   CONNECT BY, PRIOR and START WITH.........................197
   LEVEL..198
   ORDER SIBLINGS BY..199
   PRIOR..201
   SYS_CONNECT_BY_PATH..202
   CONNECT_BY_ROOT...203
   CONNECT BY LOOP..206
   CONNECT BY NOCYCLE and CONNECT_BY_ISCYCLE.......206
   CONNECT BY without PRIOR..207
   CONNECT_BY_IS_LEAF..208
   WHERE and JOIN..208
   Aggregation..211
  Conclusion...216
  Exercises..217
  Solutions..219
Chapter 7: SQL For Modeling..**224**

SQL for Modeling..224
   Partitions, dimensions and measures..................................224
   Update..228
   Upsert..229
   CV...231
   Conditions...232
   FOR loops...235
   Iterations..239
   Reference Model...240
   Aggregation..244
   Analytics..246
   Ordered Rows..247
  Conclusion...249
  Exercises..250
  Solutions..253

Appendix A: SQL*Plus **260**

  Starting SQL*Plus 260

    SQL*Plus Statements *261*

    Formatting *264*

    Substitution Variables *272*

    HTML *279*

Index **280**

About Laurent Schneider **285**

About Chen Shapira **286**

About Tom Routen **287**

Using the Online Code Depot

Purchase of this book provides complete access to the online code depot that contains sample code scripts. Any code depot scripts in this book are located at the following URL in zip format and ready to load and use:

rampant.cc/adv_sql_pgm.htm

If technical assistance is needed with downloading or accessing the scripts, please contact Rampant TechPress at rtp@rampant.cc.

Oracle Script Collection

www.oracle-script.com

Packed with over 600 ready-to-use Oracle scripts, this is the definitive collection for every Oracle professional DBA. It would take many years to develop these scripts from scratch, making this download the best value in the Oracle industry.

It's only $79.95.
For purchase and download go to:

Conventions Used in this Book

It is critical for any technical publication to follow rigorous standards and employ consistent punctuation conventions to make the text easy to read. However, this is not an easy task. Within database terminology, there are many types of notation that can confuse a reader. For example, some Oracle utilities such as STATSPACK and TKPROF are always spelled in CAPITAL letters, while Oracle parameters and procedures have varying naming conventions in the database documentation. It is also important to remember that many database commands are case sensitive, and are always left in their original executable form, and never altered with italics or capitalization.

Hence, all Rampant TechPress books follow these conventions:

Parameters – All database parameters will be *lowercase italics*. Exceptions to this rule are parameter arguments that are commonly capitalized (KEEP pool, TKPROF), these will be left in ALL CAPS.

Variables – All procedural language (e.g. PL/SQL) program variables and arguments will also remain in *lowercase italics* (*dbms_job, dbms_utility*).

Tables & dictionary objects – All data dictionary objects are referenced in lowercase italics (*dba_indexes, v$sql*). This includes all *v$* and *x$* views (*x$kcbcbh, v$parameter*) and dictionary views (*dba_tables, user_indexes*).

SQL – All SQL is formatted for easy use in the code depot, and all SQL is displayed in lowercase. The main SQL terms (select, from, where, group by, order by, having) will always appear on a separate line.

Programs & Products – All products and programs that are known to the author are capitalized according to the vendor specifications (CentOS, VMware, Oracle, etc). All names known by Rampant TechPress to be trademark names appear in this text as initial caps. References to UNIX are always made in uppercase.

Are you ready to tune?

ION for Oracle is the premier Oracle tuning tool. ION provides unparallel capability for time-series Oracle tuning, unavailable anywhere else.

ION can quickly find and plot performance signatures allowing you to see hidden trends, fast. ION interfaces with STATSPACK or AWR to provide unprecedented proactive tuning insights. Get Ion for Oracle now!

www.ion-dba.com

Acknowledgements

This type of highly technical reference book requires the dedicated efforts of many people. Even though we are the authors, our work ends when we deliver the content. After each chapter is delivered, several Oracle DBAs carefully review and correct the technical content. After the technical review, experienced copy editors polish the grammar and syntax.

The finished work is then reviewed as page proofs and turned over to the production manager, who arranges the creation of the online code depot and manages the cover art, printing distribution, and warehousing.

In short, the authors play a small role in the development of this book, and we need to thank and acknowledge everyone who helped bring this book to fruition:

Chen Shapira, who spent more time in reviewing than I spent in writing.

My readers, faithful to my blog and my forum postings.

Don Burleson, who selected me as an author.

Lutz Hartmann, who was on my side from the very beginning of this mission.

Andrew Clarke and Tom Routen, who did an amazing job in technical and grammatical reviewing.

Marco Gralike, who helped me in the XML chapter.

Diana Lorentz, from Oracle who received and answered hundreds of comments on the SQL documentation.

Robin Rademacher, for the production management, including the coordination of the cover art, page proofing, printing, and distribution.

Teri Wade, for help in the production of the page proofs.

Janet Burleson, for exceptional cover design and graphics.

John Lavender, for assistance with the web site, and for creating the code depot and the online shopping cart for this book.

Last but not least, my whole family who supported me in this quest: my aunt Irène; my kids Dora and Loïc; and, my wife Bertille.

With my sincerest thanks,

Laurent Schneider

Oracle SQL Query Overview

Introduction

Developers, database administrators and end users apply SELECT queries to select data from a database that contains schemas with tables, views, and functions. Oracle adds more capabilities than any other engine to the SQL language, such as Top-N queries, scalar subqueries, analytics, modeling and hundreds of functions from ABS to XMLTRANSFORM.

A single SELECT query sometimes contains more business logic than a package a thousand lines long. This chapter provides a review of the syntax of the various elements composing the query.

Syntax Review

SELECT and FROM

SELECT and FROM can be used to select columns from a table containing employee and salary information and might appear as follows:

```
SELECT
    ENAME,
    SAL
FROM
    EMP;
```

The results would look like the following:

```
ENAME             SAL
---------- ----------
SMITH             800
ALLEN            1600
WARD             1250
JONES            2975
MARTIN           1250
BLAKE            2850
CLARK            2450
SCOTT            3000
KING             5000
TURNER           1500
ADAMS            1100
JAMES             950
FORD             3000
MILLER           1300
```

All rows are selected and each name is displayed with the corresponding salary. In SQL*Plus, the execution plan can be displayed automatically by setting AUTOTRACE.

```
SET AUTOTRACE ON EXPLAIN
```

The execution plan of the query above looks like this:

```
-------------------------------------------------------------------
| Id | Operation         | Name | Rows | Bytes | Cost (%CPU)| Time     |
-------------------------------------------------------------------
|  0 | SELECT STATEMENT  |      |   14 |   140 |    3   (0)| 00:00:01 |
|  1 |  TABLE ACCESS FULL| EMP  |   14 |   140 |    3   (0)| 00:00:01 |
-------------------------------------------------------------------
```

The employee table used here is the one originally created for demonstration purposes by Bruce Scott, one of Oracle's first employees. The tables EMP and DEPT will be widely used in this book.

The Empdept.sql script below can be used to create the tables in a user schema:

💾 Empdept.sql

```
-- **************************************************
-- Copyright © 2008 by Rampant TechPress
-- This script is free for non-commercial purposes
-- with no warranties.  Use at your own risk.
--
-- To license this script for a commercial purpose,
-- contact rtp@rampant.cc
```

```
-- ****************************************************
-- Id     : $Id: empdept.sql,v 1.5 2007/12/07 11:05:31 lsc Exp $
-- Author : $Author: lsc $
-- Date   : $Date: 2007/12/07 11:05:31 $
--
-- Create EMP and DEPT in current schema
--

REM -- only create table and quota on default tablespace is needed
REM --
REM GRANT
REM    CREATE SESSION,
REM    CREATE TABLE,
REM    UNLIMITED TABLESPACE
REM TO
REM    SCOTT
REM IDENTIFIED BY
REM    TIGER;
REM CONNECT SCOTT/TIGER

WHENEVER SQLERROR EXIT

EXEC EXECUTE IMMEDIATE 'DROP TABLE EMP'; EXCEPTION WHEN OTHERS THEN NULL
EXEC EXECUTE IMMEDIATE 'DROP TABLE DEPT'; EXCEPTION WHEN OTHERS THEN NULL

-- create the department table
CREATE TABLE
   DEPT
(
   DEPTNO NUMBER(2)
      CONSTRAINT
         PK_DEPT
      PRIMARY KEY,
   DNAME VARCHAR2(14) ,
   LOC VARCHAR2(13)
)
/

-- create the employee table
CREATE TABLE
   EMP
(
   EMPNO NUMBER(4)
      CONSTRAINT
         PK_EMP
      PRIMARY KEY,
   ENAME VARCHAR2(10),
   JOB VARCHAR2(9),
   MGR NUMBER(4),
   HIREDATE DATE,
   SAL NUMBER(7,2),
   COMM NUMBER(7,2),
   DEPTNO NUMBER(2)
      CONSTRAINT
         FK_DEPTNO
      REFERENCES
         DEPT
)
```

```
/
-- fill the DEPT table
INSERT INTO
   DEPT
(
   DEPTNO,
   DNAME,
   LOC
)
VALUES
(
   10,
   'ACCOUNTING',
   'NEW YORK'
)
/
INSERT INTO
   DEPT
(
   DEPTNO,
   DNAME,
   LOC
)
VALUES
(
   20,
   'RESEARCH',
   'DALLAS'
)
/
INSERT INTO
   DEPT
(
   DEPTNO,
   DNAME,
   LOC
)
VALUES
(
   30,
   'SALES',
   'CHICAGO'
)
/
INSERT INTO
   DEPT
(
   DEPTNO,
   DNAME,
   LOC
)
VALUES
(
   40,
   'OPERATIONS',
   'BOSTON'
)
/
```

```
-- fill the EMP table
INSERT INTO
    EMP
(
    EMPNO,
    ENAME,
    JOB,
    MGR,
    HIREDATE,
    SAL,
    COMM,
    DEPTNO
)
VALUES
(
    7369,
    'SMITH',
    'CLERK',
    7902,
    DATE '1980-12-17',
    800,
    NULL,
    20
)
/
INSERT INTO
    EMP
(
    EMPNO,
    ENAME,
    JOB,
    MGR,
    HIREDATE,
    SAL,
    COMM,
    DEPTNO
)
VALUES
(
    7499,
    'ALLEN',
    'SALESMAN',
    7698,
    DATE '1981-02-20',
    1600,
    300,
    30
)
/
INSERT INTO
    EMP
(
    EMPNO,
    ENAME,
    JOB,
    MGR,
    HIREDATE,
    SAL,
    COMM,
```

```
    DEPTNO
)
VALUES
(
    7521,
    'WARD',
    'SALESMAN',
    7698,
    DATE '1981-02-22',
    1250,
    500,
    30
)
/
INSERT INTO
    EMP
(
    EMPNO,
    ENAME,
    JOB,
    MGR,
    HIREDATE,
    SAL,
    COMM,
    DEPTNO
)
VALUES
(
    7566,
    'JONES',
    'MANAGER',
    7839,
    DATE '1981-04-02',
    2975,
    NULL,
    20
)
/
INSERT INTO
    EMP
(
    EMPNO,
    ENAME,
    JOB,
    MGR,
    HIREDATE,
    SAL,
    COMM,
    DEPTNO
)
VALUES
(
    7654,
    'MARTIN',
    'SALESMAN',
    7698,
    DATE '1981-09-28',
    1250,
    1400,
```

```
    30
)
/
INSERT INTO
    EMP
(
    EMPNO,
    ENAME,
    JOB,
    MGR,
    HIREDATE,
    SAL,
    COMM,
    DEPTNO
)
VALUES
(
    7698,
    'BLAKE',
    'MANAGER',
    7839,
    DATE '1981-05-01',
    2850,
    NULL,
    30
)
/
INSERT INTO
    EMP
(
    EMPNO,
    ENAME,
    JOB,
    MGR,
    HIREDATE,
    SAL,
    COMM,
    DEPTNO
)
VALUES
(
    7782,
    'CLARK',
    'MANAGER',
    7839,
    DATE '1981-06-09',
    2450,
    NULL,
    10
)
/
INSERT INTO
    EMP
(
    EMPNO,
    ENAME,
    JOB,
    MGR,
    HIREDATE,
```

```
    SAL,
    COMM,
    DEPTNO
)
VALUES
(
    7788,
    'SCOTT',
    'ANALYST',
    7566,
    DATE '1987-04-19',
    3000,
    NULL,
    20
)
/
INSERT INTO
    EMP
(
    EMPNO,
    ENAME,
    JOB,
    MGR,
    HIREDATE,
    SAL,
    COMM,
    DEPTNO
)
```

```
VALUES
(
    7839,
    'KING',
    'PRESIDENT',
    NULL,
    DATE '1981-11-17',
    5000,
    NULL,
    10
)
/
INSERT INTO
    EMP
(
    EMPNO,
    ENAME,
    JOB,
    MGR,
    HIREDATE,
    SAL,
    COMM,
    DEPTNO
)
```

```sql
VALUES
(
    7844,
    'TURNER',
    'SALESMAN',
    7698,
    DATE '1981-09-08',
    1500,
    0,
    30
)
/
INSERT INTO
    EMP
(
    EMPNO,
    ENAME,
    JOB,
    MGR,
    HIREDATE,
    SAL,
    COMM,
    DEPTNO
)
VALUES
(
    7876,
    'ADAMS',
    'CLERK',
    7788,
    DATE '1987-05-23',
    1100,
    NULL,
    20
)
/
INSERT INTO
    EMP
(
    EMPNO,
    ENAME,
    JOB,
    MGR,
    HIREDATE,
    SAL,
    COMM,
    DEPTNO
)
VALUES
(
    7900,
    'JAMES',
    'CLERK',
    7698,
    DATE '1981-12-03',
    950,
    NULL,
    30
)
```

```
/
INSERT INTO
    EMP
(
    EMPNO,
    ENAME,
    JOB,
    MGR,
    HIREDATE,
    SAL,
    COMM,
    DEPTNO
)
VALUES
(
    7902,
    'FORD',
    'ANALYST',
    7566,
    DATE '1981-12-03',
    3000,
    NULL,
    20
)
/
INSERT INTO
    EMP
(
    EMPNO,
    ENAME,
    JOB,
    MGR,
    HIREDATE,
    SAL,
    COMM,
    DEPTNO
)
VALUES
(
    7934,
    'MILLER',
    'CLERK',
    7782,
    DATE '1982-01-23',
    1300,
    NULL,
    10
)
/
COMMIT;
```

DUAL

In Oracle, a special table called DUAL is always available. This table has
just one row and one column of one character. Its purpose is to enable

one to select expressions; whereas other RDBMS engines do not require a FROM clause in a query, Oracle does.

The following statements display the contents of the table as shown below:

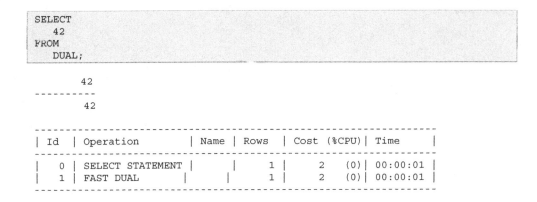

```
SELECT
   42
FROM
   DUAL;
```

```
        42
----------
        42
```

```
-------------------------------------------------------------------
| Id  | Operation         | Name | Rows  | Cost (%CPU)| Time      |
-------------------------------------------------------------------
|   0 | SELECT STATEMENT  |      |     1 |     2   (0)| 00:00:01  |
|   1 |  FAST DUAL        |      |     1 |     2   (0)| 00:00:01  |
-------------------------------------------------------------------
```

The optimizer knows that the table contains only one row and, in the query above, the table will not be accessed. In Oracle 10g, the FAST DUAL operation does not select any data from the table.

DISTINCT

The DISTINCT or UNIQUE keyword removes duplicate values, as shown below:

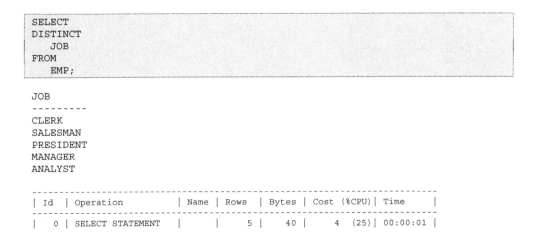

```
SELECT
DISTINCT
   JOB
FROM
   EMP;
```

```
JOB
---------
CLERK
SALESMAN
PRESIDENT
MANAGER
ANALYST
```

```
-------------------------------------------------------------------
| Id  | Operation         | Name | Rows  | Bytes | Cost (%CPU)| Time      |
-------------------------------------------------------------------
|   0 | SELECT STATEMENT  |      |     5 |    40 |     4  (25)| 00:00:01  |
```

```
|   1 |   HASH UNIQUE       |      |    5 |     40 |    4   (25)| 00:00:01 |
|   2 |    TABLE ACCESS FULL| EMP  |   14 |    112 |    3    (0)| 00:00:01 |
```

 It is a bad practice to abuse the DISTINCT keyword. If the column is supposed to be unique, using DISTINCT may affect performance since an additional operation is required.

 It is also incorrect to assume DISTINCT sorts the rows. Especially in 10gR2 and later, DISTINCT often uses hashing instead of sorting to remove duplicates.

WHERE

Conditions are added in the WHERE clause to restrict the number of rows returned. The following statements will only return rows in which the salary is greater than 2900:

```
SELECT
    ENAME,
    SAL
FROM
    EMP
WHERE
    SAL > 2900;
```

```
ENAME              SAL
---------- ----------
JONES             2975
SCOTT             3000
KING              5000
FORD              3000
```

```
-------------------------------------------------------------------
| Id | Operation          | Name | Rows | Bytes | Cost (%CPU)| Time     |
-------------------------------------------------------------------
|  0 | SELECT STATEMENT   |      |    9 |    90 |    3    (0)| 00:00:01 |
|* 1 |  TABLE ACCESS FULL| EMP  |    9 |    90 |    3    (0)| 00:00:01 |
-------------------------------------------------------------------
   1 - filter("SAL">2900)
```

The following script will return only the information for employee number 7782:

```
SELECT
    ENAME
FROM
    EMP
WHERE
    EMPNO=7782;
```

```
ENAME
----------
CLARK
```

```
---------------------------------------------------------------------
| Id  | Operation                   | Name   | Rows  | Bytes | Cost (%CPU)| Time     |
---------------------------------------------------------------------
|   0 | SELECT STATEMENT            |        |   1   |   10  |   1  (0)| 00:00:01 |
|   1 |  TABLE ACCESS BY INDEX ROWID| EMP    |   1   |   10  |   1  (0)| 00:00:01 |
|*  2 |   INDEX UNIQUE SCAN         | PK_EMP |   1   |       |   0  (0)| 00:00:01 |
---------------------------------------------------------------------
   2 - access("EMPNO"=7782)
```

EMPNO is the primary key of EMP and table access is done using the primary key index.

ORDER BY

The clause ORDER BY sorts the rows returned by the query. The following script orders by salary amount:

```
SELECT
    ENAME,
    SAL
FROM
    EMP
ORDER BY
    SAL;
```

```
ENAME           SAL
----------  ----------
SMITH              800
JAMES              950
ADAMS             1100
WARD              1250
MARTIN            1250
MILLER            1300
TURNER            1500
ALLEN             1600
CLARK             2450
BLAKE             2850
JONES             2975
SCOTT             3000
FORD              3000
KING              5000
```

```
-----------------------------------------------------------------------
| Id  | Operation            | Name | Rows  | Bytes | Cost (%CPU)| Time     |
-----------------------------------------------------------------------
|   0 | SELECT STATEMENT     |      |   14  |  140  |   4  (25)| 00:00:01 |
|   1 |  SORT ORDER BY       |      |   14  |  140  |   4  (25)| 00:00:01 |
|   2 |   TABLE ACCESS FULL  | EMP  |   14  |  140  |   3   (0)| 00:00:01 |
-----------------------------------------------------------------------
```

The rows are returned starting with the lowest salary and increasing from there. That is, by default, rows are returned in ascending order. When no ORDER BY clause is used, the rows are returned in no specific order.

Appending the DESC keyword to a field specification causes the sort to be in descending order. Using the ASC keyword is an explicit way of achieving ascending order.

```
SELECT
    DEPTNO,
    ENAME
FROM
    EMP
ORDER BY
    1 ASC,
    SAL DESC;
```

```
DEPTNO ENAME
------ ------
    10 KING
    10 CLARK
    10 MILLER
    20 SCOTT
    20 FORD
    20 JONES
    20 ADAMS
    20 SMITH
    30 BLAKE
    30 ALLEN
    30 TURNER
    30 WARD
    30 MARTIN
    30 JAMES
```

Id	Operation	Name	Rows	Bytes	Cost (%CPU)	Time
0	SELECT STATEMENT		14	182	4 (25)	00:00:01
1	SORT ORDER BY		14	182	4 (25)	00:00:01
2	TABLE ACCESS FULL	EMP	14	182	3 (0)	00:00:01

In the ORDER BY clause, it is possible to use column positions (1), column aliases, or any other expression (SAL). The rows are returned ordered by the first expression, 1, DEPTNO, ascending. For duplicate values of DEPTNO, the rows are ordered by the salary, descending. This is a nested sort.

In the example query shown above, it is possible to order by a column that is not selected. However, this is not always the case. For instance, when using DISTINCT, all sort columns must be selected.

CONNECT BY

Hierarchical queries are characterized by the CONNECT BY clause. Chapter 5 is dedicated to CONNECT BY queries.

GROUP BY

The GROUP BY clause aggregates rows. Aggregation is detailed in Chapter 3.

MODEL

The MODEL clause allows inter-rows calculation and row generation. Chapter 6 covers modeling.

Subquery Inline view

In the FROM clause below, a subquery acts as a table:

```
SELECT
    ENAME
FROM
(
    SELECT
        EMPNO,
        ENAME,
        SAL
    FROM
        EMP
    WHERE
        DEPTNO=10
)
WHERE
    SAL<2500;
```

```
ENAME
----------
CLARK
MILLER
```

```
---------------------------------------------------------------------
| Id | Operation          | Name | Rows | Bytes | Cost (%CPU)| Time     |
---------------------------------------------------------------------
|  0 | SELECT STATEMENT   |      |    1 |    13 |    3  (0)| 00:00:01 |
|* 1 |  TABLE ACCESS FULL | EMP  |    1 |    13 |    3  (0)| 00:00:01 |
---------------------------------------------------------------------

    1 - filter("DEPTNO"=10 AND "SAL"<2500)
```

The subquery returns all employees of department 10, and the main query returns only those with a salary less than 2500.

The subquery could be saved as a view, providing the necessary privileges are granted. In fact, a subquery in the FROM clause is called an inline view and might look like the following where the view is created before the selection. The selection starts with the WITH statement:

```
CREATE VIEW
    DEPT10
AS
SELECT
    EMPNO,
    ENAME,
    SAL
FROM
    EMP
WHERE
    DEPTNO=10
/
SELECT
    ENAME
FROM
    DEPT10
WHERE
    SAL<2500;
WITH
    DEPT10
AS
(
    SELECT
        EMPNO,
        ENAME,
        SAL
    FROM
        EMP
    WHERE
        DEPTNO=10
)
```

```
SELECT
    ENAME
FROM
    DEPT10
WHERE
    SAL<2500;
```

Subquery factoring was introduced in Oracle 9i. Instead of using a subquery, the two conditions, salary less than 2500 and department equal 10, could be combined by an AND logical operator.

Nested subquery

Subqueries can be used in logical statements like =ALL, >SOME, <ANY, IN, EXIST. SOME and ANY are equivalent. By using an operator like <, <=, =, !=, >=, > followed by SOME, ANY or ALL, the left operand is compared with multiple values of the subquery. IN checks if the left value is in the subquery. NOT IN checks if the left value is not in the subquery. With IN and NOT IN, it is possible to have an expression list on the left side. The number of columns of the subquery must match the number of expressions in the left expression list. EXISTS has no left operand and checks if the subquery returns at least one row. The number of columns is irrelevant, so star (*) is just fine. NOT EXISTS is true when the subquery returns no rows.

The three queries that follow create the same result and the same plan:

Example query 1

```
SELECT
    DEPTNO
FROM
    DEPT
WHERE
    DEPTNO!=ALL
    (
        SELECT
            EMP.DEPTNO
        FROM
            EMP
        WHERE
            EMP.DEPTNO IS NOT NULL
    );
```

```
    DEPTNO
----------
       40
```

```
-------------------------------------------------------------------------
| Id  | Operation          | Name    | Rows | Bytes | Cost (%CPU)| Time     |
-------------------------------------------------------------------------
|   0 | SELECT STATEMENT   |         |    3 |    18 |    5  (20)| 00:00:01 |
|*  1 |  HASH JOIN ANTI    |         |    3 |    18 |    5  (20)| 00:00:01 |
|   2 |   INDEX FULL SCAN  | PK_DEPT |    4 |    12 |    1   (0)| 00:00:01 |
|*  3 |   TABLE ACCESS FULL| EMP     |   14 |    42 |    3   (0)| 00:00:01 |
-------------------------------------------------------------------------
```

```
   1 - access("DEPTNO"="EMP"."DEPTNO")
   3 - filter("EMP"."DEPTNO" IS NOT NULL)
```

Example query 2

```
SELECT
   DEPTNO
FROM
   DEPT
WHERE
   DEPTNO NOT IN
   (
      SELECT
         EMP.DEPTNO
      FROM
         EMP
      WHERE
         EMP.DEPTNO IS NOT NULL
   );
```

```
    DEPTNO
----------
       40
```

```
-------------------------------------------------------------------------
| Id  | Operation          | Name    | Rows | Bytes | Cost (%CPU)| Time     |
-------------------------------------------------------------------------
|   0 | SELECT STATEMENT   |         |    3 |    18 |    5  (20)| 00:00:01 |
|*  1 |  HASH JOIN ANTI    |         |    3 |    18 |    5  (20)| 00:00:01 |
|   2 |   INDEX FULL SCAN  | PK_DEPT |    4 |    12 |    1   (0)| 00:00:01 |
|*  3 |   TABLE ACCESS FULL| EMP     |   14 |    42 |    3   (0)| 00:00:01 |
-------------------------------------------------------------------------
```

```
   1 - access("DEPTNO"="EMP"."DEPTNO")
   3 - filter("EMP"."DEPTNO" IS NOT NULL)
```

Example query 3

```
SELECT
   DEPTNO
FROM
   DEPT
WHERE
   NOT EXISTS
   (
      SELECT
         *
      FROM
         EMP
      WHERE
```

```
        EMP.DEPTNO=DEPT.DEPTNO
   );
```

```
    DEPTNO
----------
        40
```

```
-------------------------------------------------------------------------
| Id | Operation         | Name    | Rows | Bytes | Cost (%CPU)| Time     |
-------------------------------------------------------------------------
|  0 | SELECT STATEMENT  |         |    3 |    18 |    5  (20) | 00:00:01 |
|* 1 |  HASH JOIN ANTI   |         |    3 |    18 |    5  (20) | 00:00:01 |
|  2 |   INDEX FULL SCAN | PK_DEPT |    4 |    12 |    1   (0) | 00:00:01 |
|  3 |   TABLE ACCESS FULL| EMP    |   14 |    42 |    3   (0) | 00:00:01 |
-------------------------------------------------------------------------
    1 - access("EMP"."DEPTNO"="DEPT"."DEPTNO")
```

From the department table, the department that is different from all departments in EMP is returned.

A subquery in the WHERE clause is called a nested subquery. The join between the two tables is an antijoin.

It is important to note the NOT NULL condition in NOT IN and !=ALL. If one department is null in EMP, it should not exclude department 40:

Example query 1

```
SELECT
    DEPTNO
FROM
    DEPT
WHERE
    DEPTNO=SOME
    (
        SELECT
            EMP.DEPTNO
        FROM
            EMP
    );
```

```
    DEPTNO
----------
        10
        20
        30
```

```
-----------------------------------------------------------------------
| Id  | Operation          | Name    | Rows | Bytes | Cost (%CPU)| Time     |
-----------------------------------------------------------------------
|   0 | SELECT STATEMENT   |         |    3 |    18 |    4  (25)| 00:00:01 |
|   1 |  NESTED LOOPS      |         |    3 |    18 |    4  (25)| 00:00:01 |
|   2 |   SORT UNIQUE      |         |   14 |    42 |    3   (0)| 00:00:01 |
|   3 |    TABLE ACCESS FULL| EMP    |   14 |    42 |    3   (0)| 00:00:01 |
| * 4 |    INDEX UNIQUE SCAN | PK_DEPT|    1 |     3 |    0   (0)| 00:00:01 |
-----------------------------------------------------------------------
```

```
   4 - access("DEPTNO"="EMP"."DEPTNO")
```

Example query 2

```
SELECT
    DEPTNO
FROM
    DEPT
WHERE
    DEPTNO IN
    (
        SELECT
            EMP.DEPTNO
        FROM
            EMP
    );
```

```
    DEPTNO
----------
        10
        20
        30
```

```
-----------------------------------------------------------------------
| Id  | Operation          | Name    | Rows | Bytes | Cost (%CPU)| Time     |
-----------------------------------------------------------------------
|   0 | SELECT STATEMENT   |         |    3 |    18 |    4  (25)| 00:00:01 |
|   1 |  NESTED LOOPS      |         |    3 |    18 |    4  (25)| 00:00:01 |
|   2 |   SORT UNIQUE      |         |   14 |    42 |    3   (0)| 00:00:01 |
|   3 |    TABLE ACCESS FULL| EMP    |   14 |    42 |    3   (0)| 00:00:01 |
| * 4 |    INDEX UNIQUE SCAN | PK_DEPT|    1 |     3 |    0   (0)| 00:00:01 |
-----------------------------------------------------------------------
```

```
   4 - access("DEPTNO"="EMP"."DEPTNO")
```

Example query 3

```
SELECT
    DEPTNO
FROM
    DEPT
WHERE
    EXISTS
    (
        SELECT
            *
        FROM
            EMP
        WHERE
```

```
        EMP.DEPTNO=DEPT.DEPTNO
    );
```

```
    DEPTNO
----------
        10
        20
        30
```

```
---------------------------------------------------------------------------
| Id | Operation           | Name    | Rows | Bytes | Cost (%CPU)| Time     |
---------------------------------------------------------------------------
|  0 | SELECT STATEMENT    |         |    3 |    18 |    4  (25)| 00:00:01 |
|  1 |  NESTED LOOPS       |         |    3 |    18 |    4  (25)| 00:00:01 |
|  2 |   SORT UNIQUE       |         |   14 |    42 |    3   (0)| 00:00:01 |
|  3 |    TABLE ACCESS FULL| EMP     |   14 |    42 |    3   (0)| 00:00:01 |
|* 4 |   INDEX UNIQUE SCAN | PK_DEPT |    1 |     3 |    0   (0)| 00:00:01 |
---------------------------------------------------------------------------
    4 - access("EMP"."DEPTNO"="DEPT"."DEPTNO")
```

This type of join is called a semijoin.

Again, from the department table, the department that is different from all departments in EMP is returned. Also, it does not matter which syntax is used. This was not the case in previous versions. Nowadays, statistics are used by Oracle to choose the best plan, irrespective of query syntax.

Scalar subquery

Scalar subqueries return, at most, one row. If the subquery returns no row, the value NULL is passed to the main query:

```
SELECT
    (
        SELECT
            COUNT(*)
        FROM
            EMP
    )+(
        SELECT
            COUNT(*)
        FROM
            DEPT
    ) as "rows in dept + rows in emp"
FROM
    DUAL;
```

```
rows in dept + rows in emp
--------------------------
                        18
```

```
-----------------------------------------------------------------------
| Id | Operation          | Name    | Rows | Cost (%CPU)| Time     |
-----------------------------------------------------------------------
|  0 | SELECT STATEMENT   |         |    1 |    2   (0) | 00:00:01 |
|  1 |  SORT AGGREGATE    |         |    1 |            |          |
|  2 |   INDEX FULL SCAN  | PK_EMP  |   14 |    1   (0) | 00:00:01 |
|  3 |    SORT AGGREGATE  |         |    1 |            |          |
|  4 |     INDEX FULL SCAN| PK_DEPT |    4 |    1   (0) | 00:00:01 |
|  5 |  FAST DUAL         |         |    1 |    2   (0) | 00:00:01 |
-----------------------------------------------------------------------
```

A scalar subquery can be used in SQL expressions. It is sometimes called a single-row subquery.

Correlated subquery

Nested subqueries are correlated if they reference a column of the main query. Scalar subqueries in the SELECT clause may be related to a table in the FROM clause.

```
SELECT
   EMP.ENAME,
   (
      SELECT
         DEPT.DNAME
      FROM
         DEPT
      WHERE
         DEPT.DEPTNO=EMP.DEPTNO
   ) as DNAME
FROM
   EMP;
```

```
ENAME      DNAME
---------- --------------
SMITH      RESEARCH
ALLEN      SALES
WARD       SALES
JONES      RESEARCH
MARTIN     SALES
BLAKE      SALES
CLARK      ACCOUNTING
SCOTT      RESEARCH
KING       ACCOUNTING
TURNER     SALES
ADAMS      RESEARCH
JAMES      SALES
FORD       RESEARCH
MILLER     ACCOUNTING
```

```
---------------------------------------------------------------------------------
| Id  | Operation                    | Name    | Rows  | Bytes | Cost (%CPU)| Time     |
---------------------------------------------------------------------------------
|   0 | SELECT STATEMENT             |         |    14 |   126 |    3   (0)| 00:00:01 |
|   1 |  TABLE ACCESS BY INDEX ROWID | DEPT    |     1 |    13 |    1   (0)| 00:00:01 |
|*  2 |   INDEX UNIQUE SCAN          | PK_DEPT |     1 |       |    0   (0)| 00:00:01 |
|   3 |  TABLE ACCESS FULL           | EMP     |    14 |   126 |    3   (0)| 00:00:01 |
---------------------------------------------------------------------------------

   2 - access("DEPT"."DEPTNO"=:B1)
```

The department is retrieved for each row:

```
SELECT
    E1.ENAME,
    E1.JOB
FROM
    EMP E1
WHERE
    NOT EXISTS
    (
        SELECT
            *
        FROM
            EMP E2
        WHERE
            E1.JOB = E2.JOB
            AND
            E1.EMPNO != E2.EMPNO
    );
```

```
ENAME      JOB
---------- ----------
KING       PRESIDENT
```

```
---------------------------------------------------------------------------
| Id  | Operation           | Name | Rows  | Bytes | Cost (%CPU)| Time     |
---------------------------------------------------------------------------
|   0 | SELECT STATEMENT    |      |    14 |   420 |    7  (15)| 00:00:01 |
|*  1 |  HASH JOIN ANTI     |      |    14 |   420 |    7  (15)| 00:00:01 |
|   2 |   TABLE ACCESS FULL | EMP  |    14 |   252 |    3   (0)| 00:00:01 |
|   3 |   TABLE ACCESS FULL | EMP  |    14 |   168 |    3   (0)| 00:00:01 |
---------------------------------------------------------------------------

   1 - access("E1"."JOB"="E2"."JOB")
       filter("E1"."EMPNO"<>"E2"."EMPNO")
```

The main table has an alias E1 and is referenced in the subquery.

Joins

A join is used to select data from more than one table.

Equijoin

An equijoin is a join where keys of both tables are matched using the equal comparison operator:

```
SELECT
    e.ENAME,
    d.DEPTNO,
    d.LOC
FROM
    EMP e,
    DEPT d
WHERE
    e.DEPTNO=d.DEPTNO;
```

```
ENAME        DEPTNO LOC
---------- ---------- -------------
SMITH            20 DALLAS
ALLEN            30 CHICAGO
WARD             30 CHICAGO
JONES            20 DALLAS
MARTIN           30 CHICAGO
BLAKE            30 CHICAGO
CLARK            10 NEW YORK
SCOTT            20 DALLAS
KING             10 NEW YORK
TURNER           30 CHICAGO
ADAMS            20 DALLAS
JAMES            30 CHICAGO
FORD             20 DALLAS
MILLER           10 NEW YORK
```

```
----------------------------------------------------------------------------
| Id  | Operation                    | Name    | Rows | Bytes | Cost (%CPU)| Time     |
----------------------------------------------------------------------------
|   0 | SELECT STATEMENT             |         |   14 |   280 |   6  (17) | 00:00:01 |
|   1 |  MERGE JOIN                  |         |   14 |   280 |   6  (17) | 00:00:01 |
|   2 |   TABLE ACCESS BY INDEX ROWID| DEPT    |    4 |    44 |   2   (0) | 00:00:01 |
|   3 |    INDEX FULL SCAN           | PK_DEPT |    4 |       |   1   (0) | 00:00:01 |
| * 4 |   SORT JOIN                  |         |   14 |   126 |   4  (25) | 00:00:01 |
|   5 |    TABLE ACCESS FULL         | EMP     |   14 |   126 |   3   (0) | 00:00:01 |
----------------------------------------------------------------------------

Predicate Information (identified by operation id):
---------------------------------------------------

   4 - access("E"."DEPTNO"="D"."DEPTNO")
       filter("E"."DEPTNO"="D"."DEPTNO")
```

Both EMP and DEPT contain a reference to DEPTNO. Some columns from both tables are returned. An alternative syntax does exactly the same thing using the JOIN keyword. The following is an example of a NATURAL JOIN.

```
SELECT
    e.ENAME,
    DEPTNO,
    d.LOC
FROM
    EMP e
NATURAL JOIN
DEPT d;
```

> 🔔 When selecting from more than one table, the best practice is to prefix all columns. Not only does this improve readability, but it also helps Oracle to parse the query quicker.

The join columns are not defined. Natural join matches all columns with the same name. In EMP and DEPT, there is only one column with the same name and it is called DEPTNO.

The second syntax is JOIN with USING:

```
SELECT
    e.ENAME,
    DEPTNO,
    d.LOC
FROM
    EMP e
JOIN
    DEPT d
USING
(
    DEPTNO
);
```

The USING clause helps by specifying the join column. The join column cannot be prefixed.

The third syntax is JOIN with ON. It is the most robust syntax as it allows prefixing:

```
SELECT
    e.ENAME,
    d.DEPTNO,
    d.LOC
FROM
    EMP e
JOIN
    DEPT d
ON
    e.DEPTNO=d.DEPTNO;
```

The join columns are defined in the ON clause.

Outer join

A left or right outer join is a join where rows in one table that do not
have a matching row in the second table are selected with null values for
the unknown columns:

Example query 1

```
SELECT
    e.ENAME,
    d.DEPTNO,
    d.LOC
FROM
    EMP e,
    DEPT d
WHERE
    e.DEPTNO(+)=d.DEPTNO;
```

```
ENAME           DEPTNO LOC
---------- ---------- -------------
SMITH              20 DALLAS
ALLEN              30 CHICAGO
WARD               30 CHICAGO
JONES              20 DALLAS
MARTIN             30 CHICAGO
BLAKE              30 CHICAGO
CLARK              10 NEW YORK
SCOTT              20 DALLAS
KING               10 NEW YORK
TURNER             30 CHICAGO
ADAMS              20 DALLAS
JAMES              30 CHICAGO
FORD               20 DALLAS
MILLER             10 NEW YORK
                   40 BOSTON
```

```
-------------------------------------------------------------------------------
| Id  | Operation                    | Name    | Rows | Bytes | Cost (%CPU)| Time     |
-------------------------------------------------------------------------------
|   0 | SELECT STATEMENT             |         |   14 |   280 |   6   (17)| 00:00:01 |
|   1 |  MERGE JOIN OUTER            |         |   14 |   280 |   6   (17)| 00:00:01 |
|   2 |   TABLE ACCESS BY INDEX ROWID| DEPT    |    4 |    44 |   2    (0)| 00:00:01 |
|   3 |    INDEX FULL SCAN           | PK_DEPT |    4 |       |   1    (0)| 00:00:01 |
|*  4 |   SORT JOIN                  |         |   14 |   126 |   4   (25)| 00:00:01 |
|   5 |    TABLE ACCESS FULL         | EMP     |   14 |   126 |   3    (0)| 00:00:01 |
-------------------------------------------------------------------------------

Predicate Information (identified by operation id):
-------------------------------------------------------

   4 - access("E"."DEPTNO"(+)="D"."DEPTNO")
       filter("E"."DEPTNO"(+)="D"."DEPTNO")
```

Example query 2

```
SELECT
    e.ENAME,
    d.DEPTNO,
    d.LOC
```

```
FROM
    EMP e
RIGHT JOIN
    DEPT d
ON
    e.DEPTNO=d.DEPTNO
```

Example query 3

```
SELECT
    e.ENAME,
    d.DEPTNO,
    d.LOC
FROM
    DEPT d
LEFT JOIN
    EMP e
ON
    e.DEPTNO=d.DEPTNO
```

The right/left outer join selects departments with or without employees. As there is no employee in department 40 yet, department 40 is returned with a NULL value for the ENAME column of EMP.

Full outer join

A full outer join retrieves rows from both tables, whether or not they have a matching row:

```
WITH
    EMP
AS
(
    SELECT
        'JOEL' ENAME,
        40 DEPTNO
    FROM
        DUAL
    UNION ALL
    SELECT
        'MARY' ENAME,
        50 DEPTNO
    FROM
        DUAL
)
SELECT
    e.ENAME,
    d.DNAME
FROM
    EMP e
FULL JOIN
    DEPT d
```

```
USING
(
   DEPTNO
);
```

```
ENAM DNAME
---- --------------
JOEL OPERATIONS
MARY
      SALES
      RESEARCH
      ACCOUNTING
```

```
-------------------------------------------------------------------------
| Id  | Operation             | Name      | Rows | Bytes | Cost (%CPU)| Time     |
-------------------------------------------------------------------------
|   0 | SELECT STATEMENT      |           |    8 |   120 |   8  (13)| 00:00:01 |
|   1 |  VIEW                 | VW_FOJ_0  |    8 |   120 |   8  (13)| 00:00:01 |
| * 2 |   HASH JOIN FULL OUTER|           |    8 |   176 |   8  (13)| 00:00:01 |
|   3 |    VIEW               |           |    2 |    18 |   4   (0)| 00:00:01 |
|   4 |     UNION-ALL         |           |      |       |          |          |
|   5 |      FAST DUAL        |           |    1 |       |   2   (0)| 00:00:01 |
|   6 |      FAST DUAL        |           |    1 |       |   2   (0)| 00:00:01 |
|   7 |     TABLE ACCESS FULL | DEPT      |    4 |    52 |   3   (0)| 00:00:01 |
-------------------------------------------------------------------------
```

```
Predicate Information (identified by operation id):
---------------------------------------------------

   2 - access("E"."DEPTNO"="D"."DEPTNO")
```

The full outer join selects employees with a department, employees without a department and departments without employees. In releases prior to 11g, it does a UNION ALL of a left JOIN and a RIGHT JOIN to include all non-matched rows.

In 11g, the full outer join is much faster than before as the optimizer uses a new operation called HASH JOIN FULL OUTER that scans each table only once instead of doing a union of two joins.

Compare the same results with those from 10gR2:

```
-------------------------------------------------------------------------
---
| Id  | Operation                 | Name      | Rows | Bytes | Cost (%CPU)| Time     |
|
-------------------------------------------------------------------------
---
|   0 | SELECT STATEMENT          |           |    5 |    75 |  13  (24)|
00:00:01 |
|   1 |  TEMP TABLE TRANSFORMATION|           |      |       |          |
|
|   2 |   LOAD AS SELECT          |           |      |       |          |
|
|   3 |    UNION-ALL              |           |      |       |          |
|
|   4 |     FAST DUAL             |           |    1 |       |   2   (0)|
00:00:01 |
|   5 |     FAST DUAL             |           |    1 |       |   2   (0)|
00:00:01 |
```

```
|   6 |   VIEW                    |                             |   5 |   75 |    9  (12)|
00:00:01 |
|   7 |    UNION-ALL             |                             |     |      |           |
|
|*  8 |     HASH JOIN OUTER      |                             |   2 |   44 |    5  (20)|
00:00:01 |
|   9 |      VIEW                |                             |   2 |   18 |    2   (0)|
00:00:01 |
|  10 |       TABLE ACCESS FULL  | SYS_TEMP_0FD9D6601_2C2CE3   |   2 |   38 |    2   (0)|
00:00:01 |
|  11 |      TABLE ACCESS FULL   | DEPT                        |   4 |   52 |    2   (0)|
00:00:01 |
|* 12 |     HASH JOIN ANTI       |                             |   3 |   48 |    5  (20)|
00:00:01 |
|  13 |      TABLE ACCESS FULL   | DEPT                        |   4 |   52 |    2   (0)|
00:00:01 |
|  14 |      VIEW                |                             |   2 |    6 |    2   (0)|
00:00:01 |
|  15 |       TABLE ACCESS FULL  | SYS_TEMP_0FD9D6601_2C2CE3   |   2 |   38 |    2   (0)|
00:00:01 |
   8 - access("E"."DEPTNO"="D"."DEPTNO"(+))
  12 - access("E"."DEPTNO"="D"."DEPTNO")
```

Cross join

A cross join computes all rows from the one table to the rows of the other table:

```sql
SELECT
    d1.DNAME,
    d2.DNAME
FROM
    DEPT d1,
    DEPT d2;
```

```
DNAME            DNAME
---------------  ---------------
ACCOUNTING       ACCOUNTING
ACCOUNTING       OPERATIONS
ACCOUNTING       RESEARCH
ACCOUNTING       SALES
OPERATIONS       ACCOUNTING
OPERATIONS       OPERATIONS
OPERATIONS       RESEARCH
OPERATIONS       SALES
RESEARCH         ACCOUNTING
RESEARCH         OPERATIONS
RESEARCH         RESEARCH
RESEARCH         SALES
SALES            ACCOUNTING
SALES            OPERATIONS
SALES            RESEARCH
SALES            SALES
```

Id	Operation	Name	Rows	Bytes	Cost (%CPU)	Time
0	SELECT STATEMENT		16	320	5 (0)	00:00:01
1	MERGE JOIN CARTESIAN		16	320	5 (0)	00:00:01
2	TABLE ACCESS FULL	DEPT	4	40	2 (0)	00:00:01
3	BUFFER SORT		4	40	3 (0)	00:00:01
4	TABLE ACCESS FULL	DEPT	4	40	1 (0)	00:00:01

Advanced Oracle SQL Programming

The syntax CROSS JOIN is useful when combined with other joins:

```
WITH
    JOBS
AS
(
    SELECT
    DISTINCT
        JOB
    FROM
        EMP
)
SELECT
    JOBS.JOB,
    DEPT.DEPTNO,
    COUNT(EMP.EMPNO)
FROM
    EMP
RIGHT JOIN
(
    JOBS
CROSS JOIN
    DEPT
)
ON
(
    JOBS.JOB=EMP.JOB
    AND
    DEPT.DEPTNO=EMP.DEPTNO
)
GROUP BY
    JOBS.JOB,
    DEPT.DEPTNO;
```

```
JOB        DEPTNO COUNT(EMP.EMPNO)
---------  ------ ----------------
ANALYST        10                0
ANALYST        20                2
ANALYST        30                0
ANALYST        40                0
CLERK          10                1
CLERK          20                2
CLERK          30                1
CLERK          40                0
MANAGER        10                1
MANAGER        20                1
MANAGER        30                1
MANAGER        40                0
PRESIDENT      10                1
PRESIDENT      20                0
PRESIDENT      30                0
PRESIDENT      40                0
SALESMAN       10                0
SALESMAN       20                0
SALESMAN       30                4
SALESMAN       40                0
```

```
---------------------------------------------------------------------------
| Id  | Operation              | Name    | Rows | Bytes | Cost (%CPU)| Time     |
---------------------------------------------------------------------------
|   0 | SELECT STATEMENT       |         |   15 |   555 |   10  (30)| 00:00:01 |
|   1 |  HASH GROUP BY         |         |   15 |   555 |   10  (30)| 00:00:01 |
| * 2 |   HASH JOIN OUTER      |         |   20 |   740 |    9  (23)| 00:00:01 |
|   3 |    VIEW                |         |   20 |   440 |    6  (17)| 00:00:01 |
|   4 |     MERGE JOIN CARTESIAN|        |   20 |   180 |    6  (17)| 00:00:01 |
|   5 |      VIEW              |         |    5 |    30 |    3  (34)| 00:00:01 |
|   6 |       HASH UNIQUE      |         |    5 |    40 |    3  (34)| 00:00:01 |
|   7 |        TABLE ACCESS FULL| EMP    |   14 |   112 |    2   (0)| 00:00:01 |
|   8 |      BUFFER SORT       |         |    4 |    12 |    6  (17)| 00:00:01 |
|   9 |       INDEX FAST FULL SCAN| PK_DEPT |  4 |    12 |    1   (0)| 00:00:01 |
|  10 |    TABLE ACCESS FULL   | EMP     |   14 |   210 |    2   (0)| 00:00:01 |
---------------------------------------------------------------------------

 2 - access("DEPT"."DEPTNO"="EMP"."DEPTNO"(+) AND
           "JOBS"."JOB"="EMP"."JOB"(+))
```

The cross product of jobs and departments is joined to the table of employees.

Partitioned outer join

The partitioned outer join (10g) selects the partition key of the outer table even where there are no matching rows:

```
SELECT
    d.DEPTNO,
    e.JOB,
    COUNT(e.EMPNO)
FROM
    EMP e
PARTITION BY
    (e.JOB)
RIGHT JOIN
    DEPT d
ON
    (e.DEPTNO=d.DEPTNO)
GROUP BY
    d.DEPTNO,
    e.JOB
ORDER BY
    d.DEPTNO,
    e.JOB;
```

```
    DEPTNO JOB       COUNT(E.EMPNO)
---------- --------- --------------
        10 ANALYST                0
        10 CLERK                  1
        10 MANAGER                1
        10 PRESIDENT              1
        10 SALESMAN               0
        20 ANALYST                2
        20 CLERK                  2
        20 MANAGER                1
        20 PRESIDENT              0
        20 SALESMAN               0
        30 ANALYST                0
```

Advanced Oracle SQL Programming

```
30  CLERK                    1
30  MANAGER                  1
30  PRESIDENT                0
30  SALESMAN                 4
40  ANALYST                  0
40  CLERK                    0
40  MANAGER                  0
40  PRESIDENT                0
40  SALESMAN                 0
```

```
---------------------------------------------------------------------------
| Id  | Operation                     | Name    | Rows | Bytes | Cost (%CPU)| Time     |
---------------------------------------------------------------------------
|   0 | SELECT STATEMENT               |         |   11 |   682 |  11  (28) | 00:00:01 |
|   1 |  SORT GROUP BY                 |         |   11 |   682 |  11  (28) | 00:00:01 |
|   2 |   VIEW                         |         |   20 |  1240 |  10  (20) | 00:00:01 |
|   3 |    MERGE JOIN PARTITION OUTER  |         |   20 |   360 |  10  (20) | 00:00:01 |
|   4 |     SORT JOIN                  |         |    4 |    12 |   2  (50) | 00:00:01 |
|   5 |      INDEX FULL SCAN           | PK_DEPT |    4 |    12 |   1   (0) | 00:00:01 |
|*  6 |     SORT PARTITION JOIN        |         |   14 |   210 |   3  (34) | 00:00:01 |
|   7 |      TABLE ACCESS FULL         | EMP     |   14 |   210 |   2   (0) | 00:00:01 |
---------------------------------------------------------------------------

   6 - access("E"."DEPTNO"="D"."DEPTNO")
       filter("E"."DEPTNO"="D"."DEPTNO")
```

For each job of EMP and for each department of DEPT, there will be a matching row. This looks like a cross join query, but it is much more efficient here because the employee table is selected only once. The job is a column of EMP and is selected even when there is no matching row in EMP. Only left and right partitioned joins are supported to date.

 ANSI syntax is recommended by Oracle. It has more capabilities, like outer joining with more than one table and with OR predicates, but it also has several limitations, one of which is that it cannot be used in fast refreshable materialized views.

Sets

UNION ALL

UNION ALL selects all rows from all queries:

```
SELECT
    1 N
FROM
    DUAL
UNION ALL
SELECT
    2 N
FROM
```

```
    DUAL
UNION ALL
SELECT
    2 N
FROM
    DUAL;
```

```
         N
---------
         1
         2
         2
```

```
----------------------------------------------------------------
| Id  | Operation       | Name | Rows | Cost (%CPU)| Time       |
----------------------------------------------------------------
|   0 | SELECT STATEMENT|      |    3 |    6  (67) | 00:00:01   |
|   1 |   UNION-ALL     |      |      |           |            |
|   2 |    FAST DUAL    |      |    1 |    2  (0)  | 00:00:01   |
|   3 |    FAST DUAL    |      |    1 |    2  (0)  | 00:00:01   |
|   4 |    FAST DUAL    |      |    1 |    2  (0)  | 00:00:01   |
----------------------------------------------------------------
```

All rows are returned. Each query must have the same number of columns and the datatypes must be the same or compatible.

The partition views feature (Oracle 7.3) does not allow inserts or updates and the partitioning is done manually.

🖫 partview.sql

```
-- ************************************************
-- Copyright © 2008 by Rampant TechPress
-- This script is free for non-commercial purposes
-- with no warranties.  Use at your own risk.
--
-- To license this script for a commercial purpose,
-- contact rtp@rampant.cc
-- ************************************************
-- Id     : $Id: partview.sql,v 1.3 2008/01/18 17:16:30 lsc Exp $
-- Author : $Author: lsc $
-- Date   : $Date: 2008/01/18 17:16:30 $
--
-- Create EMP10 to EMP40 in current schema
--

WHENEVER SQLERROR EXIT

EXEC EXECUTE IMMEDIATE 'DROP TABLE EMP10'; EXCEPTION WHEN OTHERS THEN NULL
EXEC EXECUTE IMMEDIATE 'DROP TABLE EMP20'; EXCEPTION WHEN OTHERS THEN NULL
EXEC EXECUTE IMMEDIATE 'DROP TABLE EMP30'; EXCEPTION WHEN OTHERS THEN NULL
EXEC EXECUTE IMMEDIATE 'DROP TABLE EMP40'; EXCEPTION WHEN OTHERS THEN NULL
```

```
CREATE TABLE
    EMP10
AS SELECT
    *
FROM
    EMP
WHERE
    DEPTNO=10
/
CREATE TABLE
    EMP20
AS SELECT
    *
FROM
    EMP
WHERE
    DEPTNO=20
/
CREATE TABLE
    EMP30
AS SELECT
    *
FROM
    EMP
WHERE
    DEPTNO=30
/
CREATE TABLE
    EMP40
AS SELECT
    *
FROM
    EMP
WHERE
    DEPTNO=40
/
ALTER TABLE
    EMP10
ADD CONSTRAINT
    EMP10_PK
PRIMARY KEY
    (EMPNO)
/
ALTER TABLE
    EMP10
ADD CONSTRAINT
    CHECK10
CHECK
    (DEPTNO=10)
/
ALTER TABLE
    EMP20
ADD CONSTRAINT
    EMP20_PK
PRIMARY KEY
    (EMPNO)
/
ALTER TABLE
```

```
    EMP20
ADD CONSTRAINT
    CHECK20
CHECK
    (DEPTNO=20)
/
ALTER TABLE
    EMP30
ADD CONSTRAINT
    EMP30_PK
PRIMARY KEY
    (EMPNO)
/
ALTER TABLE
    EMP30
ADD CONSTRAINT
    CHECK30
CHECK
    (DEPTNO=30)
/
ALTER TABLE
    EMP40
ADD CONSTRAINT
    EMP40_PK
PRIMARY KEY
    (EMPNO)
/
ALTER TABLE
    EMP40
ADD CONSTRAINT
    CHECK40
CHECK
    (DEPTNO=40)
/
CREATE OR REPLACE VIEW
    V_EMP
AS
    SELECT
        *
    FROM
        EMP10
    UNION ALL
    SELECT
        *
    FROM
        EMP20
    UNION ALL
    SELECT
        *
    FROM
        EMP30
    UNION ALL
    SELECT
        *
    FROM
        EMP40
/
```

Four tables and a view are created. The optimizer recognizes this view as a partition view and chooses an efficient plan to retrieve data.

```
SELECT
    ENAME
FROM
    V_EMP
WHERE
    DEPTNO=20
    AND
    SAL>2000;
```

```
ENAME
----------
JONES
SCOTT
FORD
```

```
-----------------------------------------------------------------------------
| Id  | Operation             | Name  | Rows  | Bytes | Cost (%CPU)| Time     |
-----------------------------------------------------------------------------
|   0 | SELECT STATEMENT      |       |     4 |    56 |     3   (0)| 00:00:01 |
|   1 |  VIEW                 | V_EMP |     4 |    56 |     3   (0)| 00:00:01 |
|   2 |   UNION-ALL PARTITION |       |       |       |            |          |
|*  3 |    FILTER             |       |       |       |            |          |
|*  4 |     TABLE ACCESS FULL | EMP10 |     1 |    13 |     2   (0)| 00:00:01 |
|*  5 |     TABLE ACCESS FULL | EMP20 |     2 |    26 |     2   (0)| 00:00:01 |
|*  6 |    FILTER             |       |       |       |            |          |
|*  7 |     TABLE ACCESS FULL | EMP30 |     1 |    14 |     2   (0)| 00:00:01 |
|*  8 |    FILTER             |       |       |       |            |          |
|*  9 |     TABLE ACCESS FULL | EMP40 |     1 |    33 |     2   (0)| 00:00:01 |
-----------------------------------------------------------------------------

   3 - filter(NULL IS NOT NULL)
   4 - filter("DEPTNO"=20 AND "SAL">2000)
   5 - filter("SAL">2000 AND "DEPTNO"=20)
   6 - filter(NULL IS NOT NULL)
   7 - filter("DEPTNO"=20 AND "SAL">2000)
   8 - filter(NULL IS NOT NULL)
   9 - filter("DEPTNO"=20 AND "SAL">2000)
```

Note the UNION-ALL PARTITION operation.

Table partitioning (Oracle 8.0 and later) is much more efficient.

🖫 parttable.sql

```
-- Id      : $Id: parttable.sql,v 1.3 2008/01/18 17:52:53 lsc Exp $
-- Author  : $Author: lsc $
-- Date    : $Date: 2008/01/18 17:52:53 $
--
-- Create EMP_PART in current schema
--

WHENEVER SQLERROR EXIT
```

```
EXEC EXECUTE IMMEDIATE 'DROP TABLE EMP_PART'; EXCEPTION WHEN OTHERS THEN
NULL

CREATE TABLE
    EMP_PART
PARTITION BY LIST
(
    DEPTNO
)
(
    PARTITION EMP_P10 VALUES(10),
    PARTITION EMP_P20 VALUES(20),
    PARTITION EMP_P30 VALUES(30),
    PARTITION EMP_P40 VALUES(40)
)
AS SELECT
    *
FROM
    EMP
/
ALTER TABLE
    EMP_PART
ADD CONSTRAINT
    EMP_PART_PK
PRIMARY KEY
    (EMPNO)
/
```

Only one table is created with four partitions. The optimizer avoids accessing partitions:

```
SELECT
    ENAME
FROM
    EMP_PART
WHERE
    DEPTNO=20
    AND
    SAL>2000;
```

```
ENAME
----------
JONES
SCOTT
FORD
```

Id	Operation	Name	Rows	Bytes	Cost (%CPU)	Time	Pstart	Pstop
0	SELECT STATEMENT		3	39	2 (0)	00:00:01		
1	PARTITION LIST SINGLE		3	39	2 (0)	00:00:01	2	2
* 2	TABLE ACCESS FULL	EMP_PART	3	39	2 (0)	00:00:01	2	2

```
    2 - filter("SAL">2000)
```

Only a single partition is accessed.

UNION

The UNION set operator selects all rows and removes duplicates:

```
SELECT
   1 N
FROM
   DUAL
UNION
SELECT
   2 N
FROM
   DUAL
UNION
SELECT
   2 N
FROM
   DUAL;
```

```
         N
----------
         1
         2
```

```
-------------------------------------------------------------
| Id | Operation        | Name | Rows | Cost (%CPU)| Time     |
-------------------------------------------------------------
|  0 | SELECT STATEMENT |      |    3 |    9  (78)| 00:00:01 |
|  1 |  SORT UNIQUE     |      |    3 |    9  (78)| 00:00:01 |
|  2 |   UNION-ALL      |      |      |           |          |
|  3 |    FAST DUAL     |      |    1 |    2   (0)| 00:00:01 |
|  4 |    FAST DUAL     |      |    1 |    2   (0)| 00:00:01 |
|  5 |    FAST DUAL     |      |    1 |    2   (0)| 00:00:01 |
-------------------------------------------------------------
```

All unique rows are returned. The UNION is shown actually doing a UNION ALL operation before removing the duplicates with a SORT UNIQUE. Due to that additional operation, UNION ALL performs better.

MINUS

The MINUS set operator selects the rows that are not in the second query from the first query and removes any duplicates:

```
SELECT
   DEPTNO
FROM
   DEPT
MINUS
SELECT
```

```
    DEPTNO
FROM
    EMP;
```

```
    DEPTNO
----------
        40
```

Id	Operation	Name	Rows	Bytes	Cost (%CPU)	Time
0	SELECT STATEMENT		4	54	5 (80)	00:00:01
1	MINUS					
2	SORT UNIQUE NOSORT		4	12	2 (50)	00:00:01
3	INDEX FULL SCAN	PK_DEPT	4	12	1 (0)	00:00:01
4	SORT UNIQUE		14	42	3 (34)	00:00:01
5	TABLE ACCESS FULL	EMP	14	42	2 (0)	00:00:01

Only department 40 remains because the other ones exist in EMP.

INTERSECT

INTERSECT selects the distinct rows from the queries:

```
SELECT
    DEPTNO
FROM
    EMP
INTERSECT
SELECT
    DEPTNO
FROM
    DEPT;
```

```
    DEPTNO
----------
        10
        20
        30
```

Id	Operation	Name	Rows	Bytes	Cost (%CPU)	Time
0	SELECT STATEMENT		4	54	5 (60)	00:00:01
1	INTERSECTION					
2	SORT UNIQUE		14	42	3 (34)	00:00:01
3	TABLE ACCESS FULL	EMP	14	42	2 (0)	00:00:01
4	SORT UNIQUE NOSORT		4	12	2 (50)	00:00:01
5	INDEX FULL SCAN	PK_DEPT	4	12	1 (0)	00:00:01

Departments 10, 20 and 30 are in both tables. Intersect is particularly useful when a very large number of columns must be compared. This way, the optimizer does not have to figure out how to join the tables and the parsing can be quicker.

SQL expressions

Columns are not the only possible SQL expressions. Literals, functions, and pseudo columns are also valid SQL expressions.

Column

A column from a table, view or subquery can be used as a SQL expression.

```
SELECT
    ENAME as "Employee name"
FROM
    EMP;
```

The non-prefixed column ENAME is aliased as "Employee name."

```
SELECT
    EMP.ENAME
FROM
    EMP;
```

The column ENAME is prefixed by the table name.

```
SELECT
    SCOTT.EMP.ENAME
FROM
    SCOTT.EMP;
```

The column ENAME is prefixed by the table name and owner.

Star

* is a joker which selects all columns from the table(s):

```
SELECT
    *
FROM
    EMP
JOIN
    DEPT
USING
    (DEPTNO);
```

All columns are returned.

```
SELECT
    e.*
FROM
    EMP e
JOIN
    DEPT d
ON
    (e.DEPTNO=d.DEPTNO);
```

All columns from EMP are returned.

> Using e.* instead of EMPNO, ENAME, JOB, MGR, HIREDATE, SAL, COMM, or DEPTNO is often a bad idea since adding a column or changing the order of the columns in the employee table will affect the result.

Literal

Another valid expression is a date, number or character literal.

```
SELECT
    12,
    -34,
    .5
    -1.2e-10,
    100000000,
    1e200d,
    1e30f
FROM
    DUAL;
```

Numeric literals can be selected with various notations.

Suffixes D and F indicate binary double and binary float (10g). Binary doubles and binary floats offer better performance, allow numbers larger than 10^{126} and smaller than 10^{-131} and NaN (Not A Number) and Inf (Infinity).

```
SELECT
    POWER(2d,1000d) "2^1000",
    POWER(2d,10000d) "2^10000",
    POWER(-2d,10001d) "(-2)^10001",
    SQRT(-1d)
```

```
FROM
   DUAL;


    2^1000     2^10000 (-2)^10001  SQRT(-1D)
---------- ---------- ---------- ----------
1.072E+301        Inf       -Inf        Nan
```

Binary doubles and binary floats offer additional literal values for NaN and Inf:

```
SELECT
   BINARY_DOUBLE_INFINITY,
   BINARY_DOUBLE_NAN,
   BINARY_FLOAT_INFINITY,
   BINARY_FLOAT_NAN
FROM
   DUAL;

BINARY_DOUBLE_INF BINARY_DOUBLE_NAN BINARY_FLOAT_INF BINARY_FLOAT_NAN
----------------- ----------------- ---------------- ----------------
              Inf               Nan              Inf              Nan
```

Infinities and Not-a-Number values are returned. There are additional tests for NaN and Inf:

```
SELECT
   1/0D,
   -1/0D,
   0/0D,
   1/1D,
   1/2D
FROM
   DUAL
WHERE
   1/0D IS INFINITE
   AND
   -1/0D IS INFINITE
   AND
   0/0D IS NAN
   AND
   1/1D IS NOT INFINITE
   AND
   1/2D IS NOT NAN;

     1/0D      -1/0D       0/0D       1/1D       1/2D
--------- --------- --------- --------- ---------
      Inf       -Inf        Nan  1.0E+000  5.0E-001
```

Checks are performed to test for NaN or Inf.

When BINARY_DOUBLE and BINARY_FLOAT are stored in an IEEE 754 conform binary format, NUMBER is stored in an Oracle proprietary format. Numbers offer a better precision than binary double and use space more efficiently in a varying length from 1 to 21 bytes:

```
SELECT
   VSIZE(1),
   VSIZE(1d)
FROM
   DUAL;
```

```
 VSIZE(1) VSIZE(1D)
--------- ---------
        2         8
```

```
SELECT
   1234567890d/9999999999d,
   1234567890/9999999999
FROM
   DUAL;
```

```
1234567890D/9999999999D                         1234567890/9999999999
----------------------- --------------------------------------------------
 .12345678901234568000   .12345678901234567890123456789012345678900000
```

Oracle offers various date formats.

```
SELECT
   DATE '2000-01-01',
   TIMESTAMP '2000-01-01 00:00:00.000',
   TIMESTAMP '2000-01-01 00:00:00.000 Europe/Zurich',
   TIME '00:00:00.000 Europe/Zurich',
   INTERVAL '1-01' YEAR(4) TO MONTH,
   INTERVAL '0.000000001' SECOND(6,9),
   INTERVAL '-1 12' DAY(6) TO HOUR
FROM
   DUAL
```

DATE is an Oracle proprietary format. The granularity is one second and the range is from 01-Jan-4712 B.C. to 31-Dec-9999 A.D. at 23h59m59s.

The unit when adding a numeric literal is one day:

```
SELECT
   DATE '2007-12-31' + 60
FROM
   DUAL;
```

```
DATE'2007
---------
29-FEB-08
```

The sixtieth day in 2008 is a leap year day.

Timestamp offers a finer granularity up to the nanosecond. Timestamp optionally contains a time zone.

```
SELECT
    TIMESTAMP '2009-01-01 00:00:00.000000001 Europe/Zurich'
        AT TIME ZONE 'US/Central'
FROM
    DUAL;
```

```
TIMESTAMP'2009-01-0100:00:00.000000001EUROPE/ZURICH'ATTIMEZONE'US/CENTRAL'
------------------------------------------------------------------------
2008-12-31 17:00:00.000000001 US/CENTRAL
```

The syntax above converts a timestamp to a different time zone. One type of interval is the day-to-month interval. The granularity is one month and the range is from minus one billion year to plus one billion year, exclusively:

```
SELECT
    INTERVAL '1' YEAR + 2 * INTERVAL '6' MONTH
FROM
    DUAL;
```

```
INTERVAL'1'YEAR+2*INTERVAL'6'MONTH
----------------------------------
+000000002-00
```

Addition and multiplication of intervals is possible, but aggregate functions like SUM and AVG cannot be used with this datatype. The second type of interval is the day-to-second interval. The granularity is a nanosecond and the range is from minus one billion day (-10^9 days) to plus one billion day ($+10^9$ days), exclusively:

```
SELECT
    TIMESTAMP '2008-03-30 01:59:59 Europe/Zurich' + INTERVAL '1' SECOND
FROM
    DUAL;
```

```
TIMESTAMP'2008-03-3001:59:59EUROPE/ZURICH'+INTERVAL'1'SECOND
-----------------------------------------------------------
2008-03-30 03:00:00 EUROPE/ZURICH
```

> 🔔 The reader may be used to literals like '01-JAN-08'. However, this is not a
> date literal but rather a string that may be converted to a date according to
> the NLS settings.

Interval can be added to timestamp. In the example above, the daylight saving time capabilities of timestamp are shown.

Another basic datatype of Oracle is the character datatype, of which there are two: CHAR and VARCHAR2. Oracle recommends using VARCHAR2. A literal is always CHAR. Both VARCHAR2 and CHAR could be stored in the default character set or in Unicode as National Char (NCHAR) or Varchar2 (NVARCHAR2). VARCHAR2 saves disk space and, therefore, usually enhance performance as fewer blocks must be read.

```
SELECT
    'Hello',
    n'World',
    q'[it's Friday]',
    nq'{'!'}',
    '''text in quotes'''
FROM
    DUAL;
```

```
'HELL N'WOR Q'[IT'SFRID NQ' '''TEXTINQUOTES'
----- ----- ----------- --- ----------------
Hello World it's Friday '!' 'text in quotes'
```

A string literal is always in single quotes. A quote within the string is doubled, like in '5 O"Clock'.

Oracle 10g introduced the prefix q. When prefixed by q, the string uses special characters to delimit the string. N prefixes a national character set string (Unicode).

Compounded expression

An expression can be composed of multiple expressions. The operators available in Oracle are addition, subtraction, multiplication, division and concatenation.

The string concatenation operator is formed by two pipe symbols:

```
SELECT
    'X'||'Y'
FROM
    DUAL;
```

```
'X
--
XY
```

Another alternative that accomplishes the same thing is shown below.

```
SELECT
    CONCAT('X','Y')
FROM
    DUAL;
```

```
CO
--
XY
```

The internal string concatenation operator's equivalent function is CONCAT.

The numerical operators are +, -, * and /:

```
SELECT
    1+1,
    3-2,
    5*5,
    10/4
FROM
    DUAL;
```

```
       1+1        3-2        5*5       10/4
---------- ---------- ---------- ----------
         2          1         25        2.5
```

Those operators can be used with date and time expressions.

```
SELECT
   DATE '1582-10-15' - DATE '1582-10-04'
FROM
   DUAL;
```

```
DATE'1582-10-15'-DATE'1582-10-04'
---------------------------------
                                1
```

This example displayed the difference in days between the last day of the Julian calendar to the first day of the Gregorian calendar.

```
SELECT
   DATE '2000-02-29' + INTERVAL '1' MONTH
FROM
   DUAL;
```

```
DATE'2000-02-29'+IN
-------------------
29.03.2000 00:00:00
```

This example displayed one month after February 29th, 2000.

```
SELECT
   2*INTERVAL '7' MONTH,
   INTERVAL '1' / 7
FROM
   DUAL;
```

```
2*INTERVAL'7'MONTH  INTERVAL'1'DAY/7
------------------  ------------------------------
+000000001-02       +000000000 03:25:42.857142857
```

Two periods of seven months is 1 year + 2 months. A seventh of a day is close to 3 hours and 26 minutes.

NULL

NULL is a special expression that represents the absence of a value:

```
SELECT
   TO_DATE(NULL),
   TO_CHAR(NULL),
   TO_NUMBER(NULL)
FROM
   DUAL;
```

```
TO_DATE(NULL)  TO_CHAR(NULL)  TO_NUMBER(NULL)
-------------  -------------  ---------------
<NULL>         <NULL>         <NULL>
```

To display nulls as something more visible than an empty string in SQL*Plus, it is possible to set it to a specific string like '<NULL>':

```
SET NULL "<NULL>"
```

Null has no type in itself; it also has no length and no value. When comparing NULL with NULL, the result is NULL.

```
BEGIN
    IF (NULL=NULL) IS NULL
    THEN
        DBMS_OUTPUT.PUT_LINE('(NULL=NULL) IS NULL');
    END IF;
    IF (NULL!=NULL) IS NULL
    THEN
        DBMS_OUTPUT.PUT_LINE('(NULL!=NULL) IS NULL');
    END IF;
    IF (NULL OR FALSE) IS NULL
    THEN
        DBMS_OUTPUT.PUT_LINE('(NULL OR FALSE) IS NULL');
    END IF;
    IF (NULL OR TRUE)=TRUE
    THEN
        DBMS_OUTPUT.PUT_LINE('(NULL OR TRUE) IS TRUE');
    END IF;
    IF (NULL AND TRUE) IS NULL
    THEN
        DBMS_OUTPUT.PUT_LINE('(NULL AND TRUE) IS NULL');
    END IF;
    IF (NULL AND FALSE)=FALSE
    THEN
        DBMS_OUTPUT.PUT_LINE('(NULL AND FALSE) IS FALSE');
    END IF;
    IF (NOT(NULL)) IS NULL
    THEN
        DBMS_OUTPUT.PUT_LINE('(NOT(NULL)) IS NULL');
    END IF;
END;
/
```

```
(NULL=NULL) IS NULL
(NULL!=NULL) IS NULL
(NULL OR FALSE) IS NULL
(NULL OR TRUE) IS TRUE
(NULL AND TRUE) IS NULL
(NULL AND FALSE) IS FALSE
(NOT(NULL)) IS NULL
```

The logical operations with NULL are spelled out.

Pseudo column

A pseudo column is an expression that has a special meaning in Oracle but is neither a function nor a literal or a column:

```
SELECT
    ROWNUM,
    DNAME
FROM
    DEPT
```

```
    ROWNUM DNAME
---------- --------------
         1 ACCOUNTING
         2 RESEARCH
         3 SALES
         4 OPERATIONS
```

ROWNUM is probably the most common pseudo column. It is used to enumerate the rows. A common usage of ROWNUM is to select a limited number of rows.

```
SELECT
    ENAME,
    SAL
FROM
    (
        SELECT
            *
        FROM
            EMP
        ORDER BY SAL DESC
    )
WHERE
    ROWNUM<=5;
```

```
ENAME             SAL
----------  ----------
KING             5000
SCOTT            3000
FORD             3000
JONES            2975
BLAKE            2850
```

```
---------------------------------------------------------------------------
| Id  | Operation             | Name | Rows | Bytes | Cost (%CPU)| Time     |
---------------------------------------------------------------------------
|  0  | SELECT STATEMENT      |      |    5 |   100 |    3  (34) | 00:00:01 |
|* 1  |  COUNT STOPKEY        |      |      |       |           |          |
|  2  |   VIEW                |      |   14 |   280 |    3  (34) | 00:00:01 |
|* 3  |    SORT ORDER BY STOPKEY|    |   14 |   518 |    3  (34) | 00:00:01 |
|  4  |     TABLE ACCESS FULL | EMP  |   14 |   518 |    2   (0) | 00:00:01 |
---------------------------------------------------------------------------

   1 - filter(ROWNUM<=5)
   3 - filter(ROWNUM<=5)
```

In this example, the top 5 rows were returned.

```
SELECT
    ENAME,
    SAL
FROM
    (
      SELECT
          E.*,
          ROWNUM R
      FROM
          (
             SELECT
                 *
             FROM
                 EMP
             ORDER BY
                 SAL DESC
          ) E
      WHERE ROWNUM<=10
    )
WHERE
    R>5;
```

```
ENAME              SAL
----------    ----------
CLARK             2450
ALLEN             1600
TURNER            1500
MILLER            1300
WARD              1250
```

```
---------------------------------------------------------------------------
| Id | Operation                | Name | Rows | Bytes | Cost (%CPU)| Time     |
---------------------------------------------------------------------------
|  0 | SELECT STATEMENT         |      |  10  |  330  |  3  (34) | 00:00:01 |
|* 1 |  VIEW                    |      |  10  |  330  |  3  (34) | 00:00:01 |
|* 2 |   COUNT STOPKEY          |      |      |       |          |          |
|  3 |    VIEW                  |      |  14  |  280  |  3  (34) | 00:00:01 |
|* 4 |     SORT ORDER BY STOPKEY|      |  14  |  518  |  3  (34) | 00:00:01 |
|  5 |      TABLE ACCESS FULL   | EMP  |  14  |  518  |  2  (0)  | 00:00:01 |
---------------------------------------------------------------------------

   1 - filter("R">5)
   2 - filter(ROWNUM<=10)
   4 - filter(ROWNUM<=10)
```

The rows 6 to 10 were returned.

> 🔔 WHERE ROWNUM>1 is always false, because ROWNUM is evaluated
> after the WHERE condition, but before GROUP BY, HAVING and ORDER
> BY. It is incremented only for returned rows, so if ROWNUM 1 is not
> returned, no rows are returned.

ROWID is useful when accessing a single row of a table:

```
SELECT
    *
FROM
    EMP
WHERE
    ROWID
IN
(
    SELECT
        ROWID
    FROM
        (
            SELECT
                ROWID
            FROM
                EMP
            ORDER BY
                EMPNO
        )
    WHERE
        ROWNUM=1
);
```

```
 EMPNO ENAME        JOB         MGR HIREDATE    SAL  COMM DEPTNO
 ----- ----------  ----------  ----- ---------  ----- ----- ------
  7369 SMITH        CLERK        7902 17-DEC-80  1300         20
```

```
-------------------------------------------------------------------------------
| Id  | Operation                     | Name    | Rows | Bytes | Cost (%CPU)| Time     |
-------------------------------------------------------------------------------
|   0 | SELECT STATEMENT              |         |    1 |    49 |   3  (34) | 00:00:01 |
|   1 |  NESTED LOOPS                 |         |    1 |    49 |   3  (34) | 00:00:01 |
|   2 |   VIEW                        | VW_NSO_1|    1 |    12 |   1   (0) | 00:00:01 |
|   3 |    HASH UNIQUE                |         |    1 |    12 |           |          |
| * 4 |     COUNT STOPKEY             |         |      |       |           |          |
|   5 |      VIEW                     |         |    1 |    12 |   1   (0) | 00:00:01 |
|   6 |       INDEX FULL SCAN         | PK_EMP  |    1 |    16 |   1   (0) | 00:00:01 |
|   7 |   TABLE ACCESS BY USER ROWID  | EMP     |    1 |    37 |   1   (0) | 00:00:01 |
-------------------------------------------------------------------------------
    4 - filter(ROWNUM=1)
```

The primary key index returned ROWID. The first entry is selected to access the table. Note the operation TABLE ACCESS BY USER ROWID. Now compare the results with the following:

```
SELECT
    *
FROM
(
    SELECT
        *
    FROM
        EMP
    ORDER BY
        EMPNO
)
WHERE
    ROWNUM=1;
```

```
 EMPNO ENAME        JOB         MGR HIREDATE    SAL  COMM DEPTNO
 ----- ----------  ----------  ----- ---------  ----- ----- ------
  7369 SMITH        CLERK        7902 17-DEC-80  1300         20
```

```
-------------------------------------------------------------------------------
| Id  | Operation                    | Name    | Rows | Bytes | Cost (%CPU)| Time     |
-------------------------------------------------------------------------------
|   0 | SELECT STATEMENT             |         |    1 |    87 |   2   (0) | 00:00:01 |
| * 1 |  COUNT STOPKEY               |         |      |       |           |          |
|   2 |   VIEW                       |         |    1 |    87 |   2   (0) | 00:00:01 |
|   3 |    TABLE ACCESS BY INDEX ROWID| EMP     |   14 |   518 |   2   (0) | 00:00:01 |
|   4 |     INDEX FULL SCAN          | PK_EMP  |    1 |       |   1   (0) | 00:00:01 |
-------------------------------------------------------------------------------
    1 - filter(ROWNUM=1)
```

The second query may be less efficient, depending on the size of the table and the size of the index because the STOPKEY operation is executed after the table access.

ROWID is often used by the database administrator to identify the block or the datafile where a row is physically stored; for example, in

---

case of a block corruption. The package *dbms_rowid* contains some useful conversion functions.

Table expression

Table expressions could be a view, a table, a collection or a remote table:

```
SELECT
    *
FROM
    EMP;
```

EMP is a table:

```
SELECT
    *
FROM
    TABLE
    (
        SYS.ODCINUMBERLIST(1,2,3)
    );
```

```
COLUMN_VALUE
------------
          1
          2
          3
```

```
-----------------------------------------------------------------------------
| Id | Operation                          | Name | Rows | Bytes | Cost (%CPU)| Time     |
-----------------------------------------------------------------------------
|  0 | SELECT STATEMENT                   |      | 8168 | 16336 |   29   (0)| 00:00:01 |
|  1 |  COLLECTION ITERATOR CONSTRUCTOR FETCH|    |      |       |           |          |
-----------------------------------------------------------------------------
```

SYS.ODCINUMBERLIST is a varying array (or varray) of NUMBER. ODCIDATELIST (10g) is an array of DATE, ODCIRAWLIST (10g) is an array of RAW(2000) and ODCIVARCHAR2LIST (10g) is an array of VARCHAR2(4000).

Note the inaccurate row count!

TABLE is a function that transforms the collection in a table. It can be used with NESTED TABLES or VARRAY columns, with type constructs, and with functions returning a collection:

```
SELECT
    COUNT(*)
FROM
    EMP@DB02;
```

```
COUNT(*)
----------
        14
```

```
------------------------------------------------------------------------
| Id | Operation             | Name   | Rows | Cost (%CPU)| Time     | Inst  |
------------------------------------------------------------------------
|  0 | SELECT STATEMENT REMOTE|        |    1 |    1   (0)| 00:00:01 |       |
|  1 |   SORT AGGREGATE       |        |    1 |           |          |       |
|  2 |    INDEX FULL SCAN     | PK_EMP |   14 |    1   (0)| 00:00:01 | LSC01 |
------------------------------------------------------------------------
```

DB02 is a database link. EMP@DB02 is a remote table. Note the Inst column and the SELECT STATEMENT REMOTE operation:

```
SELECT
    ENAME
FROM
    EMP_PART
PARTITION
(
    EMP_P10
);
```

```
ENAME
----------
CLARK
KING
MILLER
```

```
------------------------------------------------------------------------------------
| Id | Operation              | Name     | Rows | Bytes | Cost (%CPU)| Time     | Pstart| Pstop |
------------------------------------------------------------------------------------
|  0 | SELECT STATEMENT       |          |    3 |   108 |    3   (0)| 00:00:01 |       |       |
|  1 |   PARTITION LIST SINGLE|          |    3 |   108 |    3   (0)| 00:00:01 |     1 |     1 |
|  2 |    TABLE ACCESS FULL    | EMP_PART |    3 |   108 |    3   (0)| 00:00:01 |     1 |     1 |
------------------------------------------------------------------------------------
```

EMP_P10 is a partition of the EMP_PART table.

Conclusion

The SELECT syntax contains the expressions to be selected, the tables and subquery to select from, the conditions where rows are returned, the group by clause that aggregate rows, the connect by clause to use hierarchy, and the model clause. The join can be written in Oracle or in ANSI syntax and the outer join can select columns of one table even when there is no matching row. The commonly used set operators are UNION, UNION ALL and MINUS.

Exercises

1. Point out the offending line of code in the following query.

    ```
    SELECT
        DEPTNO,
        ENAME
    FROM
        EMP
    GROUP BY
        DEPTNO
    ```

2. Which two of the following expressions are not valid?

    ```
    SELECT
        ROWID,
        DATE '01-JAN-08',
        DEPTNO,
        1/2,
        2^10,
        (
            WITH
                T
            AS
            (
                SELECT
                    13
                FROM
                    DUAL
            )
            SELECT
                T.*
            FROM
                T
        )
    FROM
        DEPT
    ```

3. Table A has 5 rows and table B has 3 rows. How many rows will be returned? Specify a range. The query will return from ... to ... rows.

    ```
    SELECT
        X
    FROM
        A
    UNION
    SELECT
        X
    FROM
        B
    ```

4. Describe the purpose of the following query. Try to rewrite the query using the (+) syntax.

```
SELECT
    d.DNAME,
    e.ENAME,
    e.JOB
FROM
    EMP e
RIGHT JOIN
    DEPT d
ON
(
    e.DEPTNO=d.DEPTNO
    AND
    e.JOB IN ('MANAGER','PRESIDENT')
)
```

5. King earns $5000 a month. What does the following query return?

```
SELECT
    CASE
        WHEN
            SAL>2000
        THEN
            1
        WHEN
            SAL>4000
        THEN
            2
        WHEN
            SAL>6000
        THEN
            3
        ELSE
            4
    END "N"
FROM
    EMP
WHERE
    ENAME='KING'
```

6. How many rows will the following query return (10g/11g)?

```
SELECT
    COLUMN_VALUE
FROM
    TABLE
    (
        SYS.ODCIDATELIST(DATE '2000-01-01',DATE '2000-01-31')
    )
```

Solutions

1. Line 3: ENAME is not a group by expression.

   To order the rows, use order by!

```
SELECT
    DEPTNO,
    ENAME
FROM
    EMP
GROUP BY
    DEPTNO
    ENAME
    *
ERROR at line 3:
ORA-00979: not a GROUP BY expression
```

2. DATE '01-JAN-08' is not a proper date literal. 2^10 is not valid.

   A date literal is always in the format DATE 'YYYY-MM-SS', regardless of the NLS settings. 2^10 must be replaced by POWER(2,10). ROWID is a pseudo column, DEPTNO is a column, 1/2 is a compounded expression and the last column is a scalar subquery returning 13.

```
SELECT
    ROWID,
    DATE '01-JAN-08',
    DEPTNO,
    1/2,
    2^10,
    (
        WITH
            T
        AS
        (
            SELECT
                13
            FROM
                DUAL
        )
        SELECT
            T.*
        FROM
            T
    )
FROM
    DEPT
```

3. Table A has 5 rows and table B has 3 rows. The union contains 1 to 8 rows.

```
SELECT
    *
FROM
    TABLE(SYS.ODCINUMBERLIST(1,2,3,4,5))
UNION
SELECT
    *
FROM
    TABLE(SYS.ODCINUMBERLIST(6,7,8))
```

```
COLUMN_VALUE
------------
           1
           2
           3
           4
           5
           6
           7
           8
```

8 rows selected.

```
SELECT
    *
FROM
    TABLE(SYS.ODCINUMBERLIST(1,1,1,1,1))
UNION
SELECT
    *
FROM
    TABLE(SYS.ODCINUMBERLIST(1,1,1));
```

```
COLUMN_VALUE
------------
           1
```

1 row selected.

4. The following query returns the managers and president of each department. If there is no manager and no president, the name and jobs are set to NULL.

```
SELECT
    d.DNAME,
    e.ENAME,
    e.JOB
FROM
    EMP e
RIGHT JOIN
    DEPT d
ON
(
```

```
    e.DEPTNO=d.DEPTNO
    AND
    e.JOB IN ('MANAGER','PRESIDENT')
)
```

```
DNAME           ENAME       JOB
--------------- ----------- ---------
ACCOUNTING      CLARK       MANAGER
ACCOUNTING      KING        PRESIDENT
RESEARCH        JONES       MANAGER
SALES           BLAKE       MANAGER
OPERATIONS
```

It is not possible to use the (+) syntax with an IN predicate, therefore a subquery is required. For example:

```
SELECT
    d.DNAME,
    e.ENAME,
    e.JOB
FROM
    (
        SELECT
            e1.ENAME,
            e1.DEPTNO,
            e1.JOB
        FROM
            EMP e1
        WHERE
            e1.JOB IN ('MANAGER','PRESIDENT')
    ) e,
    DEPT d
WHERE
    e.DEPTNO (+)=d.DEPTNO
```

5. King earns $5000 a month. Case returns the first expression that fulfills the condition, and that is "1".

```
SELECT
    CASE
        WHEN
            SAL>2000
        THEN
            1
        WHEN
            SAL>4000
        THEN
            2
        WHEN
            SAL>6000
        THEN
            3
        ELSE
            4
    END as "N"
```

```
FROM
    EMP
WHERE
    ENAME='KING'
```

```
         N
----------
         1
```

6. TABLE transforms the collection into a table. Two rows are returned.

```
SELECT
    COLUMN_VALUE
FROM
    TABLE
    (
        SYS.ODCIDATELIST(DATE '2000-01-01',DATE '2000-01-31')
    )
```

```
COLUMN_VALU
-----------
01-JAN-2000
31-JAN-2000
```

Oracle SQL Functions   CHAPTER

2

Oracle SQL functions

Oracle has many SQL functions such as mathematic, binary, and modulo functions. This chapter will cover the basics of each function, note the improvements in 11g, and give examples.

Mathematic functions

Oracle contains numerous mathematic functions.

```
SELECT
    SIN(4),
    COS(4),
    TAN(4)
FROM
    DUAL;
```

```
SIN(4) COS(4) TAN(4)
------ ------ ------
-.7568 -.6536 1.1578
```

The sine, cosine and the tangent of an angle of four radians are returned. The functions can accept more than one datatype. For trigonometric functions, both BINARY_DOUBLE and NUMBER are supported. If the argument is BINARY_FLOAT, the expression is converted to double.

The mathematic functions perform much faster with BINARY_DOUBLE than with NUMBER.

```
SET TIMING ON
DECLARE
    X NUMBER := 1;
BEGIN
```

```
      FOR I IN 1 .. 1000000
      LOOP
         X := SIN(X);
      END LOOP;
END;
/

PL/SQL procedure successfully completed.

Elapsed: 00:00:25.58
SET TIMING ON
DECLARE
   X BINARY_DOUBLE := 1d;
BEGIN
   FOR I IN 1 .. 1000000
   LOOP
      X := SIN(X);
   END LOOP;
END;
/

PL/SQL procedure successfully completed.

Elapsed: 00:00:00.76
```

Binary functions

```
SELECT
   BITAND
   (
      BIN_TO_NUM(1,1,0,1),
      BIN_TO_NUM(1,0,1,1)
   )
FROM
   DUAL;
```

```
BITAND(BIN_TO_NUM(1,1,0,1),BIN_TO_NUM(1,0,1,1))
------------------------------------------------
                                               9
```

BIN_TO_NUM converts a list of 0 and 1 to an integer, as $(1,1,0,1)$ is $1*8+1*4+0*2+1$. BITAND selects the bits that are sets in both arguments, so 1101_2 & $1011_2 = 1001_2 = 9_{10}$.

Signs functions

```
SELECT
   SIGN(-10), SIGN(0), SIGN(+10),
   ABS(-10), ABS(0), ABS(-10)
FROM
   DUAL;
```

```
SIGN(-10)    SIGN(0)   SIGN(+10)   ABS(-10)     ABS(0)    ABS(-10)
---------- ---------- ---------- ---------- ---------- ----------
        -1          0          1         10          0         10
```

SIGN returns -1, 0 and 1 for a negative, zero and positive value. ABS returns the absolute value. Both functions accept NUMBER, BINARY_FLOAT and BINARY_DOUBLE.

Rounding and truncating functions

```
SELECT
    X.COLUMN_VALUE X,
    ROUND(X.COLUMN_VALUE)  "ROUND(X)",
    TRUNC(X.COLUMN_VALUE)  "TRUNC(X)",
    FLOOR(X.COLUMN_VALUE)  "FLOOR(X)",
    CEIL(X.COLUMN_VALUE)  "CEIL(X)"
FROM
    TABLE(SYS.ODCINUMBERLIST(-9.9,-1.1,-0.5,0.5,1.1,9.9)) X;
```

```
         X   ROUND(X)   TRUNC(X)   FLOOR(X)    CEIL(X)
---------- ---------- ---------- ---------- ----------
      -9.9        -10         -9        -10         -9
      -1.1         -1         -1         -2         -1
      -.5          -1          0         -1          0
       .5           1          0          0          1
       1.1          1          1          1          2
       9.9         10          9          9         10
```

TRUNC removes the decimal part for both negatives and positives. Therefore, TRUNC(-x) is equal to -TRUNC(x). ROUND returns the closest value and when both upper and lower values are equidistant, it rounds up to the higher positive value or the lower negative value, i.e. ROUND(-x)=-ROUND(x).

FLOOR(x) returns the highest integer that is not greater than x (the lower bound) and CEIL(x) returns the lowest integer that is not less than x (the upper bound).

ROUND and TRUNC accept a second argument to round or truncate at another decimal place than the default unit:

```
SELECT
    X.COLUMN_VALUE X,
    ROUND(X.COLUMN_VALUE, -2) "ROUND(X,-2)",
    TRUNC(X.COLUMN_VALUE, -2) "TRUNC(X,-2)",
```

```
   ROUND(X.COLUMN_VALUE, 0) "ROUND(X)",
   TRUNC(X.COLUMN_VALUE, 0) "TRUNC(X)",
   ROUND(X.COLUMN_VALUE, 2) "ROUND(X,2)",
   TRUNC(X.COLUMN_VALUE, 2) "TRUNC(X,2)",
FROM
   TABLE(SYS.ODCINUMBERLIST(1234.4321,-9876.6789)) X;
```

```
        X ROUND(X,-2) TRUNC(X,-2)   ROUND(X)   TRUNC(X) ROUND(X,2)
TRUNC(X,2)
---------- ----------- ----------- ---------- ---------- ---------- --------
--
1234.4321        1200        1200       1234       1234    1234.43 1234.43
-9876.6789      -9900       -9800      -9877      -9876   -9876.68 -
9876.67
```

The second argument is an integer that defines at which decimal place the rounding takes place, so ROUND(x, 2) will round to the hundredth.

ROUND and TRUNC also work for dates:

```
SELECT
   SYSDATE,
   ROUND(SYSDATE),
   TRUNC(SYSDATE)
FROM
   DUAL;
```

```
SYSDATE              ROUND(SYSDATE)       TRUNC(SYSDATE)
------------------- ------------------- -------------------
25.01.2008 21:08:26 26.01.2008 00:00:00 25.01.2008 00:00:00
```

Unfortunately, TIMESTAMP is cast to DATE when using TRUNC and ROUND.

TRUNC and ROUND accept a second argument to truncate or round to a specific period of time:

```
SELECT
   D.COLUMN_VALUE "D",
   FMT.COLUMN_VALUE "FMT",
   ROUND(D.COLUMN_VALUE, FMT.COLUMN_VALUE) "ROUND(D,FMT)",
   TRUNC(D.COLUMN_VALUE, FMT.COLUMN_VALUE) "TRUNC(D,FMT)"
FROM
   TABLE(SYS.ODCIDATELIST(TIMESTAMP '1994-08-18 12:30:30.00')) D,
   TABLE
   (
      SYS.ODCIVARCHAR2LIST
      (
         'MI', 'HH', 'DD', 'D', 'W', 'WW', 'IW', 'MM', 'Q', 'Y', 'IY', 'CC'
      )
```

```
   ) FMT;
```

```
D                    FMT ROUND(D,FMT)        TRUNC(D,FMT)
-------------------- --- -------------------- --------------------
18.08.1994 12:30:30  MI  18.08.1994 12:31:00  18.08.1994 12:30:00
18.08.1994 12:30:30  HH  18.08.1994 13:00:00  18.08.1994 12:00:00
18.08.1994 12:30:30  DD  19.08.1994 00:00:00  18.08.1994 00:00:00
18.08.1994 12:30:30  D   21.08.1994 00:00:00  14.08.1994 00:00:00
18.08.1994 12:30:30  W   22.08.1994 00:00:00  15.08.1994 00:00:00
18.08.1994 12:30:30  WW  20.08.1994 00:00:00  13.08.1994 00:00:00
18.08.1994 12:30:30  IW  22.08.1994 00:00:00  15.08.1994 00:00:00
18.08.1994 12:30:30  MM  01.09.1994 00:00:00  01.08.1994 00:00:00
18.08.1994 12:30:30  Q   01.10.1994 00:00:00  01.07.1994 00:00:00
18.08.1994 12:30:30  Y   01.01.1995 00:00:00  01.01.1994 00:00:00
18.08.1994 12:30:30  IY  02.01.1995 00:00:00  03.01.1994 00:00:00
18.08.1994 12:30:30  CC  01.01.2001 00:00:00  01.01.1901 00:00:00
```

MI truncates to the minute, HH to the hour, DD to the day, MM to the month, Q to the quarter, Y to the year and CC to the century. When rounding, MM rounds up from the 16th day and Q from the 16th day of the second month. IW is fairly useful as it truncates to Monday regardless of session parameters.

D is the first day of the week, which is Sunday when the territory is America. W is the week of the month and WW is the week of year.

```
SELECT
    DATE '2008-01-01',
    DATE '2008-02-01'
FROM
    DUAL;
```

```
DATE'2008-01-01'     DATE'2008-02-01'
-------------------- --------------------
Tuesday   01 January Friday    01 February
```

2008 starts on a Tuesday, February starts on a Friday and the territory is set to America:

```
SELECT
    TRUNC(DATE '2008-02-14','IW') IW,
    TRUNC(DATE '2008-02-14','W') W,
    TRUNC(DATE '2008-02-14','WW') WW,
    TRUNC(DATE '2008-02-14','D') D
FROM
    DUAL;
```

```
IW           W            WW          D
----------   ----------   ----------  ----------
Mon 11 Feb  Fri 8 Feb    Tue 12 Feb  Sun 10 Feb
```

IW truncates to Monday (always), W to Friday (1st day of month), WW to Tuesday (1st day of year) and D to Sunday (in America).

Rather than using TO_NUMBER(TO_CHAR(d, 'D')) to get the day of the week, it is possible to use TRUNC:

```
SELECT
    TRUNC(SYSDATE)-TRUNC(SYSDATE,'IW') "DAY"
FROM
    DUAL;
```

```
TRUNC(SYSDATE)-TRUNC(SYSDATE,'IW')
----------------------------------
                                 4
```

Monday is 0 and Sunday is 6. The main advantage of this method is that it can be used in materialized views, function-based indexes and session-independent views and procedures.

```
SELECT
    COLUMN_VALUE N,
    ROUND(COLUMN_VALUE*20)/20 "ROUND(N)"
FROM
    TABLE(SYS.ODCINUMBERLIST(1.12, 2.53, 5.25));
```

```
         N     ROUND(N)
----------   -------------
      1.12          1.10
      2.53          2.55
      5.25          5.25
```

The value is multiplied by 20 before rounding. The rounding is then done at a five-hundredths granularity.

```
SELECT
    COLUMN_VALUE D,
    DATE '2000-01-01'+
        TRUNC((COLUMN_VALUE - DATE '2000-01-01')*96)/96 "TRUNC(D)"
FROM
    TABLE(SYS.ODCIDATELIST(
        TIMESTAMP '2009-02-21 05:25:45',
        TIMESTAMP '2009-02-25 06:31:30'
    ));
```

```
D                     TRUNC(D)
------------------    ------------------
2009-02-21 05:25:45   2009-02-21 05:15:00
2009-02-25 06:31:30   2009-02-25 06:30:00
```

The difference with an arbitrary date is multiplied by 96 to split the day in 96 periods of 15 minutes (24 hours times 4 quarters = 96 periods).

Some periods could be switched to default calendar periods by adding a period before the TRUNC:

```
SELECT
   COLUMN_VALUE D,
   TO_CHAR(TRUNC(ADD_MONTHS(COLUMN_VALUE, 3), 'Y'), '"FY"YY') "FY"
FROM
   TABLE
   (
      SYS.ODCIDATELIST(
         DATE '2008-09-30',
         DATE '2008-12-21',
         DATE '2009-02-25'
      )
   );
```

```
D            FY
----------   ----
2008-09-30   FY08
2008-12-21   FY09
2009-02-25   FY09
```

The fiscal year starts in October, three months before the calendar year. This three-month period is added before truncating the date.

Modulo functions

```
SELECT
   X.COLUMN_VALUE X,
   Y.COLUMN_VALUE Y,
   MOD(X.COLUMN_VALUE, Y.COLUMN_VALUE) "MOD(X,Y)",
   REMAINDER(X.COLUMN_VALUE, Y.COLUMN_VALUE) "REMAINDER(X,Y)"
FROM
   TABLE(SYS.ODCINUMBERLIST(-30,-20,20,30)) X,
   TABLE(SYS.ODCINUMBERLIST(-7,7)) Y;
```

X	Y	MOD(X,Y)	REMAINDER(X,Y)
-30	-7	-2	-2
-30	7	-2	-2
-20	-7	-6	1
-20	7	-6	1
20	-7	6	-1
20	7	6	-1
30	-7	2	2
30	7	2	2

MOD and REMAINDER return the rest of the integer division. Here 30/7=4 remains 2. MOD truncates the quotient and REMAINDER rounds it. 20/7 is equal to 2.857. For MOD, 20/7=2 remains 6. For REMAINDER, 20/7=3 remains -1. For negative numbers, the sign of the first argument determines the sign of the modulo and the remainder.

```
SELECT
   MOD(5, 0)
FROM
   DUAL;
```

```
 MOD(5,0)
----------
        5
```

Another special case is modulo 0. In Perl or in C, modulo 0 is illegal. REMAINDER returns an error for modulo 0 but MOD returns the first argument.

Functions to search and modify strings

```
SELECT
   ENAME,
   SUBSTR(ENAME, 1, 2)
FROM
   EMP;
```

```
ENAME      SU
---------- --
SMITH      SM
ALLEN      AL
WARD       WA
JONES      JO
MARTIN     MA
BLAKE      BL
CLARK      CL
SCOTT      SC
KING       KI
TURNER     TU
```

```
ADAMS      AD
JAMES      JA
FORD       FO
MILLER     MI
```

SUBSTR returns a substring of the employee name, starting at position 1. The third parameter is the maximum length; by default, the rest of the string is returned.

```
SELECT
   INSTR
   (
      'Advanced Oracle SQL Programming',
      'ra',
      1,
      2
   ) RA
FROM
   DUAL;
```

```
        RA
----------
        25
```

INSTR returns the position of the second match of the string 'ra', starting at position 1.

SUBSTR and INSTR are often used together:

```
SELECT
   SUBSTR
   (
      COLUMN_VALUE,
      INSTR
      (
         COLUMN_VALUE,
         ' '
      )+1,
      INSTR
      (
         COLUMN_VALUE,
         ' ',
         1,
         2
      )-
      INSTR
      (
         COLUMN_VALUE,
         ' '
      )-1
   ) "WORD2"
```

```
FROM
   TABLE(SYS.ODCIVARCHAR2LIST('Advanced Oracle SQL Programming'));

WORD2
----------
Oracle
```

The second word is the substring starting right after the first space and for a length equal to the difference between the position of the first space and the position of the second space.

LENGTH returns the length of a string. LPAD and RPAD are left and right padding functions.

```
SELECT
   LPAD(DNAME, 20, '.') LEFT,
   RPAD(DNAME, 20, '.') RIGHT,
   RPAD(LPAD(DNAME, 10+LENGTH(DNAME)/2, '.'), 20, '.') MIDDLE
FROM
   DEPT;
```

```
LEFT                 RIGHT                MIDDLE
-------------------- -------------------- --------------------
..........ACCOUNTING ACCOUNTING.......... .....ACCOUNTING.....
............RESEARCH RESEARCH............ ......RESEARCH......
...............SALES SALES............... ........SALES.......
..........OPERATIONS OPERATIONS.......... .....OPERATIONS.....
```

By default, the padding character is a space. LPAD adds the character to the left and RPAD to the right. To get the center effect, the string is first padded to 10 + half of the length of the string, and then padded to 20.

To remove characters from the left and from the right, three functions are available - TRIM, LTRIM and RTRIM. By default, TRIM removes trailing and leading spaces.

```
SELECT
   ENAME,
   TRIM(LEADING 'S' FROM ENAME),
   TRIM(TRAILING 'S' FROM ENAME),
   TRIM(BOTH 'S' FROM ENAME)
FROM
   EMP
WHERE
   ENAME LIKE '%S%';
```

```
ENAME       TRIM(LEADI TRIM(TRAIL TRIM(BOTH'
---------- ---------- ---------- ----------
SMITH      MITH       SMITH      MITH
JONES      JONES      JONE       JONE
SCOTT      COTT       SCOTT      COTT
ADAMS      ADAMS      ADAM       ADAM
JAMES      JAMES      JAME       JAME
```

TRIM removes either spaces, by default, or any other single character from the string by taking them from either the left, the right or from both sides (default). The leading and trailing Ss are removed from the employee names:

```
SELECT
    ENAME,
    LTRIM(ENAME, 'BCDFGHJKLMNPQRSTVWXZ'),
    RTRIM(ENAME, 'BCDFGHJKLMNPQRSTVWXZ')
FROM
    EMP
WHERE
    ROWNUM<6;
```

```
ENAME       LTRIM(ENAM RTRIM(ENAM
---------- ---------- ----------
SMITH      ITH        SMI
ALLEN      ALLEN      ALLE
WARD       ARD        WA
JONES      ONES       JONE
MARTIN     ARTIN      MARTI
```

LTRIM and RTRIM remove either spaces, by default, or any other character from a character string from the left or from the right. The consonants left and right of the name are trimmed. Note that TRIM does not support the removal of more than one character while LTRIM and RTRIM support removing character from a list of character, i.e. a string:

```
SELECT
    *
FROM
    TABLE(SYS.ODCIVARCHAR2LIST('123','ABC456','789GHI','JKL'))
WHERE
    LTRIM(COLUMN_VALUE,'0123456789') IS NULL;
```

```
COL
---
123
```

> ⚠ For VARCHAR2 and CHAR, an empty string is null and has a length of NULL. For CLOB, the empty string is not null and has a length of 0.

The LTRIM functions returns an empty string where the string contains only digits.

TRANSLATE substitutes one character for another character and REPLACE substitutes a string for another string:

```
SELECT
    LOC,
    REPLACE(LOC,'YORK','ORLEANS'),
    TRANSLATE(LOC,'AOIEY ','@013 ')
FROM
    DEPT;
```

```
LOC             REPLACE(LOC,'YO  TRANSLATE(LOC
-------------   ---------------  -------------
NEW YORK        NEW ORLEANS      N3W0RK
DALLAS          DALLAS           D@LL@S
CHICAGO         CHICAGO          CH1C@G0
BOSTON          BOSTON           B0ST0N
```

The string 'YORK' is searched and replaced by the string 'ORLEANS'. When the last argument is omitted, the searched string is deleted from the original string.

TRANSLATE substitutes each 'A', 'O', 'E', 'T', 'Y' and ' ' with '@', '0', '3', '1', NULL and NULL, respectively. When the third argument is shorter than the second, the characters from the first string that have no correspondence are removed. The third argument is not optional and if it is NULL, TRANSLATE returns NULL.

UPPER, LOWER and INITCAP change the case of the string:

```
SELECT
    UPPER(COLUMN_VALUE),
    LOWER(COLUMN_VALUE),
    INITCAP(COLUMN_VALUE)
FROM
    TABLE(SYS.ODCIVARCHAR2LIST('JoHn sMiTh'));
```

```
UPPER(COLU LOWER(COLU INITCAP(CO
---------- ---------- ----------
JOHN SMITH john smith John Smith
```

UPPER returns everything in uppercase, LOWER in lowercase and INITCAP capitalizes the first letter of each word and sets the other letters to lowercase.

Regular expression functions

Oracle 10g introduced regular expression functions in SQL with the functions REGEXP_SUBSTR, REGEXP_REPLACE, REGEXP_INSTR and REGEXP_LIKE. Oracle 11g extends the set of available expressions with REGEXP_COUNT.

```
SELECT
    ENAME,
    REGEXP_SUBSTR(ENAME,'DAM') SUBSTR,
    REGEXP_INSTR(ENAME, 'T') INSTR,
    REGEXP_REPLACE(ENAME,'AM','@') REPLACE,
    REGEXP_COUNT(ENAME, 'A') COUNT
FROM
    EMP
WHERE
    REGEXP_LIKE(ENAME,'S');
```

```
ENAME      SUBSTR      INSTR REPLACE       COUNT
---------- ---------- ---------- ---------- ----------
SMITH                      4 SMITH             0
JONES                      0 JONES             0
SCOTT                      4 SCOTT             0
ADAMS      DAM             0 AD@S              2
JAMES                      0 J@ES              1
```

REGEXP_SUBSTR returns the substring DAM if found, REGEXP_INSTR returns the position of the first 'T', REGEXP_REPLACE replaces the strings 'AM' with '@' and REGEXP_COUNT counts the occurrences of 'A'. REGEXP_LIKE returns the strings that contain the pattern 'S'.

```
SELECT
    REGEXP_SUBSTR('Advanced Oracle SQL Programming','[[:alpha:]]+',1,2)
FROM
    DUAL;
```

```
REGEXP
------
Oracle
```

'[[:alpha:]]' is a POSIX regular expression that matches any letter. The second set of consecutive word characters is returned. The '+' specifies that the number of characters to be matched is one or more. '.' matches exactly one character; '.?' matches zero or one character; '.*' match zero, one or more character; '.+' matches one or more character; '.{3}' matches exactly three characters; '.{4,6}' matches 4, 5 or 6 characters; '.{7,}' matches 7 or more characters. The third argument is the starting position. The default 1 means the pattern will be searched from the beginning of the substring. The fourth argument in 11g represents the occurrence of the substring.

```
SELECT
   REGEXP_SUBSTR('Advanced Oracle SQL Programming','\w+',1,2)
FROM
   DUAL;
```

```
REGEXP
------
Oracle
```

Oracle 10gR2 introduced Perl-influenced regular expressions. '\w' represents any letter, number and the underscore. Unfortunately, in comparison to the old-style approach with INSTR and SUBSTR, the 10g regular expressions perform poorly.

```
SET TIMING ON
DECLARE
   X VARCHAR2(40);
BEGIN
   FOR I IN 1..10000000 LOOP
      X := 'Advanced Oracle SQL Programming';
      X := SUBSTR(X,
         INSTR(X, ' ')+1,
         INSTR(X, ' ', 1,2)-INSTR(X, ' ')-1);
   END LOOP;
END;
/
PL/SQL procedure successfully completed.

Elapsed: 00:00:20.40
SET TIMING ON
DECLARE
   X VARCHAR2(40);
```

```
BEGIN
   FOR I IN 1..10000000 LOOP
      X := 'Advanced Oracle SQL Programming';
      X := REGEXP_SUBSTR(X,'\w+',1,2);
   END LOOP;
END;
/
PL/SQL procedure successfully completed.

Elapsed: 00:02:10.82
```

REPLACE replaces all occurrence of a string. REGEXP_REPLACE has the same behavior by default, but when the fifth parameter, OCCURRENCE, is set to a value greater than zero, the substitution is not global.

```
SELECT
   REGEXP_REPLACE
   (
      'Advanced Oracle SQL Programming',
      '([[:alpha:]]+)[[:space:]]([[:alpha:]]+)',
      '\2: \1',
      1,
      1
   )
FROM
   DUAL;
```

```
REGEXP_REPLACE('ADVANCEDORACLESQ
--------------------------------
Oracle: Advanced SQL Programming
```

The search pattern contains a group of one or more alphabetic characters, followed by a space, then followed by a group of one or more alphabetic characters. This pattern is present more than once in the string, but only the first occurrence is affected. The replace pattern contains a reference to the second word, followed by a column and a space, followed by the first string.

```
SELECT
   REGEXP_SUBSTR
   (
      'Advanced Oracle SQL Programming',
      '(\w).*?\1',
      1,
      1,
      'i'
   )
FROM
```

```
    DUAL;
```

```
REGE
----
Adva
```

The search pattern contains any alphabetic character followed by a non-greedy number of characters followed by the same character as in the group. The search starts at the character one and looks for the first match of the pattern. The modifier 'i' indicates a case insensitive search. Non-greedy expressions appeared in 10gR2. The difference between a non-greedy expression like '.*?', '.+?', '.??', '.{2}?', '.{3,5}?' or '.{6,}?' and a greedy expression like '.*', '.+', '.?', '.{2}', '.{3,5}' or '.{6,}' is that the non-greedy searches for the smallest possible string and the greedy for the largest possible string.

```
SELECT
    REGEXP_SUBSTR
    (
        'Oracle',
        '.{2,4}?'
    ) NON_GREEDY,
    REGEXP_SUBSTR
    (
        'Oracle',
        '.{2,4}'
    ) GREEDY
FROM
    DUAL;
```

```
NON_GREEDY GREEDY
---------- ------
Or         Orac
```

Both patterns select from two to four characters. In this case, it could be 'Or', 'Ora' or 'Orac'. The non-greedy pattern returns two and the greedy four:

```
SELECT
    ENAME,
    REGEXP_SUBSTR(ENAME,'^K') "^K",
    REGEXP_SUBSTR(ENAME,'T$') "T$",
    REGEXP_SUBSTR(ENAME,'^[ABC]') "^[ABC]",
    REGEXP_SUBSTR(ENAME,'^.?M') "^.?M",
    REGEXP_SUBSTR(ENAME,'(RD|ES)$') "(RD|ES)$",
    REGEXP_SUBSTR(ENAME,'(..R){2}') "(..R){2}",
    REGEXP_SUBSTR(ENAME,'^.{4}[^A-E]') "^.{4}[^A-E]"
FROM
```

```
    EMP;
```

```
ENAME        ^K T$ ^[ABC] ^.?M (RD|ES)$ (..R){2} ^.{4}[^A-E
---------- -- -- ------ ---- -------- -------- ----------
SMITH                    SM                      SMITH
ALLEN           A                                ALLEN
WARD                          RD
JONES                    ES                      JONES
MARTIN               M                           MARTI
BLAKE           B
CLARK           C                                CLARK
SCOTT        T                                   SCOTT
KING      K
TURNER                                  TURNER
ADAMS           A                                ADAMS
JAMES                         ES                  JAMES
FORD                          RD
MILLER               M
```

The function REGEXP_SUBSTR matches ENAME to a pattern and
returns the matched string. The first pattern checks if the name starts
with 'K,' the second checks if it ends with 'T,' the third checks if it starts
with A, B or C, the fourth checks if the string start with one or zero
characters followed by M, which means the first or second character is a
'M,' the fifth checks if it ends with either ES or RD, the sixth checks if
the pattern "one character + one character + the letter R" is found twice
consecutively and the last pattern checks if the fifth character (the
character following 4 characters at the beginning of the string) is not in
the range A-E. Note that KING is not matched because the fifth
character is not a character different from A-E. To test a string less than
five characters, the pattern ^.{1,4}$ could be used.

Conversion functions

Implicit conversion exists between numeric, date-time and character
datatypes.

```
SELECT
    LENGTH(999),
    SINH('000'),
    LAST_DAY('01-FEB-2008')
FROM
    DUAL;
```

```
LENGTH(999) SINH('000') LAST_DAY(
----------- ----------- ---------
          3           0 29-FEB-08
```

The length function converts number 999 to a string, hyperbolic sine converts string '000' to a number and last day of month converts string '01-FEB-2008' to a date, providing the session NLS setting is appropriate (DD-MON-YYYY). Explicit conversion is preferred.

A number can be converted to a character and inversely:

```
SELECT
    CHR(65),
    ASCII('Z')
FROM
    DUAL;
```

```
C ASCII('Z')
- ----------
A         90
```

The CHR converts a number to an ASCII character and the inverse function ASCII converts a character to its corresponding ASCII value.

```
SELECT
    DUMP
    (
        HEXTORAW
        (
            '4F5241434C45'
        ),
        17
    ) DUMP,
    VSIZE
    (
        HEXTORAW
        (
            '4F5241434C45'
        )
    ) VSIZE
FROM
    DUAL;
```

```
DUMP                             VSIZE
-------------------------------- -----
Typ=23 Len=6: O,R,A,C,L,E           6
```

HEXTORAW converts a string that represents a hexadecimal number to raw data. HEXTORAW is useful when comparing a raw value from a table or a function to a literal. DUMP provides octal (8), decimal (10), hexadecimal (16) or character (17) dump.

The type 23 represents the RAW datatype. The length is 6 bytes. The function VSIZE also returns the length in bytes.

```
SELECT
    TO_NUMBER
    (
        RAWTOHEX
        (
            SYS_GUID()
        ),
        'XXXXXXXXXXXXXXXXXXXXXXXXXXXXXXXX'
    )
FROM
    DUAL;
```

```
TO_NUMBER(RAWTOHEX(SYS_GUID()),'XXXXXXXXXXXXXXXXXXXXXXXXXXXXXXXX')
-----------------------------------------------------------------
              94677074495605736132992199838641691196
```

The inverse function RAWTOHEX converts raw data to a string containing hexadecimals. SYS_GUID generates 32 bytes of raw data. The globally unique identifier is transformed to a hexadecimal string by RAWTOHEX and then to an integer by TO_NUMBER.

```
SELECT
    SYSDATE,
    EXTRACT(YEAR FROM SYSDATE) YYYY,
    EXTRACT(MONTH FROM SYSDATE) MM,
    EXTRACT(DAY FROM SYSDATE) DD
FROM
    DUAL;
```

```
SYSDATE      YYYY  MM  DD
----------   ----- --- ---
2008-02-08   2008   2   8
```

EXTRACT with a date returns numeric values for the year, the month or the day. It is not possible to extract the time out of the date datatype with this function.

```
SELECT
    CURRENT_TIMESTAMP,
    EXTRACT(HOUR FROM CURRENT_TIMESTAMP) HH,
    EXTRACT(MINUTE FROM CURRENT_TIMESTAMP) MI,
    EXTRACT(SECOND FROM CURRENT_TIMESTAMP) SS,
    EXTRACT(TIMEZONE_HOUR FROM CURRENT_TIMESTAMP) TZH,
    EXTRACT(TIMEZONE_MINUTE FROM CURRENT_TIMESTAMP) TZM,
    EXTRACT(TIMEZONE_REGION FROM CURRENT_TIMESTAMP) TZR,
    EXTRACT(TIMEZONE_ABBR FROM CURRENT_TIMESTAMP) TZA
```

```
FROM
    DUAL;
```

```
CURRENT_TIMESTAMP                      HH  MI          SS TZH TZM TZR          TZA
---------------------------------      ---  ---  ----------  ---  ---  -------------  ---
2008-02-08 13:25:13 EUROPE/ZURICH      12  25  13.103363    1    0  Europe/Zurich  CET
```

EXTRACT with a timestamp returns numeric values for the year, the month, the day and also the hour, the minute and the second. The second may contain fractions of a second. The hour and minute are extracted at GMT+00:00 and the offset, if applicable, is retrieved from the time zone. The region and abbreviation are returned as strings.

```
WITH T AS
(
    SELECT
        (CURRENT_TIMESTAMP - TIMESTAMP '1970-01-01 00:00:00 +00:00')
            YEAR(2) TO MONTH Y2M
    FROM
        DUAL
)
SELECT
    Y2M,
    EXTRACT(YEAR FROM Y2M) YYYY,
    EXTRACT(MONTH FROM Y2M) MM
FROM
    T;
```

```
Y2M       YYYY  MM
------    -----  ---
+38-01      38   1
```

EXTRACT with a year-to-month interval returns numeric values for the year or the month:

```
WITH T AS
(
    SELECT
        (CURRENT_TIMESTAMP - TIMESTAMP '1970-01-01 00:00:00 +00:00')
            DAY(6) TO SECOND(6) D2S
    FROM
        DUAL
)
SELECT
    D2S,
    86400*EXTRACT(DAY FROM D2S) +
    3600*EXTRACT(HOUR FROM D2S) +
    60*EXTRACT(MINUTE FROM D2S) +
    EXTRACT(SECOND FROM D2S)
        UNIXTIME
FROM
```

```
   T;
```

```
D2S                           UNIXTIME
--------------------- ------------------
+013917 12:25:13.247043   1202473513.247043
```

EXTRACT with a day-to-second interval returns numeric values for the day, hour, minute and second. The interval between January 1st, 1970 and the current time is used to calculate a number of seconds that represents the UNIX time.

```
SELECT
    (
        TIMESTAMP '1970-01-01 00:00:00 +00:00'+
        NUMTODSINTERVAL(1202473513.247043,'SECOND')
    ) AT TIME ZONE SESSIONTIMEZONE TIMESTAMP
FROM
    DUAL;
```

```
TIMESTAMP
----------------------------------------
2008-02-08 13:25:13.247043 Europe/Zurich
```

The function NUMTODSINTERVAL converts a number of DAY, HOUR, MINUTE or SECOND to a day-to-second interval. Adding a number of seconds to January 1st, 1970 is useful for converting UNIX timestamps to Oracle timestamps.

The function NUMTOYMINTERVAL returns an interval from a number of YEAR or MONTH:

```
SELECT
    TO_DSINTERVAL('+1 2:3:4.5') D2S_SQL,
    TO_DSINTERVAL('P1DT2H3M4.5S') D2S_ISO,
    TO_YMINTERVAL('1-2') Y2M_SQL,
    TO_YMINTERVAL('P1Y2M') Y2M_ISO
FROM
    DUAL;
```

```
D2S_SQL          D2S_ISO          Y2M_SQL Y2M_ISO
---------------- ---------------- ------- -------
+01 02:03:04.50  +01 02:03:04.50  +01-02  +01-02
```

TO_DSINTERVAL and TO_YMINTERVAL create an interval from a string. The string format cannot be changed. The two possible notations are listed. A large number of possible formats for dates and numbers exist.

```
SELECT
   TO_CHAR
   (
      CURRENT_TIMESTAMP,
      'FMDay ddth Month, YYYY B.C., FMHH:MI:SSXFF AM TZH:TZM'
   ) TODAY
FROM
   DUAL;
```

```
TODAY
----------------------------------------------------------------
Friday 1st February, 2008 A.D., 05:01:02.560225 PM +01:00
```

TO_CHAR converts a date or a timestamp to a string. Note the FM formatter: by default, words like Day or Month are padded. In English, the longest month is September, so all months will be right-padded with spaces to nine characters. The numeric values are left-padded with zero. FM provides a nicer output by removing extra spaces and leading zeroes. For hours, however, 05:01:02 looks better than 5:1:2. So the second FM formatting switches back to the default padding behavior. Note the capitalization of the format elements: Day returns Friday, DAY returns FRIDAY and day returns friday.

Also note the difference between HH and HH24. HH is often used together with AM to display the time in 12 hours format (from 1 to 12), and HH24 is the 24 hours format (from 0 to 23).

A fancy option to observe is the SP suffix, which spells the element. Unfortunately, it is not possible to choose a language other than English. The TH suffix is used for ordinal numbers.

```
SELECT
   TO_CHAR
   (
      TO_TIMESTAMP
      (
         TO_CHAR
         (
            42e-9
         ),
         '.FF9'
      ),
```

```
      'ff9sp ff9spth'
   ) "42"
FROM
   DUAL;
```

```
42
---------------------
forty-two forty-second
```

The number is expressed in nanoseconds (10⁻⁹ seconds) and spelled as a cardinal and an ordinal number.

The inverse functions TO_DATE, TO_TIMESTAMP and TO_TIMESTAMP_TZ convert a string to a date, a timestamp, and a timestamp with time zone:

```
SELECT
   TO_DATE('1-VIII-1291 AD','DD-RM-YYYY BC') "DATE",
   TO_TIMESTAMP('3000000 20000 100000000','J SSSSS FF') "TIMESTAMP",
   TO_TIMESTAMP_TZ('4 02','DD HH24') "TIMESTAMP_TZ"
FROM
   DUAL;
```

```
DATE       TIMESTAMP                     TIMESTAMP_TZ
---------- ----------------------------- -----------------------------
1291-08-01 3501-08-15 05:33:20.100000000 2008-02-04 02:00 EUROPE/ZURICH
```

RM is a Roman month from I to XII, J is the Julian day, where day 1 is January 1st, 4712 BC, day 60 is March 1st, 4712 BC. Day 1 is the first supported day of the Oracle Calendar and day 5373484 is the last supported day of the Oracle Calendar, December 31st, 9999 AD. SSSSS is the number of seconds since midnight (0-86399). FF is a fraction of seconds. It is not mandatory to specify all fields. The third expression returns the 4th of the current month, at 02:00:00.00 at session time zone.

```
SELECT
   TO_DATE('2 FEB. 08','DD-MONTH-RRRR') DD_MONTH_RR,
   TO_DATE('2-JAN-1994','DD/MM/YY') DD_MM_YY,
   TO_DATE('06-06-2007', 'FXDD-MM-YYYY') FXDD_MM_YYYY,
   TO_DATE('1/1/08','FXFMDD/MM/RR') FXFMDD_MM_RR
FROM
   DUAL;
```

```
DD_MONTH_RR DD_MM_YY   FXDD_MM_YY FXFMDD_MM_RR
----------- ---------- ---------- ------------
2008-02-02  1994-01-02 2007-06-06 2008-01-01
```

Oracle SQL functions

By default, Oracle tolerates fairly different formats such as the number of spaces, the characters used as separators and the leading zeroes. RR and YY accept two digits years, where "99" represents 1999 with the RR mask and 2099 with the YY mask. RR has been used to fix the year 2000 issues at the end of the 20th century. Until 2049, RR will return dates from 1950 to 2049. As of 2050, it will return dates from 2050 to 2149. FX is the strict format checker. The separator must be identical, the format of the day and month must include a leading zero when smaller than 10, and the year must be 4 characters long. It is a good practice to always enter the year with four digits, and using the default format DD-MON-RR is a not advisable as it introduces the year 2050 bug.

```
SELECT
   TO_DATE('19-APR-03') DATE_OF_BIRTH,
   TO_DATE('18-APR-68') DATE_OF_RETIREMENT,
   (TO_DATE('18-APR-68')-TO_DATE('19-APR-03')) YEAR TO MONTH
AGE_OF_RETIREMENT
FROM
   DUAL;
```

```
DATE_OF_B DATE_OF_R AGE_OF
--------- --------- ------
19-APR-03 18-APR-68 -35-00
```

The query above shows the date of birth and date of retirement and the difference between those. The age of -35 years is due to the missing century information, which is probably the next century issue after 2000.

TO_CHAR function is used with numbers for various formatting and calculation tasks:

```
SELECT
   TO_CHAR(COLUMN_VALUE,'FMS99,999.00$') "FMS99,999.00$",
   TO_CHAR(COLUMN_VALUE,'L9G990D00MI') "L9G990D00MI",
   TO_CHAR(COLUMN_VALUE,'FMXXXXXX') "FMXXXXXX",
   TO_CHAR(COLUMN_VALUE,'RM') "RM",
   TO_CHAR(COLUMN_VALUE,'0.99EEEE') "0.99999EEEE ",
   TO_CHAR(COLUMN_VALUE,'9999V99') "9999V99"
FROM
   TABLE(SYS.ODCINUMBERLIST(-1.234, 1899, 1234*5678));
```

FMS99,999.0	L9G990D00MI	FMXXXXX	RM	0.99999EEE	9999V99
-----------	------------	-------	----------	----------	-------
-$1.23	SFr.1.23-	######	##########	-1.23E+00	-123
+$1,899.00	SFr.1'899.00	76B	MDCCCXCIX	1.90E+03	189900
##########	############	6AE9BC	##########	7.01E+06	#######

By default, a number is left padded up to the maximum length. The maximum length of '99' is 3, as it may contain numbers from -99 to 99. The FM formatter removes the leading spaces. '$', ',' and '.' represent the dollar currency symbol, the comma thousand separator and the decimal point. 'L', 'G' and 'D' is the locale equivalency to '$', ',' and '.'. X is a hexadecimal digit from 0 to F. RM is the Roman representation of integers from 1 to 3999. Its maximum length of 15 is reached by MMMDCCCLXXXVIII. EEEE forces scientific notation. V is an invisible dot. Any number longer than the output pattern is returned as a chain of hashes.

The inverse functions are TO_NUMBER, TO_BINARY_FLOAT and TO_BINARY_DOUBLE:

```
SELECT
    TO_NUMBER('2008+','9999S') "9999S",
    TO_BINARY_FLOAT('Inf') "Inf",
    TO_BINARY_DOUBLE('9.876543E+210','9.999999EEEE') "9.99999EEEE"
FROM
    DUAL;
```

```
     9999S        Inf 9.99999EEEE
---------- ---------- -----------
      2008        Inf  9.877E+210
```

The S is a trailing positive or negative sign. Inf is the positive infinity when using BINARY_FLOAT or BINARY_DOUBLE. NaN is an undefined number (Not A Number), like SQRT(-1). Note the infinity symbol that represents the infinity for a number datatype is '~'. It is, however, not possible to convert a string to positive infinity with TO_NUMBER.

```
SELECT
    TO_CHAR(9.9999999999999999999999999999999999999e125)
FROM
    DUAL;
T
-
~
```

Numbers very close to 1E126 are displayed with '~'.

TO_CHAR, TO_DATE, TO_NUMBER, TO_BINARY_DOUBLE, TO_BINARY_FLOAT, TO_TIMESTAMP and TO_TIMESTAMP_TZ support a third parameter that overrides the default locale behavior.

```
SELECT
   TO_CHAR
   (
      -1E5/81,
      '9G999D99',
      'NLS_NUMERIC_CHARACTERS='','''''''
   ) "9G999D99",
   TO_NUMBER
   (
      '1,20SFr.',
      '999D99L',
      'NLS_CURRENCY=''SFr.'' NLS_NUMERIC_CHARACTERS='',.'''
   ) "999D99L",
   TO_CHAR
   (
      TO_DATE('AVRIL','MONTH','NLS_DATE_LANGUAGE=FRENCH'),
      'MONTH',
      'NLS_DATE_LANGUAGE=''LATIN UZBEK'''
   ) "MONTH"
FROM
   DUAL;
```

```
9G999D99    999D99L MONTH
---------  ---------- --------
-1'234,57      1.2 APREL
```

The formatting also depends on the territory; there is no NLS_DATE_TERRITORY yet, which means the setting must be changed at the session level. It is not possible to have two functions within the same statements using different territories.

```
SELECT
   TO_CHAR
   (
      SYSDATE,
      'DL'
   ) "DL",
   TO_CHAR
   (
      SYSDATE,
      'DAY=D'
   ) "D",
   VALUE "NLS_TERRITORY"
FROM
   NLS_SESSION_PARAMETERS
WHERE
```

```
    PARAMETER='NLS_TERRITORY';

DL                           D            NLS_TERRITORY
---------------------------- ----------- -------------
wednesday, 20 february 2008  WEDNESDAY=6 BANGLADESH
```

Many parameters, like currencies or numeric characters, are derived from NLS_TERRITORY when not explicitly set. Settings like 'DL' (long date, 10g), 'TS' (short time, 10g) or 'D' (day of week) depend on the territory.

It is possible to convert to large objects:

```
SELECT
    TO_BLOB
    (
        HEXTORAW
        (
            '42'
        )
    ) BLOB,
    TO_CLOB
    (
        '42'
    ) CLOB
FROM
    DUAL;
```

```
BLOB CLOB
---- ----
42   42
```

TO_BLOB converts raw data to blob and TO_CLOB converts character data to clob. Note that only the 11g SQL*Plus client can display blob.

The final conversion function is cast:

```
SELECT
    CAST
    (
        'Inf'
        AS
        BINARY_FLOAT
    ),
    CAST
    (
        BINARY_DOUBLE_NAN
        AS
        VARCHAR2(3)
    ),
    CAST
```

```
   (
      NULL
      AS
      NUMBER(6,2)
   )
FROM
   DUAL;
```

```
CAST('INF'ASBINARY_FLOAT) CAS CAST(NULLASNUMBER(6,2))
------------------------- --- ----------------------
                      Inf Nan <NULL>
```

CAST enables conversion from any type. It is useful in statements like
CREATE TABLE AS SELECT to specify the length and the datatype
of a column.

NLS functions

NLS_UPPER, NLS_LOWER and NLS_INITCAP use the setting
NLS_SORT to define what is the uppercase of a specific character.

```
SELECT
   NLS_UPPER
   (
      'Ich weiß es nicht',
      'NLS_SORT=XSWISS'
   ),
   NLS_INITCAP
   (
      'éléphant',
      'NLS_SORT=XFRENCH'
   )
FROM
   DUAL;
```

```
NLS_UPPER('ICHWEIß NLS_INIT
------------------ --------
ICH WEISZ ES NICHT Éléphant
```

The locale uppercase of a Swiss-German sentence and initial
capitalization of a French word are returned. It is possible to modify an
existing linguistic sort or add a new one using the Oracle Locale Builder
graphical tool:

```
SELECT
   *
FROM
   TABLE
```

```
    (
      SYS.ODCIVARCHAR2LIST
      (
        'privé',
        'priver',
        'privation'
      )
    )
ORDER BY
    NLSSORT(COLUMN_VALUE,'NLS_SORT=Xfrench');
```

```
COLUMN_VALUE
------------
privation
privé
priver
```

In French, the sort is accent insensitive:

```
CREATE INDEX
    ENAME_CI
ON
    EMP(NLSSORT(ENAME,'NLS_SORT=BINARY_CI'));
ALTER SESSION
SET
    NLS_COMP=LINGUISTIC
    NLS_SORT=BINARY_CI;
SELECT
    EMPNO,
    ENAME
FROM
    EMP
WHERE
    ENAME='Scott';
```

```
     EMPNO ENAME
---------- ----------
      7788 SCOTT
----------------------------------------------------------------------------
| Id  | Operation                   | Name     | Rows | Bytes | Cost (%CPU)| Time     |
----------------------------------------------------------------------------
|   0 | SELECT STATEMENT            |          |    1 |    37 |    2   (0)| 00:00:01 |
|   1 |  TABLE ACCESS BY INDEX ROWID| EMP      |    1 |    37 |    2   (0)| 00:00:01 |
|*  2 |   INDEX RANGE SCAN          | ENAME_CI |    1 |       |    1   (0)| 00:00:01 |
----------------------------------------------------------------------------

Predicate Information (identified by operation id):
---------------------------------------------------

   2 - access(NLSSORT("ENAME",'nls_sort=''BINARY_CI''')=HEXTORAW('73636F747400'))
```

The comparison is done linguistically and the sort is binary case insensitive (10g). The function-based index is scanned to find the appropriate rows that match the sorting pattern.

National character set

Unicode and multi-byte functions are available to do conversions and use different length semantics. As INSTR, LENGTH and SUBSTR work best with single-byte character sets, a multi-byte character may use bytes or char semantics.

```
SELECT
   LENGTHB(UNISTR('X')) LENGTHB,
   LENGTHC(UNISTR('X')) LENGTHC
FROM
   DUAL;
```

```
  LENGTHB    LENGTHC
---------- ----------
        2          1
```

UNISTR returns a Unicode string and is the inverse function of ASCIISTR. LENGTHB returns the length in bytes, where LENGTHC returns the length in characters. LENGTH2 and LENGTH4 are for fixed width character sets. LENGTH, INSTR and SUBSTR also have Unicode variations INSTRB, INSTRC, INSTR2, INSTR4 and SUBSTRB, SUBSTRC, SUBSTR2 and SUBSTR4.

```
SELECT
   CONVERT(UPPER('Chryséléphantin'),'US7ASCII')
FROM
   DUAL;
```

```
CONVERT(UPPER('
---------------
CHRYSELEPHANTIN
```

The string is converted to a non-accentuated string.

NCHR is similar to CHR, but it returns a national character (NCHAR). TO_CHAR and TO_NCHAR convert characters to and from the national character set. TO_NCLOB converts LOB or strings to Unicode large objects.

Logical functions with true or false values

There is no support for the Boolean datatype in Oracle; nevertheless, Oracle implements a few functions to perform logical operations.

```
SELECT
    ENAME,
    SAL,
    DECODE
    (
        GREATEST(SAL,2800),
        SAL,
        DECODE
        (
            JOB,
            'PRESIDENT',
            TO_NUMBER(NULL),
            1
        )
    ) DECODE,
    CASE
        WHEN SAL>=2800 AND JOB!='PRESIDENT'
        THEN 1
    END CASE
FROM
    EMP;
```

ENAME	SAL	DECODE	CASE
SMITH	800		
ALLEN	1600		
WARD	1250		
JONES	2975	1	1
MARTIN	1250		
BLAKE	2850	1	1
CLARK	2450		
SCOTT	3000	1	1
KING	5000		
TURNER	1500		
ADAMS	1100		
JAMES	950		
FORD	3000	1	1
MILLER	1300		

DECODE is checking for equivalency between the first and the second argument. GREATEST returns the greatest of its arguments and LEAST the smallest.

CASE is more powerful as it does check for any kind of comparison. As in the query above, CASE appears to be more readable. CASE is more of a SQL expression than a SQL function.

Nevertheless, CASE has an additional interesting property regarding indexing. The CASE SQL expression could be used in a function-based index; therefore, any condition could be indexed.

```
CREATE INDEX
    CLERK_OR_LOWSAL
ON
    EMP
    (
        CASE WHEN JOB='CLERK' OR SAL<1260 THEN 1 END
    );
SELECT
    ENAME,
    JOB,
    SAL
FROM
    EMP
WHERE
    CASE WHEN JOB='CLERK' OR SAL<1260 THEN 1 END = 1;
```

```
ENAME        JOB           SAL
---------- ---------- ----------
SMITH        CLERK         800
WARD         SALESMAN     1250
MARTIN       SALESMAN     1250
ADAMS        CLERK        1100
JAMES        CLERK         950
MILLER       CLERK        1300
```

```
-------------------------------------------------------------------------------------
| Id  | Operation                    | Name            | Rows  | Bytes | Cost (%CPU)| Time     |
-------------------------------------------------------------------------------------
|   0 | SELECT STATEMENT             |                 |     5 |   100 |     2   (0)| 00:00:01 |
|   1 |  TABLE ACCESS BY INDEX ROWID| EMP             |     5 |   100 |     2   (0)| 00:00:01 |
|*  2 |   INDEX RANGE SCAN           | CLERK_OR_LOWSAL |     5 |       |     1   (0)| 00:00:01 |
-------------------------------------------------------------------------------------

Predicate Information (identified by operation id):
---------------------------------------------------

   2 - access(CASE  WHEN ("JOB"='CLERK' OR "SAL"<1260) THEN 1 END =1)
```

The clerks and employees with a salary lower than 1260 are returned. The condition is integrated in a case statement and indexed.

Null functions

Null functions can translate NULL into a value and a value into NULL. Any type can contain NULL: number, dates, or strings.

```
WITH
    X
AS
(
    SELECT
        COLUMN_VALUE X
    FROM
        TABLE(SYS.ODCIVARCHAR2LIST('X',NULL))
),
    Y
AS
(
    SELECT
        COLUMN_VALUE Y
    FROM
        TABLE(SYS.ODCIVARCHAR2LIST('Y',NULL))
),
    Z
AS
(
    SELECT
        COLUMN_VALUE Z
    FROM
        TABLE(SYS.ODCIVARCHAR2LIST('Z',NULL))
)
SELECT
    X,
    Y,
    Z,
    NVL(X,Y),
    NVL2(X,Y,Z),
    COALESCE(X,Y,Z)
FROM
    X,Y,Z;
```

```
X       Y       Z       NVL(X,Y) NVL2(X,Y,Z) COALESCE(X,Y,Z)
------  ------  ------  -------- ----------- ----------------
X       Y       Z       X        Y           X
X       Y       <NULL>  X        Y           X
X       <NULL>  Z       X        <NULL>      X
X       <NULL>  <NULL>  X        <NULL>      X
<NULL>  Y       Z       Y        Z           Y
<NULL>  Y       <NULL>  Y        <NULL>      Y
<NULL>  <NULL>  Z       <NULL>   Z           Z
<NULL>  <NULL>  <NULL>  <NULL>   <NULL>      <NULL>
```

NVL returns Y when X is null and X when X is not null. NVL2 returns Y when X is not null and Z when X is null. COALESCE returns the first non-null expression.

```
SELECT
    ENAME,
    COMM,
    NULLIF(COMM,0)
FROM
    EMP
WHERE
    DEPTNO=30;
```

```
ENAME            COMM NULLIF(COMM,0)
---------- ---------- --------------
ALLEN             300            300
WARD              500            500
MARTIN           1400           1400
BLAKE          <NULL>         <NULL>
TURNER              0         <NULL>
JAMES          <NULL>         <NULL>
```

NULLIF returns NULL if both arguments are equal; otherwise, it returns the first argument.

```
SELECT
    ENAME,
    SAL,
    COMM
FROM
    EMP
WHERE
    SAL<=1550
    AND
    LNNVL(COMM!=0);
```

```
ENAME             SAL       COMM
---------- ---------- ----------
SMITH             800 <NULL>
TURNER           1500          0
ADAMS            1100 <NULL>
JAMES             950 <NULL>
MILLER           1300 <NULL>
```

LNNVL is a function that returns TRUE when the condition passed as parameter is either FALSE or NULL.

Conclusion

This chapter covered many SQL functions available in Oracle. They included mathematic, binary, and modulo functions. A brief description of each function was provided as well as examples of use. This chapter also noted where Oracle 11g introduced improvements to various functions. The next chapter gets into Aggregate functions in SQL.

Exercises

1. Binary

   What is the result of the following expression?

   ```
   1024 + 1025 - 2 * BITAND(1024, 1025)
   ```

2. Sign

   Prior to Oracle 8i, developers were often coding expressions like:

   ```
   DECODE(SIGN(X - Y), 1, ...)
   ```

   What is the DECODE expression checking?

3. Formatting

   Which string is returned by the following expressions?

   ```
   TO_CHAR(SYSDATE, 'CCYY')
   ```

   And:

   ```
   TO_CHAR(
       1E5,
       'L999G990D00',
       'NLS_CURRENCY=''NPR ''NLS_NUMERIC_CHARACTERS='.'''''''
   )
   ```

4. Searching

   What is the position returned by the following expression?

   ```
   INSTR('MISSISSIPI', 'I', -1, 2)
   ```

5. Regular expression

   Which expression matches integers from 0 to 1000?

   ```
   '^(10{3}|\d{1,3}?)$'
   ```

   Or:

```
'(^1000$|^[[:digit:]][[:digit:]]?[[:digit:]]?$)'
```

Or:

```
'^(10{3}|[0-9]{0,2}[0123456789])$'
```

6. Nulls

When is the following condition true?

```
WHERE NVL2(X,NULLIF(X,Y),Y) IS NULL
```

Solutions

1. Binary

   ```
   1024 + 1025 - 2 * BITAND(1024, 1025)
   ```

   1, A+B-(A AND B)-(A AND B) is equivalent to (A XOR B)

2. Sign

   ```
   DECODE(SIGN(X - Y), 1, ...)
   ```

   Decode is checking if X>Y. Prior to 8i, there is no CASE SQL expression.

3. Formatting

   ```
   TO_CHAR(SYSDATE, 'CCYY')
   ```

   2108, CC is the century, current century is 21st :

   ```
   TO_CHAR(
       1E5,
       'L999G990D00',
       'NLS_CURRENCY=''NPR ''NLS_NUMERIC_CHARACTERS=''.'''''''
   )

   NPR 100'000.00
   ```

   L is the local currency, defined as 'NPR ', the dot is '.' and the group separator is a single quote.

4. Searching

   ```
   INSTR('MISSISSIPI', 'I', -1, 2)
   ```

   8, the second 'I' starting from the right is in the eighth position, counting from the left.

5. Regular expression

   Which expression matches integers from 0 to 1000?

   ```
   '^(10{3}|\d{1,3}?)$'
   ```

Or:

```
'(^1000$|^[[:digit:]][[:digit:]]?[[:digit:]]?$)'
```

Or:

```
'^(10{3}|[0-9]{0,2}[0123456789])$'
```

All three expressions matches integer from 0 to 1000.

6. Nulls

When is the following condition true?

```
WHERE NVL2(X,NULLIF(X,Y),Y) IS NULL
```

The condition is equivalent to:

```
WHERE X=Y OR (X IS NULL AND Y IS NULL)
```

SQL Aggregate Functions

Aggregate functions

An aggregate function in SQL is a function that returns a single value from multiple rows.

Standard Aggregate Functions

An aggregate function can be used over the whole table to return a single value:

```
SELECT
    COUNT(ENAME)
FROM
    EMP;
```

```
COUNT(ENAME)
------------
          14
```

```
-----------------------------------------------------------------
| Id  | Operation          | Name | Rows  | Bytes | Cost (%CPU)| Time     |
-----------------------------------------------------------------
|   0 | SELECT STATEMENT   |      |     1 |     6 |     3   (0)| 00:00:01 |
|   1 |  SORT AGGREGATE    |      |     1 |     6 |            |          |
|   2 |   TABLE ACCESS FULL| EMP  |    14 |    84 |     3   (0)| 00:00:01 |
-----------------------------------------------------------------
```

The number of employees in the EMP table is returned.

```
SELECT
    DEPTNO,
    SUM(SAL)
FROM
    EMP
GROUP BY
    DEPTNO;
```

```
    DEPTNO    SUM(SAL)
---------- ----------
        30        9400
        20       10875
        10        8750
```

```
---------------------------------------------------------------------
| Id | Operation          | Name | Rows | Bytes | Cost (%CPU)| Time     |
---------------------------------------------------------------------
|  0 | SELECT STATEMENT   |      |    3 |    21 |    4  (25)| 00:00:01 |
|  1 |  HASH GROUP BY     |      |    3 |    21 |    4  (25)| 00:00:01 |
|  2 |   TABLE ACCESS FULL| EMP  |   14 |    98 |    3   (0)| 00:00:01 |
---------------------------------------------------------------------
```

The group is the department. Note the operation HASH GROUP BY in the execution plan. This operation appeared in 10gR2 and requires no sorting.

```
---------------------------------------------------------------------
| Id | Operation          | Name | Rows | Bytes | Cost (%CPU)| Time     |
---------------------------------------------------------------------
|  0 | SELECT STATEMENT   |      |    3 |    21 |    4  (25)| 00:00:01 |
|  1 |  SORT GROUP BY     |      |    3 |    21 |    4  (25)| 00:00:01 |
|  2 |   TABLE ACCESS FULL| EMP  |   14 |    98 |    3   (0)| 00:00:01 |
---------------------------------------------------------------------
```

In earlier releases, the operation to group the rows was a SORT GROUP BY operation and it implied sorting. This optimization affected applications that rely on implicit sorting. In 10gR2 and later, sorting is achieved by using the ORDER BY clause.

Multiple aggregate functions can be used in the same query. For example, the maximum and the minimum salary can be returned as a single row:

```
SELECT
   MIN(SAL),
   MAX(SAL)
FROM
   EMP;
```

```
  MIN(SAL)   MAX(SAL)
---------- ----------
       800       5000
       801
```

```
--------------------------------------------------------------------
| Id  | Operation          | Name | Rows  | Bytes | Cost (%CPU)| Time     |
--------------------------------------------------------------------
|   0 | SELECT STATEMENT   |      |     1 |     4 |     3   (0)| 00:00:01 |
|   1 |  SORT AGGREGATE    |      |     1 |     4 |            |          |
|   2 |   TABLE ACCESS FULL| EMP  |    14 |    56 |     3   (0)| 00:00:01 |
--------------------------------------------------------------------
```

Both values are returned. The function AVG computes the average:

```
SELECT
    COUNT(*),
    COUNT(COMM),
    SUM(COMM),
    AVG(COMM)
FROM
    EMP;
```

```
  COUNT(*) COUNT(COMM)  SUM(COMM)  AVG(COMM)
---------- ----------- ---------- ----------
        14           4       2200        550
```

Notice the null values are ignored; only the not null values are taken to evaluate the average. Null values are never aggregated.

> 🔔 COUNT(*) is the best way to count the rows; not even COUNT(1) performs faster.

COUNT(*) is a special syntax that instructs Oracle to count all rows including nulls.

STATS_MODE is a very efficient function that returns the mode value for a column, i.e. the value that appears most frequently.

```
SELECT
    STATS_MODE(DEPTNO)
FROM
    EMP;
```

```
STATS_MODE(DEPTNO)
------------------
                30
```

The department with the most employees is returned. The function is not deterministic. In case of a tie, the chosen modal value may differ from one execution to another.

Distinct

When counting rows, the DISTINCT keyword can be used to count only distinct, i.e. unique rows.

```
SELECT
    COUNT(
        DISTINCT
        JOB
    )
FROM
    EMP;
```

```
COUNT(DISTINCTJOB)
------------------
                 5
```

The number of different jobs in the employee table is retrieved. Not all functions support this keyword.

COUNT DISTINCT does not support multiple columns. However, there is a way of achieving the effect of such a query. If the concatenated size of all columns is small, it is possible to concatenate and select the distinct strings:

```
SELECT
    COUNT(
        DISTINCT
        CONCAT
        (
            DUMP(JOB,16),
            DUMP(DEPTNO,16)
        )
    ) DISTINCTJOBDEPTNO
FROM
    EMP;
```

```
DISTINCTJOBDEPTNO
-----------------
                9
```

```
-------------------------------------------------------------------
| Id | Operation        | Name | Rows | Bytes | Cost (%CPU)| Time     |
-------------------------------------------------------------------
|  0 | SELECT STATEMENT |      |    1 |    11 |     3   (0)| 00:00:01 |
|  1 |  SORT GROUP BY   |      |    1 |    11 |            |          |
|  2 |   TABLE ACCESS FULL| EMP |   14 |   154 |     3   (0)| 00:00:01 |
-------------------------------------------------------------------
```

Another approach is to count all rows from a subquery using DISTINCT:

```
SELECT
    COUNT(*)
FROM
(
    SELECT
        DISTINCT
        JOB,
        DEPTNO
    FROM
        EMP
);
```

```
DISTINCTJOBDEPTNO
-----------------
                9
```

```
-------------------------------------------------------------------
| Id | Operation        | Name | Rows | Bytes | Cost (%CPU)| Time     |
-------------------------------------------------------------------
|  0 | SELECT STATEMENT |      |    1 |       |     4  (25)| 00:00:01 |
|  1 |  SORT AGGREGATE  |      |    1 |       |            |          |
|  2 |   VIEW           |      |   11 |       |     4  (25)| 00:00:01 |
|  3 |    HASH UNIQUE   |      |   11 |   121 |     4  (25)| 00:00:01 |
|  4 |     TABLE ACCESS FULL| EMP |   14 |   154 |     3   (0)| 00:00:01 |
-------------------------------------------------------------------
```

The first query concatenates the representation of the different columns in an unambiguous string. The second query selects distinct values of jobs and departments and counts the rows retrieved in the inner query. Note that COUNT(DISTINCT JOB) does not count the nulls.

Keep

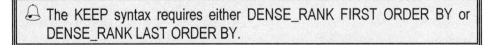

The KEEP syntax requires either DENSE_RANK FIRST ORDER BY or DENSE_RANK LAST ORDER BY.

It is possible to aggregate only the top or bottom rows using KEEP.

```
SELECT
   MIN(DEPTNO),
   SUM(SAL)
      KEEP
      (
         DENSE_RANK
            FIRST
         ORDER BY
            DEPTNO
      ) SUMDEPTNO
FROM
   EMP;
```

```
MIN(DEPTNO)  SUMDEPTNO
-----------  ----------
         10        8750
```

Before the SUM function is applied, the rows are sorted by department number and only the salaries of the first department are passed in the aggregate function. The result is the total salary of department 10.

A common query is to select the employee with the highest salary. The Oracle 8i approach is to use a nested subquery:

```
SELECT
   ENAME,
   DEPTNO,
   SAL
FROM
   EMP
WHERE
   SAL=
   (
      SELECT
         MAX(SAL)
      FROM
         EMP
   );
```

```
ENAME           DEPTNO        SAL
----------   ----------   ----------
KING              10         5000
```

```
----------------------------------------------------------------------
| Id  | Operation          | Name | Rows | Bytes | Cost (%CPU)| Time     |
----------------------------------------------------------------------
|  0  | SELECT STATEMENT   |      |   1  |   13  |    6   (0)| 00:00:01 |
|* 1  | TABLE ACCESS FULL  | EMP  |   1  |   13  |    3   (0)| 00:00:01 |
|  2  |   SORT AGGREGATE   |      |   1  |    4  |           |          |
|  3  |    TABLE ACCESS FULL| EMP |  14  |   56  |    3   (0)| 00:00:01 |
----------------------------------------------------------------------

Predicate Information (identified by operation id):
---------------------------------------------------

   1 - filter("SAL"= (SELECT MAX("SAL") FROM "EMP" "EMP"))
```

To retrieve the name of the best paid employee, the table is accessed twice, once to retrieve the maximum salary and once to retrieve the matching name and department. If there is a tie for the top salary, all rows are returned.

A more efficient approach is to use the KEEP keyword:

```
SELECT
    MAX(ENAME)
        KEEP
        (
            DENSE_RANK
                FIRST
            ORDER BY
                SAL DESC,
                EMPNO
        ) ENAME,
    MAX(DEPTNO)
        KEEP
        (
            DENSE_RANK
                FIRST
            ORDER BY
                SAL DESC,
                EMPNO
        ) DEPTNO,
    MAX(SAL) SAL
FROM
    EMP;
```

```
ENAME           DEPTNO      SAL
----------   ----------  ----------
KING               10      5000


-----------------------------------------------------------------
| Id  | Operation         | Name | Rows  | Bytes | Cost (%CPU)| Time     |
-----------------------------------------------------------------
|   0 | SELECT STATEMENT  |      |     1 |    17 |    3   (0)| 00:00:01 |
|   1 |  SORT AGGREGATE   |      |     1 |    17 |           |          |
|   2 |   TABLE ACCESS FULL| EMP |    14 |   238 |    3   (0)| 00:00:01 |
-----------------------------------------------------------------
```

The maximum salary is returned. The department and employee name for the highest salary are also returned. This time, the table is accessed only once. In case of a tie for the top salary, the one with the lowest employee number is returned. This way, only one row is returned to the aggregate function and this unique row is consistent because EMPNO is the primary key and uniquely identifies the row.

Consider the following query:

```
INSERT INTO
   EMP
   (
      EMPNO,
      ENAME,
      DEPTNO,
      SAL
   )
VALUES
(
   1001,
   'KATE',
   40,
   5000
);
SELECT
   MAX(ENAME)
      KEEP
      (
         DENSE_RANK
            FIRST
         ORDER BY
            SAL DESC
      ) ENAME,
   MAX(DEPTNO)
      KEEP
      (
         DENSE_RANK
            FIRST
         ORDER BY
            SAL DESC
      ) DEPTNO,
   MAX(SAL) SAL
```

```
FROM
    EMP;
```

```
ENAME             DEPTNO        SAL
----------    ----------    ----------
KING                  40       5000
ROLLBACK;
```

For the first rows in descending order of salaries, Kate and King are passed to the aggregate functions. The MAX functions return the highest name (KING) and the highest department (40); they do not belong to the same row.

Nested Aggregates

Aggregate functions can be nested:

```
SELECT
    AVG(
        MAX(SAL)
    )
FROM
    EMP
GROUP BY
    DEPTNO;
```

```
AVG(MAX(SAL))
-------------
  3616.66667
```

```
-----------------------------------------------------------------
| Id | Operation          | Name | Rows | Bytes | Cost (%CPU)| Time     |
-----------------------------------------------------------------
|  0 | SELECT STATEMENT   |      |    1 |    7 |    4  (25)| 00:00:01 |
|  1 |  SORT AGGREGATE    |      |    1 |    7 |    4  (25)| 00:00:01 |
|  2 |   SORT GROUP BY    |      |    1 |    7 |    4  (25)| 00:00:01 |
|  3 |    TABLE ACCESS FULL| EMP |   14 |   98 |    3   (0)| 00:00:01 |
-----------------------------------------------------------------
```

The average of the maximum salary of each department is returned. A query containing a nested aggregation requires one group by clause and returns one row.

Subtotals

The CUBE, ROLLUP and GROUPING SETS functions are used in the GROUP BY clause to generate totals and subtotals.

```
SELECT
    DEPTNO,
    SUM(SAL)
FROM
    EMP
GROUP BY
    ROLLUP(DEPTNO);
```

```
    DEPTNO    SUM(SAL)
---------- ----------
        10        8750
        20       10875
        30        9400
                 29025
```

Id	Operation	Name	Rows	Bytes	Cost (%CPU)	Time
0	SELECT STATEMENT		3	21	4 (25)	00:00:01
1	SORT GROUP BY ROLLUP		3	21	4 (25)	00:00:01
2	TABLE ACCESS FULL	EMP	14	98	3 (0)	00:00:01

The sum of salaries is aggregated per department, and then an additional row containing the total of all employees' salaries is returned.

The ROLLUP has generated the following rows:

- One for each group
- One for the department
- One for the total of all groups

ROLLUP can have more than one dimension, generating grand totals and subtotals:

```
SELECT
    DEPTNO,
    JOB,
    SUM(SAL)
FROM
    EMP
GROUP BY
    ROLLUP(DEPTNO,JOB);
```

```
    DEPTNO JOB           SUM(SAL)
-------- --------- ----------
        10 CLERK            1300
        10 MANAGER          2450
        10 PRESIDENT        5000
        10                  8750
        20 CLERK            1900
        20 ANALYST          6000
```

```
20  MANAGER            2975
20                    10875
30  CLERK              950
30  MANAGER           2850
30  SALESMAN          5600
30                    9400
                     29025
```

The sum generates a grand total, a subtotal per department and a sub-subtotal per department and job.

It also possible to mix ROLLUP groups with normal groups in the GROUP BY clause:

```
SELECT
    DEPTNO,
    JOB,
    SUM(SAL)
FROM
    EMP
GROUP BY
    DEPTNO, ROLLUP(JOB);
```

```
  DEPTNO JOB          SUM(SAL)
-------- --------- ----------
      10 CLERK           1300
      10 MANAGER         2450
      10 PRESIDENT       5000
      10                 8750
      20 CLERK           1900
      20 ANALYST         6000
      20 MANAGER         2975
      20                10875
      30 CLERK            950
      30 MANAGER         2850
      30 SALESMAN        5600
      30                 9400
```

A subtotal per department and a sub-subtotal per department and job are returned. As DEPTNO is a standard GROUP BY expression, there is no grand total.

```
SELECT
    MAX(ENAME)
    KEEP
    (
      DENSE_RANK
          FIRST
      ORDER BY
          SAL DESC
    ) ENAME,
```

```
      DEPTNO,
      JOB,
      MAX(SAL) SAL
FROM
      EMP
GROUP BY
      CUBE(DEPTNO,JOB);
```

```
ENAME        DEPTNO JOB              SAL
---------- ---------- ---------- ----------
KING                               5000
MILLER              CLERK          1300
SCOTT               ANALYST        3000
JONES               MANAGER        2975
ALLEN               SALESMAN       1600
KING                PRESIDENT      5000
KING             10                5000
MILLER           10 CLERK          1300
CLARK            10 MANAGER        2450
KING             10 PRESIDENT      5000
SCOTT            20                3000
ADAMS            20 CLERK          1100
SCOTT            20 ANALYST        3000
JONES            20 MANAGER        2975
BLAKE            30                2850
JAMES            30 CLERK           950
BLAKE            30 MANAGER        2850
ALLEN            30 SALESMAN       1600
```

```
----------------------------------------------------------------------------
| Id | Operation          | Name | Rows | Bytes | Cost (%CPU)| Time     |
----------------------------------------------------------------------------
|  0 | SELECT STATEMENT   |      |   11 |  231  |   4   (25)| 00:00:01 |
|  1 |  SORT GROUP BY     |      |   11 |  231  |   4   (25)| 00:00:01 |
|  2 |   GENERATE CUBE    |      |   11 |  231  |   4   (25)| 00:00:01 |
|  3 |    SORT GROUP BY   |      |   11 |  231  |   4   (25)| 00:00:01 |
|  4 |     TABLE ACCESS FULL| EMP |   14 |  294  |   3    (0)| 00:00:01 |
----------------------------------------------------------------------------
```

CUBE generates nine rows for the various job/departments, three rows for the subtotal per department, three rows for the subtotal per job and one row for the grand total. For each job and department, the maximum salary is returned, and for this salary, the name of the corresponding employee is returned. In case of duplicates, the MAX function is applied to the name.

With this result set, a superaggregation is performed for each dimension, the department, the job, and the overall. In addition to the rows that are aggregated by ROLLUP, CUBE also produces a row for each job.

GROUPING SETS simplifies the management of the subtotals:

```
SELECT
    DEPTNO,
    JOB,
    MIN(SAL)
FROM
    EMP
GROUP BY
    GROUPING SETS
    (
       (JOB),
       (DEPTNO)
    );
```

```
    DEPTNO JOB         MIN(SAL)
---------- --------- ----------
           ANALYST        3000
           CLERK           800
           MANAGER        2450
           PRESIDENT      5000
           SALESMAN       1250
        10                1300
        20                 800
        30                 950
```

GROUPING SETS is a subset of CUBE. The minimum salary in each job and the minimum salary in each department are returned.

Compare with:

```
SELECT
    CASE
       WHEN GROUPING_ID(JOB, DEPTNO)=1
       THEN 'Count per job'
       WHEN GROUPING_ID(JOB, DEPTNO)=2
       THEN 'Count per department'
    END " ",
    CASE
       WHEN GROUPING(JOB)=0
       THEN JOB
       ELSE '========'
    END JOB,
    CASE
       WHEN GROUPING(DEPTNO)=0
       THEN TO_CHAR(DEPTNO,'99999')
       ELSE '======'
    END DEPTNO,
    COUNT(*)
FROM
    EMP
GROUP BY
    CUBE(JOB, DEPTNO)
HAVING
    GROUPING_ID (JOB, DEPTNO) in (0,1,2);
```

```
                        JOB        DEPTNO   COUNT(*)
--------------------    ---------  ------   ----------
                        CLERK          10            1
                        CLERK          20            2
                        CLERK          30            1
                        ANALYST        20            2
                        MANAGER        10            1
                        MANAGER        20            1
                        MANAGER        30            1
                        SALESMAN       30            4
                        PRESIDENT      10            1
Count per job          CLERK      ======            4
Count per job          ANALYST    ======            2
Count per job          MANAGER    ======            3
Count per job          SALESMAN   ======            4
Count per job          PRESIDENT  ======            1
Count per department ========        10            3
Count per department ========        20            5
Count per department ========        30            6
```

CUBE generates counts in every possible dimension including overall counts. The HAVING clause evaluates the GROUPING_ID function. When no superaggregation occurs, it gets the value of 0; when the first argument group is a subtotal, it gets 1 (2^0); when the second is a subtotal, it gets 2 (2^1). If it is a grand total for both the first and the second arguments, it gets 3 (2^0+2^1). Only the 0, 1 and 2 grouping ids are returned. GROUPING returns 1 when the column is summarized and otherwise, 0.

There is one more function related to grouping that is called GROUP_ID that is useful when there are duplicate subtotals:

```
SELECT
   CASE
      WHEN GROUPING(ENAME)=0
      THEN NULL
      WHEN GROUP_ID()=0
      THEN 'SUM'
      WHEN GROUP_ID()=1
      THEN 'AVG'
   END TYPE,
   ENAME,
   DEPTNO,
   CASE
      WHEN GROUPING(ENAME)=0
      THEN NULL
      WHEN GROUP_ID()=0
      THEN SUM(SAL)
      WHEN GROUP_ID()=1
      THEN AVG(SAL)
   END VALUE
```

```
FROM
    EMP
GROUP BY
    GROUPING SETS
    (
        (ENAME,DEPTNO),
        (DEPTNO),
        (DEPTNO),
        (),
        ()
    )
    DEPTNO,
    ENAME,
    GROUP_ID();
```

```
TYP ENAME          DEPTNO      VALUE
--- ----------  ---------- ----------
    CLARK           10
    KING            10
    MILLER          10
SUM                 10       8750
AVG                 10 2916.66667
    ADAMS           20
    FORD            20
    JONES           20
    SCOTT           20
    SMITH           20
SUM                 20      10875
AVG                 20       2175
    ALLEN           30
    BLAKE           30
    JAMES           30
    MARTIN          30
    TURNER          30
    WARD            30
SUM                 30       9400
AVG                 30 1566.66667
SUM                         29025
AVG                    2073.21429
```

For each department and for the whole table, one total and one average are evaluated.

PIVOT and UNPIVOT

The function PIVOT transposes rows in columns and the function UNPIVOT transposes columns in rows. They have been added in 11g.

```
WITH
    T
AS
(
    SELECT
```

```
          DEPTNO
   FROM
          EMP
)
SELECT
   *
FROM
   T
PIVOT
(
   COUNT(*)
   FOR
      (DEPTNO)
   IN
      (10,20,30,40)
);
```

```
        10          20          30          40
---------- ---------- ---------- ----------
         3           5           6           0
```

```
-------------------------------------------------------------------------------
| Id  | Operation          | Name | Rows | Bytes | Cost (%CPU)| Time     |
-------------------------------------------------------------------------------
|  0  | SELECT STATEMENT   |      |    1 |    52 |    3   (0)| 00:00:01 |
|  1  |  VIEW              |      |    1 |    52 |    3   (0)| 00:00:01 |
|  2  |   SORT AGGREGATE   |      |    1 |     3 |           |          |
|  3  |    TABLE ACCESS FULL| EMP |   14 |    42 |    3   (0)| 00:00:01 |
-------------------------------------------------------------------------------
```

Four columns are created for the departments 10, 20, 30 and 40. For each column, the number of corresponding rows is counted.

Compare with:

```
SELECT
   DEPTNO,
   COUNT(*)
FROM
   EMP
GROUP BY
   DEPTNO;
```

```
    DEPTNO   COUNT(*)
---------- ----------
        30          6
        20          5
        10          3
```

In the first statement, one row is returned with all departments. In the second statement each department is on a different row. The columns that are not aggregated and not pivoted will return multiple rows:

Aggregate functions

```
WITH
    T
AS
(
    SELECT
        DEPTNO,
        JOB,
        SAL
    FROM
        EMP
)
SELECT
    *
FROM
    T
PIVOT
(
    MIN(SAL) AS MINSAL,
    MAX(SAL) AS MAXSAL
FOR
    (JOB)
IN
    (
        'CLERK' AS CLERK,
        'SALESMAN' AS SALES
    )
)
ORDER BY
    DEPTNO;
```

```
    DEPTNO CLERK_MINSAL CLERK_MAXSAL SALES_MINSAL SALES_MAXSAL
---------- ------------ ------------ ------------ ------------
        10         1300         1300
        20          800         1100
        30          950          950         1250         1600
```

Three rows are selected. The job is the pivot, the salaries are aggregated and the departments are returned as distinct rows. Note the different values for the pivot are explicitly listed.

The inline view T contains three columns, the salary is aggregated, the job is transposed into multiple columns, and the remaining column is used as a group for the aggregation. The remaining column is the department, which contains three distinct values; each value returns exactly one row. To specify the group by the department, it is therefore necessary to select only the department in addition to the aggregated values and to the transposed column.

UNPIVOT does the opposite operation. The columns are converted into rows:

```
SELECT
    EMPNO,
    ENAME,
    PROPERTY,
    VALUE
FROM
    EMP
UNPIVOT
EXCLUDE NULLS
(
    VALUE
    FOR
        PROPERTY
    IN
    (
        SAL,
        COMM
    )
)
WHERE
    DEPTNO=30;
```

```
   EMPNO ENAME      PROP      VALUE
---------- ---------- ---- ----------
     7499 ALLEN      SAL        1600
     7499 ALLEN      COMM        300
     7521 WARD       SAL        1250
     7521 WARD       COMM        500
     7654 MARTIN     SAL        1250
     7654 MARTIN     COMM       1400
     7698 BLAKE      SAL        2850
     7844 TURNER     SAL        1500
     7844 TURNER     COMM          0
     7900 JAMES      SAL         950
```

```
-----------------------------------------------------------------------
| Id  | Operation         | Name | Rows | Bytes | Cost (%CPU)| Time     |
-----------------------------------------------------------------------
|   0 | SELECT STATEMENT  |      |   10 |   500 |    6   (0) | 00:00:01 |
|*  1 |  VIEW             |      |   10 |   500 |    6   (0) | 00:00:01 |
|   2 |   UNPIVOT         |      |      |       |            |          |
|*  3 |    TABLE ACCESS FULL| EMP |    5 |    95 |    3   (0) | 00:00:01 |
-----------------------------------------------------------------------

Predicate Information (identified by operation id):
---------------------------------------------------

   1 - filter("unpivot_view"."VALUE" IS NOT NULL)
   3 - filter("EMP"."DEPTNO"=30)
```

For each employee in department 30, two rows are returned - one for the salary and one for the commission. The EXCLUDE NULLS clause (default) does not return rows with a salary or a commission that is null. INCLUDE NULLS includes null values.

A possible usage of UNPIVOT is to display one row in a vertical format:

```
WITH
      T
AS
(
   SELECT
      TO_CHAR(EMPNO) EMPNO,
      ENAME,
      JOB,
      TO_CHAR(MGR) MGR,
      TO_CHAR(HIREDATE) HIREDATE,
      TO_CHAR(SAL) SAL,
      TO_CHAR(COMM) COMM,
      TO_CHAR(DEPTNO) DEPTNO
   FROM
      EMP
   WHERE
      EMPNO=7788
)
SELECT
   *
FROM
   T
UNPIVOT
INCLUDE NULLS
(
   VALUE
   FOR
      COL
   IN
   (
      EMPNO,
      ENAME,
      JOB,
      MGR,
      HIREDATE,
      SAL,
      COMM,
      DEPTNO
   )
);
```

```
COL       VALUE
--------  ---------
EMPNO     7788
ENAME     SCOTT
JOB       ANALYST
MGR       7566
HIREDATE  19-APR-87
SAL       3000
COMM
DEPTNO    20
```

Each column is converted to characters and transposed as a row.

Conclusion

This chapter covered aggregate functions, which are functions that return a single value from multiple rows. Various keywords such as DISTINCT, COUNT DISTINCT and KEEP can be used to count rows in different ways. There are also other aggregate functions like CUBE, ROLLUP, and GROUPING SETS that generate subtotals and totals. PIVOT and UNPIVOT are aggregate functions that deal with the transposing of rows and columns and have been added in 11g.

Exercises

1. Counting

   What is the difference between the following queries?

   ```
   SELECT COUNT(*) FROM T;
   ```

   And:

   ```
   SELECT COUNT(*) FROM T GROUP BY 1;
   ```

   And:

   ```
   SELECT SUM(1) FROM T;
   ```

2. Group

   Which group by clause is expected in the following query?

```
SELECT EXTRACT(YEAR FROM HIREDATE), COUNT(*) FROM EMP GROUP BY
```

3. Keep

Rewrite the following query without using a subquery (consider HIREDATE to be unique).

```
SELECT DEPTNO, ENAME FROM EMP
WHERE
    (DEPTNO, HIREDATE) IN (SELECT DEPTNO,MIN(HIREDATE) FROM EMP GROUP BY
DEPTNO)
```

4. Nested aggregates

What is missing in the following query?

```
SELECT MAX(AVG(SAL)) FROM EMP
```

5. Subtotals

How many rows will be returned by the following query?

```
WITH T AS (SELECT 1 NUM, 'RED' COL, 'EMPTY' SHADE, 'CIRCLE' SYMBOL FROM
DUAL
UNION ALL SELECT 3, 'BLUE', 'FULL', 'SQUARE' FROM DUAL)
SELECT T.*, COUNT(*) FROM T GROUP BY CUBE(NUM, COL, SHADE, SYMBOL)
```

6. Pivot

Rewrite the following query using the pivot operator.

```
SELECT
    DEPTNO,
    COUNT(CASE WHEN SAL BETWEEN 0 AND 999 THEN 1 END) "0-999",
    COUNT(CASE WHEN SAL BETWEEN 1000 AND 1999 THEN 1 END) "1000-1999",
    COUNT(CASE WHEN SAL BETWEEN 2000 AND 2999 THEN 1 END) "2000-2999",
    COUNT(CASE WHEN SAL BETWEEN 3000 AND 3999 THEN 1 END) "3000-3999"
FROM EMP
GROUP BY DEPTNO
```

7. Unpivot

What is the result of the following query?

```
SELECT MAX(ROWNUM) FROM DUAL UNPIVOT(X FOR Y IN (DUMMY,DUMMY,DUMMY))
```

Solutions

1. Counting

```
SELECT COUNT(*) FROM T;
```

```
SELECT COUNT(*) FROM T GROUP BY 1;
```

```
SELECT SUM(1) FROM T;
```

The three queries above are very similar and will count the rows in the tables. The first query returns the number of rows in the table T. the expected result may be 0, 1, 14 or any positive number.

The second query groups the rows in a group and for this group, returns the number of rows. If there is no row, there will be no group and therefore, no rows will be returned.

In the third query, the value 1 is attributed to each row and the sum is the number of the rows. When no row exists, no value will be attributed and therefore, SUM will return NULL.

```
CREATE TABLE
    T
(
    X NUMBER
);
Table created.
SELECT COUNT(*) FROM T;
  COUNT(*)
----------
         0
SELECT COUNT(*) FROM T GROUP BY 1;
no rows selected
SELECT SUM(1) FROM T;
    SUM(1)
----------
<NULL>
```

2. Group

```
SELECT EXTRACT(YEAR FROM HIREDATE), COUNT(*) FROM EMP GROUP BY
```

It is syntaxically correct to group by the hire date. To group by the year, the extract function is used as a group:

```
SELECT
   EXTRACT(YEAR FROM HIREDATE),
   COUNT(*)
FROM
   EMP
GROUP BY
   HIREDATE;
```
```
EXTRACT(YEARFROMHIREDATE)    COUNT(*)
-------------------------    ----------
                     1980           1
                     1981           2
                     1981           1
                     1981           1
                     1981           1
                     1981           1
                     1981           1
                     1981           1
                     1981           1
                     1981           1
                     1982           1
                     1987           1
                     1987           1
```

```
SELECT
   EXTRACT(YEAR FROM HIREDATE),
   COUNT(*)
FROM
   EMP
GROUP BY
   EXTRACT(YEAR FROM HIREDATE;
```
```
EXTRACT(YEARFROMHIREDATE)    COUNT(*)
-------------------------    ----------
                     1980           1
                     1981          10
                     1982           1
                     1987           2
```

The second query returns the expected results.

3. Keep

```
SELECT DEPTNO, ENAME FROM EMP
WHERE
   (DEPTNO, HIREDATE) IN (SELECT DEPTNO,MIN(HIREDATE) FROM EMP GROUP BY
DEPTNO)
```

The first employee of each department of EMP can be retrieved by using the KEEP clause.

```
SELECT
    DEPTNO,
    MAX(ENAME) KEEP (DENSE_RANK FIRST ORDER BY HIREDATE)
FROM
    EMP
GROUP BY
    DEPTNO;
DEPTNO MAX(ENAME)
------ ----------
    10 CLARK
    20 SMITH
    30 ALLEN
```

4. Nested aggregates

```
SELECT MAX(AVG(SAL)) FROM EMP
SELECT MAX(AVG(SAL)) FROM EMP
            *
ERROR at line 1:
ORA-00978: nested group function without GROUP BY
```

Nested aggregate requires a GROUP BY clause.

5. Superaggregation

```
WITH T AS (SELECT 1 NUM, 'RED' COL, 'EMPTY' SHADE, 'CIRCLE' SYMBOL FROM
DUAL
UNION ALL SELECT 3, 'BLUE', 'FULL', 'SQUARE' FROM DUAL)
SELECT T.*, COUNT(*) FROM T GROUP BY CUBE(NUM, COL, SHADE, SYMBOL)
```

With four columns and one row, there are 16 rows (2^4): the group itself, 14 subtotals and the grand total. With two distinct rows with all values that are distinct, there are 16*2 rows, minus one, because the grand total is aggregating the two distinct rows in one. Therefore, 31 rows are selected.

NUM	COL	SHADE	SYMBOL	COUNT(*)
				2
			CIRCLE	1
			SQUARE	1
		FULL		1
		FULL	SQUARE	1
		EMPTY		1
		EMPTY	CIRCLE	1
	RED			1
	RED		CIRCLE	1
	RED	EMPTY		1
	RED	EMPTY	CIRCLE	1
	BLUE			1
	BLUE		SQUARE	1
	BLUE	FULL		1

```
   BLUE FULL  SQUARE          1
 1                            1
 1            CIRCLE          1
 1      EMPTY                 1
 1      EMPTY CIRCLE          1
 1 RED                        1
 1 RED        CIRCLE          1
 1 RED  EMPTY                 1
 1 RED  EMPTY CIRCLE          1
 3                            1
 3            SQUARE          1
 3      FULL                  1
 3      FULL  SQUARE          1
 3 BLUE                       1
 3 BLUE       SQUARE          1
 3 BLUE FULL                  1
 3 BLUE FULL  SQUARE          1
```

31 rows selected.

6. Pivot

```
SELECT
   DEPTNO,
   COUNT(CASE WHEN SAL BETWEEN 0 AND 999 THEN 1 END) "0-999",
   COUNT(CASE WHEN SAL BETWEEN 1000 AND 1999 THEN 1 END) "1000-1999",
   COUNT(CASE WHEN SAL BETWEEN 2000 AND 2999 THEN 1 END) "2000-2999",
   COUNT(CASE WHEN SAL BETWEEN 3000 AND 3999 THEN 1 END) "3000-3999"
FROM EMP
GROUP BY DEPTNO
```

The pivot aggregate function is COUNT and the transposed column is the salary:

```
SELECT
   *
FROM
(
   SELECT
      DEPTNO,
      TRUNC(SAL,-3) SAL
   FROM
      EMP
)
PIVOT
(
   COUNT(*)
   FOR
      (SAL)
   IN
      (0,1000,2000,3000)
);
```

```
DEPTNO              0      1000      2000      3000
---------- ---------- ---------- ---------- ----------
        30          1         4         1         0
        20          1         1         1         2
        10          0         1         1         0
```

7. Unpivot

```
SELECT MAX(ROWNUM) FROM DUAL UNPIVOT(X FOR Y IN (DUMMY,DUMMY,DUMMY))
```

For each column DUMMY, DUMMY and DUMMY, a row is generated and the highest ROWNUM is 3.

Oracle SQL Analytics

Analytics

An analytic function is calculated over multiple rows and returns the result in the current row. The multiple row function could be an aggregate function, like COUNT, or a pure analytic function like RANK.

OVER

The scope of an analytic function is defined in an OVER clause. OVER is a mandatory keyword for all analytic functions. Giving (), as the parameter to OVER, indicates the widest possible scope - "all". In the example below, the total number of departments over the whole table is counted.

```
SELECT
    DEPTNO,
    COUNT(*) OVER () "NUMBER OF DEPARTMENTS"
FROM
    DEPT;
```

```
    DEPTNO COUNT(*)OVER()
---------- --------------
        10              4
        20              4
        30              4
        40              4
```

The total count of departments is returned next to each department. Note the COUNT function is used here without the GROUP BY clause. It is possible to use the KEEP clause to retrieve additional columns.

```
SELECT
    ENAME,
```

```
   SAL,
   MIN(ENAME) KEEP (DENSE_RANK FIRST ORDER BY SAL) OVER (),
   MIN(SAL) OVER ()
FROM
   EMP;
```

```
ENAME            SAL MIN(ENAME) MIN(SAL)OVER()
---------- ---------- ---------- --------------
SMITH            800 SMITH                  800
ALLEN           1600 SMITH                  800
WARD            1250 SMITH                  800
JONES           2975 SMITH                  800
MARTIN          1250 SMITH                  800
BLAKE           2850 SMITH                  800
CLARK           2450 SMITH                  800
SCOTT           3000 SMITH                  800
KING            5000 SMITH                  800
TURNER          1500 SMITH                  800
ADAMS           1100 SMITH                  800
JAMES            950 SMITH                  800
FORD            3000 SMITH                  800
MILLER          1300 SMITH                  800
```

The name and salary of the employee with the lowest salary is returned.

PARTITION

As the aggregate functions use GROUP BY to group rows, analytic functions use PARTITION BY.

```
SELECT
   ENAME,
   SAL,
   DEPTNO,
   MAX(SAL) OVER (PARTITION BY DEPTNO) MAX_SAL_DEPTNO,
   JOB,
   MAX(SAL) OVER (PARTITION BY JOB) MAX_SAL_JOB
FROM
   EMP;
```

```
ENAME            SAL     DEPTNO MAX_SAL_DEPTNO JOB        MAX_SAL_JOB
---------- ---------- ---------- -------------- ---------- -----------
MILLER          1300         10           5000 CLERK             1300
KING            5000         10           5000 PRESIDENT         5000
CLARK           2450         10           5000 MANAGER           2975
SMITH            800         20           3000 CLERK             1300
SCOTT           3000         20           3000 ANALYST           3000
ADAMS           1100         20           3000 CLERK             1300
FORD            3000         20           3000 ANALYST           3000
JONES           2975         20           3000 MANAGER           2975
WARD            1250         30           2850 SALESMAN          1600
MARTIN          1250         30           2850 SALESMAN          1600
TURNER          1500         30           2850 SALESMAN          1600
```

```
ALLEN                1600        30        2850 SALESMAN     1600
JAMES                 950        30        2850 CLERK        1300
BLAKE                2850        30        2850 MANAGER       2975
```

Miller is the clerk of department 10. In his department, the best paid employee has a salary of 5000. Over all clerks, his salary of 1300 is the highest. The PARTITION BY reduces the scope to the current partition.

Ranking functions

The ranking family of functions use ORDER BY in the analytic clause to enumerate the rows or to retrieve previous or next rows.

```
SELECT
    ENAME,
    HIREDATE,
    ROW_NUMBER() OVER (ORDER BY HIREDATE) ROW_NUMBER,
    LAG(ENAME) OVER (ORDER BY HIREDATE) LAG,
    LEAD(ENAME) OVER (ORDER BY HIREDATE) LEAD
FROM
    EMP
ORDER BY
    HIREDATE;
```

```
ENAME       HIREDATE  ROW_NUMBER LAG         LEAD
----------  --------- ---------- ----------  ----------
SMITH       17-DEC-80          1             ALLEN
ALLEN       20-FEB-81          2 SMITH       WARD
WARD        22-FEB-81          3 ALLEN       JONES
JONES       02-APR-81          4 WARD        BLAKE
BLAKE       01-MAY-81          5 JONES       CLARK
CLARK       09-JUN-81          6 BLAKE       TURNER
TURNER      08-SEP-81          7 CLARK       MARTIN
MARTIN      28-SEP-81          8 TURNER      KING
KING        17-NOV-81          9 MARTIN      JAMES
JAMES       03-DEC-81         10 KING        FORD
FORD        03-DEC-81         11 JAMES       MILLER
MILLER      23-JAN-82         12 FORD        SCOTT
SCOTT       19-APR-87         13 MILLER      ADAMS
ADAMS       23-MAY-87         14 SCOTT
```

ROW_NUMBER returns a row number in the specified order. LAG returns the previous row and LEAD returns the next row. The LAG and LEAD functions are not deterministic; for James and Ford, the hire date is the same but the function returns different results which may differ from one execution to another.

RANK and DENSE_RANK are deterministic.

```
SELECT
    ENAME,
    HIREDATE,
    ROW_NUMBER() OVER (ORDER BY HIREDATE) ROW_NUMBER,
    RANK() OVER (ORDER BY HIREDATE) RANK,
    DENSE_RANK() OVER (ORDER BY HIREDATE) DENSE_RANK
FROM
    EMP
ORDER BY
    HIREDATE;
```

ENAME	HIREDATE	ROW_NUMBER	RANK	DENSE_RANK
SMITH	17-DEC-80	1	1	1
ALLEN	20-FEB-81	2	2	2
WARD	22-FEB-81	3	3	3
JONES	02-APR-81	4	4	4
BLAKE	01-MAY-81	5	5	5
CLARK	09-JUN-81	6	6	6
TURNER	08-SEP-81	7	7	7
MARTIN	28-SEP-81	8	8	8
KING	17-NOV-81	9	9	9
JAMES	03-DEC-81	10	10	10
FORD	03-DEC-81	11	10	10
MILLER	23-JAN-82	12	12	11
SCOTT	19-APR-87	13	13	12
ADAMS	23-MAY-87	14	14	13

ROW_NUMBER always returns distinct numbers for duplicates. Both RANK and DENSE_RANK return duplicate numbers for employees with the same hire date. The difference between them is DENSE_RANK and it does not skip numbers.

ROW_NUMBER, DENSE_RANK and RANK have different effects. Because the differences between them are quite subtle, the specification of the query must be very precise so the right one can be used.

```
SELECT
    DEPTNO,
    ENAME,
    SAL
FROM
(
    SELECT
        DEPTNO,
        ENAME,
        SAL,
        ROW_NUMBER() OVER (PARTITION BY DEPTNO ORDER BY SAL DESC) R
    FROM
```

```
      EMP
)
WHERE
   R<=3
ORDER BY
   DEPTNO,
   R;
```

```
   DEPTNO ENAME             SAL
---------- ---------- ----------
       10 KING             5000
       10 CLARK            2450
       10 MILLER           1300
       20 SCOTT            3000
       20 FORD             3000
       20 JONES            2975
       30 BLAKE            2850
       30 ALLEN            1600
       30 TURNER           1500
```

 An analytic function cannot be used in the WHERE clause, only in the SELECT or in the ORDER BY clause.

By default, LEAD and LAG return the previous and next rows. The second argument allows retrieving the nth previous and n^{th} next rows. The third argument defines a default value.

```
SELECT
   ENAME,
   SAL,
   LAG(SAL,1,0) OVER (ORDER BY SAL) LAG1,
   LAG(SAL,2,0) OVER (ORDER BY SAL) LAG2,
   LAG(SAL,3,0) OVER (ORDER BY SAL) LAG3
FROM
   EMP
ORDER BY
   SAL;
```

```
ENAME             SAL       LAG1       LAG2       LAG3
---------- ---------- ---------- ---------- ----------
SMITH             800          0          0          0
JAMES             950        800          0          0
ADAMS            1100        950        800          0
WARD             1250       1100        950        800
MARTIN           1250       1250       1100        950
MILLER           1300       1250       1250       1100
TURNER           1500       1300       1250       1250
ALLEN            1600       1500       1300       1250
CLARK            2450       1600       1500       1300
BLAKE            2850       2450       1600       1500
JONES            2975       2850       2450       1600
SCOTT            3000       2975       2850       2450
```

FORD	3000	3000	2975	2850
KING	5000	3000	3000	2975

The values of the last three rows are returned. Non-existing values default to 0.

Window

The partition clause is not the only method of limiting the scope of an analytic function. When using a ROWS BETWEEN clause, rows are ordered and a window is defined.

```
SELECT
    ENAME,
    HIREDATE,
    SAL,
    MAX
    (
        SAL
    )
    OVER
    (
        ORDER BY
            HIREDATE,
            ENAME
        ROWS BETWEEN
            UNBOUNDED PRECEDING
            AND
            1 PRECEDING
    ) MAX_BEFORE,
    MAX
    (
        SAL
    )
    OVER
    (
        ORDER BY
            HIREDATE,
            ENAME
        ROWS BETWEEN
            1 FOLLOWING
            AND
            UNBOUNDED FOLLOWING
    ) MAX_AFTER
FROM
    EMP
ORDER BY
    HIREDATE,
    ENAME;
```

```
ENAME       HIREDATE         SAL MAX_BEFORE  MAX_AFTER
----------  ---------  ----------  ----------  ----------
SMITH       17-DEC-80        800                    5000
ALLEN       20-FEB-81       1600         800         5000
WARD        22-FEB-81       1250        1600         5000
JONES       02-APR-81       2975        1600         5000
BLAKE       01-MAY-81       2850        2975         5000
CLARK       09-JUN-81       2450        2975         5000
TURNER      08-SEP-81       1500        2975         5000
MARTIN      28-SEP-81       1250        2975         5000
KING        17-NOV-81       5000        2975         3000
FORD        03-DEC-81       3000        5000         3000
JAMES       03-DEC-81        950        5000         3000
MILLER      23-JAN-82       1300        5000         3000
SCOTT       19-APR-87       3000        5000         1100
ADAMS       23-MAY-87       1100        5000
```

On each row, the highest salary before the current row and the highest salary after are returned. The ORDER BY clause is not used here for ranking but for specifying a window.

Summing with ORDER BY produces cumulative totals.

```
SELECT
    ENAME,
    SAL,
    SUM(SAL) OVER (ORDER BY ENAME ROWS UNBOUNDED PRECEDING) CUMSUM
FROM
    EMP;
```

```
ENAME            SAL     CUMSUM
----------  ----------  ----------
ADAMS           1100        1100
ALLEN           1600        2700
BLAKE           2850        5550
CLARK           2450        8000
FORD            3000       11000
JAMES            950       11950
JONES           2975       14925
KING            5000       19925
MARTIN          1250       21175
MILLER          1300       22475
SCOTT           3000       25475
SMITH            800       26275
TURNER          1500       27775
WARD            1250       29025
```

The lowest possible bound is UNBOUNDED PRECEDING (the first row), the current row is CURRENT ROW and the highest possible row is UNBOUNDED FOLLOWING (the last row).

Rows preceding and following the current row are retrieved with *n* PRECEDING and *n* FOLLOWING where *n* is the relative position to the current row.

When not specifying BETWEEN, the window implicitly ends at the CURRENT ROW.

```
SELECT
    ENAME,
    SAL,
    AVG(SAL) OVER (ORDER BY SAL ROWS 1 PRECEDING) AVG
FROM
    EMP;
```

```
ENAME           SAL         AVG
---------- ---------- ----------
SMITH           800         800
JAMES           950         875
ADAMS          1100        1025
WARD           1250        1175
MARTIN         1250        1250
MILLER         1300        1275
TURNER         1500        1400
ALLEN          1600        1550
CLARK          2450        2025
BLAKE          2850        2650
JONES          2975      2912.5
SCOTT          3000      2987.5
FORD           3000        3000
KING           5000        4000
```

The average is calculated for rows between the previous and the current row. The windows start at the position immediately preceding the current row and the current row.

RANGE is similar to ROWS but the intervals are not a number of rows. They are either numeric or date values.

```
SELECT
    ENAME,
    SAL,
    SAL*.9 LOW,
    SAL*1.1 HIGH,
    COUNT(*)
        OVER
        (
            ORDER BY
                SAL
            RANGE BETWEEN
```

```
          SAL*.1 PRECEDING
          AND
          SAL*.1 FOLLOWING
     ) COUNT
FROM
   EMP;
```

ENAME	SAL	LOW	HIGH	COUNT
SMITH	800	720	880	1
JAMES	950	855	1045	1
ADAMS	1100	990	1210	1
WARD	1250	1125	1375	3
MARTIN	1250	1125	1375	3
MILLER	1300	1170	1430	3
TURNER	1500	1350	1650	2
ALLEN	1600	1440	1760	2
CLARK	2450	2205	2695	1
BLAKE	2850	2565	3135	4
JONES	2975	2677.5	3272.5	4
SCOTT	3000	2700	3300	4
FORD	3000	2700	3300	4
KING	5000	4500	5500	1

The sort key is the salary. The count of employees with the same salary, +/- 10%, is evaluated.

When using RANGE, the result is deterministic. If two rows get the same value, they are both either included or excluded from the window.

```
SELECT
   ENAME,
   SAL,
   SUM(SAL) OVER (ORDER BY SAL ROWS UNBOUNDED PRECEDING) SUMROWS,
   SUM(SAL) OVER (ORDER BY SAL RANGE UNBOUNDED PRECEDING) SUMRANGE
FROM
   EMP;
```

ENAME	SAL	SUMROWS	SUMRANGE
SMITH	800	800	800
JAMES	950	1750	1750
ADAMS	1100	2850	2850
WARD	1250	4100	5350
MARTIN	1250	5350	5350
MILLER	1300	6650	6650
TURNER	1500	8150	8150
ALLEN	1600	9750	9750
CLARK	2450	12200	12200
BLAKE	2850	15050	15050
JONES	2975	18025	18025
SCOTT	3000	21025	24025
FORD	3000	24025	24025
KING	5000	29025	29025

For Scott and Ford, the salary is equal to 3000. The analytic function that uses RANGE is deterministic and for both returns the same value while ROWS will return a unique value for each row.

ROWS CURRENT ROW points to exactly one row; RANGE CURRENT ROW points to all rows where the sort key is equal to the current row.

When using ORDER BY with no windowing clause, the implicit window is RANGE BETWEEN UNBOUNDED PRECEDING AND CURRENT ROW for analytic functions that support a windowing clause.

With dates and timestamps, the interval could be a number of days, a day-to-seconds interval or a year-to-month interval.

```
SELECT
   ENAME,
   HIREDATE,
   SAL,
   AVG(SAL)
      OVER
      (
         ORDER BY
            TRUNC(HIREDATE,'MM')
         RANGE BETWEEN
            INTERVAL '1' MONTH PRECEDING
            AND
            INTERVAL '1' MONTH PRECEDING
   ) "PREVIOUS",
   AVG(SAL)
      OVER
      (
         ORDER BY
            TRUNC(HIREDATE,'MM')
         RANGE CURRENT ROW
   ) "CURRENT",
   AVG(SAL)
      OVER
      (
         ORDER BY
            TRUNC(HIREDATE,'MM')
         RANGE BETWEEN
            INTERVAL '1' MONTH FOLLOWING
            AND
            INTERVAL '1' MONTH FOLLOWING
   ) "NEXT",
   AVG(SAL)
      OVER
```

```
      (
         ORDER BY
             TRUNC(HIREDATE,'MM')
         RANGE BETWEEN
             INTERVAL '1' MONTH PRECEDING
             AND
             INTERVAL '1' MONTH FOLLOWING
      ) "3MONTHS"
FROM
   EMP
ORDER BY
   HIREDATE;
```

ENAME	HIREDATE	SAL	PREVIOUS	CURRENT	NEXT	3MONTHS
SMITH	17-DEC-80	800		800		800
ALLEN	20-FEB-81	1600		1425		1425
WARD	22-FEB-81	1250		1425		1425
JONES	02-APR-81	2975		2975	2850	2913
BLAKE	01-MAY-81	2850	2975	2850	2450	2758
CLARK	09-JUN-81	2450	2850	2450		2650
TURNER	08-SEP-81	1500		1375		1375
MARTIN	28-SEP-81	1250		1375		1375
KING	17-NOV-81	5000		5000	1975	2983
JAMES	03-DEC-81	950	5000	1975	1300	2563
FORD	03-DEC-81	3000	5000	1975	1300	2563
MILLER	23-JAN-82	1300	1975	1300		1750
SCOTT	19-APR-87	3000		3000	1100	2050
ADAMS	23-MAY-87	1100	3000	1100		2050

The sort key is the month of hire date. The previous column evaluates the average salary for the employees hired in the month before the current employee was hired, the current column includes the average of employees hired in the same month of the current row and the next column relates to the employees hired in the month after the hire date of the current employee.

Aggregation

Analytics can be used with aggregation. When combining analytics with aggregation, all expressions in the ORDER BY clause and column expressions have to be either part of the GROUP BY expressions or aggregate functions.

```
SELECT
   ROW_NUMBER() OVER (ORDER BY DEPTNO) "ROW_NUMBER",
   DEPTNO,
   SUM(SAL),
   TO_CHAR
```

```
   (
      100*RATIO_TO_REPORT
      (
         SUM(SAL)
      )
      OVER
      (),
      '990.00L',
      'NLS_CURRENCY=%'
   ) PCT
FROM
   EMP
GROUP BY
   DEPTNO;
```

```
ROW_NUMBER     DEPTNO    SUM(SAL)                PCT
----------  ----------  ----------  ------------------
         1          10        8750              30.15%
         2          20       10875              37.47%
         3          30        9400              32.39%
```

ROW_NUMBER is evaluated after the GROUP BY and ordered by the department number. RATIO_TO_REPORT returns the percentage of the total salary of the department to the overall total.

Used with ROLLUP, CUBE or GROUPING SETS, analytic functions can use GROUPING in the partition clause.

```
SELECT
   ENAME,
   DEPTNO,
   JOB,
   SUM(SAL),
   TO_CHAR
   (
      100*RATIO_TO_REPORT(SUM(SAL))
        OVER (PARTITION BY GROUPING(ENAME),GROUPING(DEPTNO),JOB),
      '990.00L',
      'NLS_CURRENCY=%'
   ) PCT_JOB,
   TO_CHAR
   (
      100*RATIO_TO_REPORT(SUM(SAL))
         OVER (PARTITION BY GROUPING(ENAME),GROUPING(JOB),DEPTNO),
      '990.00L',
      'NLS_CURRENCY=%'
   ) PCT_DEPTNO,
   TO_CHAR
   (
      100*RATIO_TO_REPORT(SUM(SAL))
         OVER (PARTITION BY GROUPING(ENAME),GROUPING(DEPTNO),GROUPING(JOB)),
      '990.00L',
      'NLS_CURRENCY=%'
```

```
    ) PCT_EMP
FROM
    EMP
GROUP BY
    GROUPING SETS
    (
        (ENAME,DEPTNO,JOB),
        (DEPTNO,JOB),
        (DEPTNO),
        (JOB),
        ()
    )
ORDER BY
    GROUPING(ENAME),
    GROUPING(JOB),
    GROUPING(DEPTNO),
    DEPTNO,
    JOB,
    ENAME;
```

ENAME	DEPTNO	JOB	SUM(SAL)	PCT_JOB	PCT_DEPTNO	PCT_EMP
MILLER	10	CLERK	1300	31.33%	14.86%	4.48%
CLARK	10	MANAGER	2450	29.61%	28.00%	8.44%
KING	10	PRESIDENT	5000	100.00%	57.14%	17.23%
FORD	20	ANALYST	3000	50.00%	27.59%	10.34%
SCOTT	20	ANALYST	3000	50.00%	27.59%	10.34%
ADAMS	20	CLERK	1100	26.51%	10.11%	3.79%
SMITH	20	CLERK	800	19.28%	7.36%	2.76%
JONES	20	MANAGER	2975	35.95%	27.36%	10.25%
JAMES	30	CLERK	950	22.89%	10.11%	3.27%
BLAKE	30	MANAGER	2850	34.44%	30.32%	9.82%
ALLEN	30	SALESMAN	1600	28.57%	17.02%	5.51%
MARTIN	30	SALESMAN	1250	22.32%	13.30%	4.31%
TURNER	30	SALESMAN	1500	26.79%	15.96%	5.17%
WARD	30	SALESMAN	1250	22.32%	13.30%	4.31%
	10	CLERK	1300	31.33%	14.86%	4.48%
	10	MANAGER	2450	29.61%	28.00%	8.44%
	10	PRESIDENT	5000	100.00%	57.14%	17.23%
	20	ANALYST	6000	100.00%	55.17%	20.67%
	20	CLERK	1900	45.78%	17.47%	6.55%
	20	MANAGER	2975	35.95%	27.36%	10.25%
	30	CLERK	950	22.89%	10.11%	3.27%
	30	MANAGER	2850	34.44%	30.32%	9.82%
	30	SALESMAN	5600	100.00%	59.57%	19.29%
		ANALYST	6000	100.00%	20.67%	20.67%
		CLERK	4150	100.00%	14.30%	14.30%
		MANAGER	8275	100.00%	28.51%	28.51%
		PRESIDENT	5000	100.00%	17.23%	17.23%
		SALESMAN	5600	100.00%	19.29%	19.29%
	10		8750	30.15%	100.00%	30.15%
	20		10875	37.47%	100.00%	37.47%
	30		9400	32.39%	100.00%	32.39%
			29025	100.00%	100.00%	100.00%

The result set contains rows, subtotals and grand totals for each employee, department and job with the total salary.

For SCOTT, the department is 20, the job is CLERK and the salary is 3000. 3000 represents 50% of the sum of salaries of analysts where neither the name nor the department is a subtotal. 3000 is 27.59% of the sum of salaries of department 20 where neither the name nor the department is a subtotal. 3000 is also 10.34% of the sum of salaries in the employee table where none of the name, the job, or the department are subtotals.

For the subtotals for salesmen in department 30, the sum of salaries is 5600. 5600 is 100% of the sum of the totals of salaries of salesmen per department where the name is a subtotal but the department is not a subtotal (5600). 5600 is 59.57% of the sum of the totals in department 30 per job where name is a subtotal but job is not a subtotal (950 + 2850 + 5600). 5600 is also 19.29% of the total of all subtotals per job and department (1300 + 2450 + 5000 + 600 + 1900 + 2975 + 950 + 2850 + 5600).

For the subtotal of department 10, the sum of salaries is 8750. 8750 is 30.15% of the sum of the subtotals per department where the name and the job are subtotals but the department is not a subtotal (8750 + 10875 + 9400).

FIRST_VALUE and LAST_VALUE

The discrete bounds of the current window are returned by the FIRST_VALUE and LAST_VALUE functions.

```
SELECT
    ENAME,
    HIREDATE,
    FIRST_VALUE(ENAME||'('||HIREDATE||')')
    OVER
    (
        ORDER BY
            HIREDATE
        RANGE BETWEEN
            30 PRECEDING
            AND
            30 FOLLOWING
    ) FIRST,
    LAST_VALUE(ENAME||'('||HIREDATE||')')
    OVER
    (
```

```
       ORDER BY
           HIREDATE
       RANGE BETWEEN
           30 PRECEDING
           AND
           30 FOLLOWING
   ) LAST
FROM
   EMP;
```

ENAME	HIREDATE	FIRST	LAST
SMITH	17-DEC-80	SMITH(17-DEC-80)	SMITH(17-DEC-80)
ALLEN	20-FEB-81	ALLEN(20-FEB-81)	WARD(22-FEB-81)
WARD	22-FEB-81	ALLEN(20-FEB-81)	WARD(22-FEB-81)
JONES	02-APR-81	JONES(02-APR-81)	BLAKE(01-MAY-81)
BLAKE	01-MAY-81	JONES(02-APR-81)	BLAKE(01-MAY-81)
CLARK	09-JUN-81	CLARK(09-JUN-81)	CLARK(09-JUN-81)
TURNER	08-SEP-81	TURNER(08-SEP-81)	MARTIN(28-SEP-81)
MARTIN	28-SEP-81	TURNER(08-SEP-81)	MARTIN(28-SEP-81)
KING	17-NOV-81	KING(17-NOV-81)	JAMES(03-DEC-81)
FORD	03-DEC-81	KING(17-NOV-81)	JAMES(03-DEC-81)
JAMES	03-DEC-81	KING(17-NOV-81)	JAMES(03-DEC-81)
MILLER	23-JAN-82	MILLER(23-JAN-82)	MILLER(23-JAN-82)
SCOTT	19-APR-87	SCOTT(19-APR-87)	SCOTT(19-APR-87)
ADAMS	23-MAY-87	ADAMS(23-MAY-87)	ADAMS(23-MAY-87)

The window starts 30 days before the current hire date and ends 30 days after the current hire date. Within this period, the first and last discrete values are returned. King was hired November 17, 1981. Within the period October 18 and December 17, the first record is King and the last record is James. Note that LAST_VALUE returns James because his name is alphabetically greater than Ford.

When using physical offset, duplicate entries are sorted randomly. With logical offset, FIRST_VALUE returns the lowest and LAST_VALUE the highest of the duplicate values.

In 10g and later, the IGNORE NULLS clause returns the first and last non-null values.

```
SELECT
   ENAME,
   SAL,
   COMM,
   LAST_VALUE(COMM IGNORE NULLS)
   OVER
   (
       ORDER BY
```

```
        SAL
    ROWS BETWEEN
        UNBOUNDED PRECEDING
        AND
        1 PRECEDING
  ) PREVIOUS,
  FIRST_VALUE(COMM IGNORE NULLS)
  OVER
  (
     ORDER BY
        SAL
     ROWS BETWEEN
        1 FOLLOWING
        AND
        UNBOUNDED FOLLOWING
  ) NEXT
FROM
   EMP;
```

```
ENAME           SAL       COMM    PREVIOUS       NEXT
----------  ----------  ----------  ----------  ----------
SMITH           800                                1400
JAMES           950                                1400
ADAMS          1100                                1400
MARTIN         1250       1400                      500
WARD           1250        500        1400            0
MILLER         1300                    500            0
TURNER         1500          0         500          300
ALLEN          1600        300           0
CLARK          2450                    300
BLAKE          2850                    300
JONES          2975                    300
FORD           3000                    300
SCOTT          3000                    300
KING           5000                    300
```

The last non-null value of the preceding rows and the first non-null value of the following rows are returned.

LAST_VALUE IGNORE NULLS can group consecutive periods.

🖫 tabletime.sql

```
-- ************************************************
-- Copyright © 2008 by Rampant TechPress
-- This script is free for non-commercial purposes
-- with no warranties.  Use at your own risk.
--
-- To license this script for a commercial purpose,
-- contact rtp@rampant.cc
-- ************************************************
-- Id     : $Id: tabletime.sql,v 1.1 2008/07/09 17:16:36 Laurent Exp $
-- Author : $Author: Laurent $
-- Date   : $Date: 2008/07/09 17:16:36 $
```

```
--
-- Create TIMETABLE Table in current schema
--

WHENEVER SQLERROR EXIT FAILURE

EXEC BEGIN EXECUTE IMMEDIATE 'DROP TABLE TIMETABLE'; EXCEPTION WHEN OTHERS
THEN NULL; END

CREATE TABLE
    TIMETABLE
(
    EMPNO NUMBER REFERENCES EMP,
    BEGINTIME TIMESTAMP,
    ENDTIME TIMESTAMP,
    PRIMARY KEY (EMPNO, BEGINTIME, ENDTIME)
);
INSERT INTO
    TIMETABLE
(
    EMPNO,
    BEGINTIME,
    ENDTIME
)
VALUES
(
    7499,
    TIMESTAMP '2008-07-09 08:30:00',
    TIMESTAMP '2008-07-09 12:30:00'
);
INSERT INTO
    TIMETABLE
(
    EMPNO,
    BEGINTIME,
    ENDTIME
)
VALUES
(
    7521,
    TIMESTAMP '2008-07-09 06:30:00',
    TIMESTAMP '2008-07-09 11:30:00'
);
INSERT INTO
    TIMETABLE
(
    EMPNO,
    BEGINTIME,
    ENDTIME
)
VALUES
(
    7654,
    TIMESTAMP '2008-07-09 13:00:00',
    TIMESTAMP '2008-07-09 18:00:00'
);
INSERT INTO
    TIMETABLE
```

```
(
   EMPNO,
   BEGINTIME,
   ENDTIME
)
VALUES
(
   7844,
   TIMESTAMP '2008-07-09 13:30:00',
   TIMESTAMP '2008-07-09 17:30:00'
);
INSERT INTO
   TIMETABLE
(
   EMPNO,
   BEGINTIME,
   ENDTIME
)
VALUES
(
   7521,
   TIMESTAMP '2008-07-09 14:30:00',
   TIMESTAMP '2008-07-09 17:00:00'
);
COMMIT;
```

```
    EMPNO BEGINTIME         ENDTIME
---------- ---------------- ----------------
      7499 2008-07-09 08:30 2008-07-09 12:30
      7521 2008-07-09 06:30 2008-07-09 11:30
      7521 2008-07-09 14:30 2008-07-09 17:00
      7654 2008-07-09 13:00 2008-07-09 18:00
      7844 2008-07-09 13:30 2008-07-09 17:30
```

The salesman timetable is displayed.

```
SELECT
DISTINCT
   LAST_VALUE(PERIODBEGIN IGNORE NULLS) OVER
      (ORDER BY BEGINTIME) BEGINTIME,
   FIRST_VALUE(PERIODEND IGNORE NULLS) OVER
      (ORDER BY ENDTIME RANGE BETWEEN CURRENT ROW AND UNBOUNDED FOLLOWING)
      ENDTIME
FROM
(
   SELECT
      EMPNO,
      BEGINTIME,
      ENDTIME,
      CASE
         WHEN BEGINTIME <= MAX(ENDTIME) OVER
            (ORDER BY BEGINTIME ROWS BETWEEN
               UNBOUNDED PRECEDING AND 1 PRECEDING)
         THEN NULL
         ELSE BEGINTIME
      END PERIODBEGIN,
```

```
        CASE
            WHEN ENDTIME >= MIN(BEGINTIME) OVER
                (ORDER BY ENDTIME ROWS BETWEEN
                    1 FOLLOWING AND UNBOUNDED FOLLOWING)
            THEN NULL
            ELSE ENDTIME
        END PERIODEND
    FROM
        TIMETABLE
);
```

```
BEGINTIME          ENDTIME
---------------- ----------------
2008-07-09 06:30 2008-07-09 12:30
2008-07-09 13:00 2008-07-09 18:00
```

6:30 and 13:00 are the lower bounds. There is no salesman working at 6:29 or at 12:59. 12:30 and 18:00 are the upper bounds. No salesman is working at 12:31 or 18:01.

The inner query sets PERIODBEGIN to NULL when the current BEGINTIME is smaller than the highest ENDTIME before the current row, ordered by BEGINTIME. PERIODEND is set to NULL when the current ENDTIME is bigger than the lowest BEGINTIME after the current row, ordered by ENDTIME.

The outer query replaces a null PERIODBEGIN by the last non-null value preceding and a null PERIODEND by the first non-null value following.

DISTINCT suppresses duplicates.

Conclusion

An analytic function is calculated over multiple rows and returns the result in the current row. Analytic functions use PARTITION BY, not GROUPED BY, which is used with aggregate functions. However, when combining analytics with aggregation, all expressions in the ORDER BY clause and column expressions have to be either part of the GROUP BY expressions or aggregate functions. Various clauses that are used in analytic functions, such as the OVER, KEEP, ROWS BETWEEN and RANGE are covered in more detail in this chapter.

Also, other functions such as ranking functions, FIRST_VALUE and LAST_VALUE are illustrated.

Exercises

1. OVER

💾 **tabletax.sql**

```
-- **************************************************
-- Copyright © 2008 by Rampant TechPress
-- This script is free for non-commercial purposes
-- with no warranties.  Use at your own risk.
--
-- To license this script for a commercial purpose,
-- contact rtp@rampant.cc
-- **************************************************
-- Id      : $Id: tabletax.sql,v 1.3 2008/07/10 08:50:54 Laurent Exp $
-- Author  : $Author: Laurent $
-- Date    : $Date: 2008/07/10 08:50:54 $
--
-- Create TAX and TAX_OPTION Tables in current schema
--
-- Current user needs CREATE VIEW privilege

WHENEVER SQLERROR EXIT FAILURE

EXEC BEGIN EXECUTE IMMEDIATE 'DROP TABLE TAX_EMP'; EXCEPTION WHEN OTHERS
THEN NULL; END
EXEC BEGIN EXECUTE IMMEDIATE 'DROP TABLE TAX_OPTION'; EXCEPTION WHEN
OTHERS THEN NULL; END

CREATE TABLE
   TAX_EMP
(
   EMPNO NUMBER REFERENCES EMP,
   YEAR NUMBER,
   TAX NUMBER,
   PRIMARY KEY (EMPNO, YEAR)
);
INSERT INTO
   TAX_EMP
(
   EMPNO,
   YEAR,
   TAX
)
VALUES
(
   7788,
   2008,
   5000
);
INSERT INTO
   TAX_EMP
(
   EMPNO,
```

```
   YEAR,
   TAX
)
VALUES
(
   7839,
   2009,
   10000
);
CREATE TABLE
   TAX_OPTION
(
   OPTION_ID NUMBER,
   DUEMONTH NUMBER,
   DUEDAY NUMBER,
   PRIMARY KEY (OPTION_ID, DUEMONTH, DUEDAY),
   CHECK (TO_DATE(2001*10000+DUEMONTH*100+DUEDAY,'YYYYMMDD') IS NOT
NULL)
   -- checks that it is a valid day and month
);

INSERT INTO
   TAX_OPTION
(
   OPTION_ID,
   DUEMONTH,
   DUEDAY
)
VALUES
(
   1,
   9,
   30
);
INSERT INTO
   TAX_OPTION
(
   OPTION_ID,
   DUEMONTH,
   DUEDAY
)
VALUES
(
   2,
   6,
   30
);
INSERT INTO
   TAX_OPTION
(
   OPTION_ID,
   DUEMONTH,
   DUEDAY
)
VALUES
(
   2,
   9,
   30
```

```
);
INSERT INTO
    TAX_OPTION
(
    OPTION_ID,
    DUEMONTH,
    DUEDAY
)
VALUES
(
    2,
    12,
    31
);
COMMIT;
CREATE OR REPLACE VIEW
    TAX
AS
SELECT
    e.ENAME,
    t.YEAR,
    t.TAX,
    o.OPTION_ID,
    TO_DATE(t.YEAR||'.'||o.DUEMONTH||'.'||o.DUEDAY, 'YYYY.MM.DD') DUEDATE
FROM
    EMP e
    JOIN TAX_EMP t USING (EMPNO)
    CROSS JOIN TAX_OPTION o;

SELECT * FROM TAX;
```

```
ENAME    YEAR     TAX  OPTION_ID DUEDATE
------   ------   ------ ---------- ---------
SCOTT    2008     5000          1 30-SEP-08
SCOTT    2008     5000          2 30-JUN-08
SCOTT    2008     5000          2 30-SEP-08
SCOTT    2008     5000          2 31-DEC-08
KING     2009    10000          1 30-SEP-09
KING     2009    10000          2 30-JUN-09
KING     2009    10000          2 30-SEP-09
KING     2009    10000          2 31-DEC-09
```

The tax could be paid either in one or three installments.

Determine the due amount for each date. Round the value to \$1 and, if necessary, correct the final payment to keep the overall total accurate. The expected result is:

```
ENAME   OPTION_ID DUEDATE       AMOUNT
------  ---------- ---------   ----------
SCOTT           1 30-SEP-08       5000
SCOTT           2 30-JUN-08       1667
SCOTT           2 30-SEP-08       1667
SCOTT           2 31-DEC-08       1666
```

```
KING              1 30-SEP-09      10000
KING              2 30-JUN-09       3333
KING              2 30-SEP-09       3333
KING              2 31-DEC-09       3334
```

2. RANGE

   For each employee, retrieve the previous and next hire dates. Example: James was hired on 1981-12-03, the previous hire date is 1981-11-17 and the next hire date is 1982-01-23.

3. Moving average

   Using a window of three months preceding and three months following, retrieve the average salary per hire date.

4. Cumulative totals

   Return the cumulative salary of clerks and the cumulative salary of managers for each employee from the longest-serving to the most recently hired.

Solutions

1. OVER

```
SELECT
   ENAME,
   OPTION_ID,
   DUEDATE,
   CASE
      WHEN
         COUNT(*) OVER (PARTITION BY ENAME, YEAR, OPTION_ID)=1
      THEN
         TAX
      WHEN
         ROW_NUMBER() OVER (PARTITION BY ENAME, YEAR, OPTION_ID
            ORDER BY DUEDATE DESC)=1
      THEN
         TAX-(COUNT(*) OVER (PARTITION BY ENAME, YEAR, OPTION_ID)-1)*
            ROUND(TAX/COUNT(*) OVER (PARTITION BY ENAME, YEAR,
OPTION_ID))
      ELSE
         ROUND(TAX/COUNT(*) OVER (PARTITION BY ENAME, YEAR, OPTION_ID))
   END AMOUNT
FROM
   TAX;
```

```
ENAME    OPTION_ID DUEDATE       AMOUNT
------   ---------- ---------   ----------
SCOTT            1 30-SEP-08      5000
SCOTT            2 30-JUN-08      1667
SCOTT            2 30-SEP-08      1667
SCOTT            2 31-DEC-08      1666
KING             1 30-SEP-09     10000
KING             2 30-JUN-09      3333
KING             2 30-SEP-09      3333
KING             2 31-DEC-09      3334
```

COUNT retrieves the number of periods. For one period, the result is trivial. For more than one period, the first amounts are equals to the tax divided by the count. The last amount is the difference between the tax and all previous amounts.

2. RANGE

RANGE windowing is required to retrieve an employee that was hired before and not on the same date.

```
SELECT
   ENAME,
   HIREDATE,
```

```
    LAST_VALUE(HIREDATE) OVER
    (
        ORDER BY HIREDATE
        RANGE BETWEEN UNBOUNDED PRECEDING AND INTERVAL '1' DAY PRECEDING
    ) PREVIOUS,
    FIRST_VALUE(HIREDATE) OVER
    (
        ORDER BY HIREDATE
        RANGE BETWEEN INTERVAL '1' DAY FOLLOWING AND UNBOUNDED FOLLOWING
    ) NEXT
FROM
    EMP;
```

```
    ENAME       HIREDATE  PREVIOUS   NEXT
    ----------  --------- ---------  ---------
    SMITH       17-DEC-80            20-FEB-81
    ALLEN       20-FEB-81 17-DEC-80  22-FEB-81
    WARD        22-FEB-81 20-FEB-81  02-APR-81
    JONES       02-APR-81 22-FEB-81  01-MAY-81
    BLAKE       01-MAY-81 02-APR-81  09-JUN-81
    CLARK       09-JUN-81 01-MAY-81  08-SEP-81
    TURNER      08-SEP-81 09-JUN-81  28-SEP-81
    MARTIN      28-SEP-81 08-SEP-81  17-NOV-81
    KING        17-NOV-81 28-SEP-81  03-DEC-81
    JAMES       03-DEC-81 17-NOV-81  23-JAN-82
    FORD        03-DEC-81 17-NOV-81  23-JAN-82
    MILLER      23-JAN-82 03-DEC-81  19-APR-87
    SCOTT       19-APR-87 23-JAN-82  23-MAY-87
    ADAMS       23-MAY-87 19-APR-87
```

Both James and Ford were hired on Dec 3. The previous hire date is Nov 17 and the next is Jan 23.

3. Moving average

```
SELECT
    ENAME,
    SAL,
    HIREDATE,
    AVG(SAL)
    OVER
    (
        ORDER BY
            HIREDATE
        RANGE BETWEEN
            INTERVAL '3' MONTH PRECEDING
            AND
            INTERVAL '3' MONTH FOLLOWING
    ) MOVINGAVG
FROM
    EMP;
```

```
    ENAME        SAL HIREDATE  MOVINGAVG
    ----------  ----- --------- ---------
    SMITH         800 17-DEC-80      1217
    ALLEN        1600 20-FEB-81      1895
```

```
WARD           1250 22-FEB-81          1895
JONES          2975 02-APR-81          2225
BLAKE          2850 01-MAY-81          2225
CLARK          2450 09-JUN-81          2444
TURNER         1500 08-SEP-81          2358
MARTIN         1250 28-SEP-81          2340
KING           5000 17-NOV-81          2167
JAMES           950 03-DEC-81          2167
FORD           3000 03-DEC-81          2167
MILLER         1300 23-JAN-82          2563
SCOTT          3000 19-APR-87          2050
ADAMS          1100 23-MAY-87          2050
```

The average is evaluated over a 6 month period. For instance, the moving average of Scott is the average salary of employees hired between Jan 19, 1987 and July 19, 1987.

4. Cumulative totals

```
SELECT
   ENAME,
   JOB,
   SAL,
   HIREDATE,
   SUM(DECODE(JOB,'CLERK',SAL)) OVER (ORDER BY HIREDATE) SALCLERK,
   SUM(DECODE(JOB,'MANAGER',SAL)) OVER (ORDER BY HIREDATE) SALMGR
FROM
   EMP;
```

```
ENAME       JOB            SAL HIREDATE    SALCLERK    SALMGR
----------  ---------   ------ ---------   ----------  ----------
SMITH       CLERK          800 17-DEC-80        800
ALLEN       SALESMAN      1600 20-FEB-81        800
WARD        SALESMAN      1250 22-FEB-81        800
JONES       MANAGER       2975 02-APR-81        800        2975
BLAKE       MANAGER       2850 01-MAY-81        800        5825
CLARK       MANAGER       2450 09-JUN-81        800        8275
TURNER      SALESMAN      1500 08-SEP-81        800        8275
MARTIN      SALESMAN      1250 28-SEP-81        800        8275
KING        PRESIDENT     5000 17-NOV-81        800        8275
JAMES       CLERK          950 03-DEC-81       1750        8275
FORD        ANALYST       3000 03-DEC-81       1750        8275
MILLER      CLERK         1300 23-JAN-82       3050        8275
SCOTT       ANALYST       3000 19-APR-87       3050        8275
ADAMS       CLERK         1100 23-MAY-87       4150        8275
```

The clerks' cumulative total sums the salaries of the clerks; other salaries are set to NULL by DECODE and ignored by SUM. The same mechanism is used for SALMGR.

XML

XML

XML functionality is part of the Oracle Database.

XML Instance

An instance could be a well-formed XML document. An XML document contains a root node:

```
<DOC>
   <ELEM id="1"/>
   <ELEM id="2"/>
</DOC>
```

An instance could be well-formed XML content. XML content does not require a root node:

```
<ELEM>1</ELEM>
<ELEM>2</ELEM>
```

An XML instance could also contains simple data:

```
1000
```

XMLTYPE

XMLTYPE is the datatype used to store XML data. The type constructor accepts different input like character, binary or ref cursor. The text passed to the constructor must be a well-formed document.

```
SELECT
   XMLTYPE
```

```
   (
      '<X/>'
   )
FROM
   DUAL;

XMLTYPE
-------
<X/>
```

The XMLTYPE is constructed from a character literal.

```
SELECT
   XMLTYPE
   (
      TO_BLOB
      (
         HEXTORAW ('3C696D673E3A2D293C2F696D673E')
      ),
      NLS_CHARSET_ID('WE8MSWIN1252')
   )
FROM
   DUAL;

XMLTYPE(TO_BLOB
---------------
<img>:-)</img>
```

A BLOB is passed to the XMLTYPE constructor.

NLS_CHARSET_ID returns the character set used for the encoding of
the BLOB. Oracle 9i does not support BLOB as input.

```
SELECT
   XMLTYPE
   (
      BFILENAME('TEMP', 'test.xml'),
      NLS_CHARSET_ID('WE8MSWIN1252')
   )
FROM
   DUAL;

XMLTYPE(BFILENAME('TEM
----------------------
<msg>Hello World</msg>
```

A file is passed to the XMLTYPE constructor. BFILENAME returns a
BFILE locator to the file *test.xml* in the Oracle directory TEMP.

```
SELECT
   XMLTYPE
   (
      CURSOR
      (
         SELECT
            *
         FROM
            DEPT
      )
   )
FROM
   DUAL;
```

```
XMLTYPE(CURSOR(SELECT*FROMDEPT))
--------------------------------
<?xml version="1.0"?>
<ROWSET>
 <ROW>
  <DEPTNO>10</DEPTNO>
  <DNAME>ACCOUNTING</DNAME>
  <LOC>NEW YORK</LOC>
 </ROW>
 <ROW>
  <DEPTNO>20</DEPTNO>
  <DNAME>RESEARCH</DNAME>
  <LOC>DALLAS</LOC>
 </ROW>
 <ROW>
  <DEPTNO>30</DEPTNO>
  <DNAME>SALES</DNAME>
  <LOC>CHICAGO</LOC>
 </ROW>
 <ROW>
  <DEPTNO>40</DEPTNO>
  <DNAME>OPERATIONS</DNAME>
  <LOC>BOSTON</LOC>
 </ROW>
</ROWSET>
```

XMLTYPE accepts a Ref Cursor as a parameter.

XMLELEMENT

XMLELEMENT is a function that returns an XMLTYPE. The first argument is the name of the tag. The following argument is the value and could be string, XMLTYPE, number, or date.

```
SELECT
   EMPNO,
   XMLELEMENT(NAME, ENAME) NAME
```

```
FROM
    EMP
WHERE
    ENAME LIKE 'S%';
```

```
     EMPNO NAME
---------- ------------------------------
      7369 <NAME>SMITH</NAME>
      7788 <NAME>SCOTT</NAME>
```

XMLELEMENT generates an XML type with a tag NAME and the employee name as value.

XMLELEMENT can be nested and can contain attributes:

```
SELECT
    EMPNO,
    XMLELEMENT
    (
        EMP,
        XMLATTRIBUTES
        (
            EMPNO,
            DEPTNO
        ),
        XMLELEMENT
        (
            NAME,
            ENAME
        ),
        XMLELEMENT
        (
            JOB,
            JOB
        )
    ) EMP
FROM
    EMP
WHERE
    ENAME LIKE 'S%';
```

```
EMP
----------------------------------------------------------------------
<EMP EMPNO="7369" DEPTNO="20"><NAME>SMITH</NAME><JOB>CLERK</JOB></EMP>
<EMP EMPNO="7788" DEPTNO="20"><NAME>SCOTT</NAME><JOB>ANALYST</JOB></EMP>
```

The EMP element contains two attributes - the employee number and the department number - and two sub elements, the name and the job.

Starting with 10gR2, not only the value of the element could be an expression, but also the name of the element.

```
SELECT
   XMLELEMENT
   (
      EVALNAME ENAME,
      XMLATTRIBUTES
      (
         EMPNO AS EVALNAME JOB||'_ID'
      )
   ) EMP
FROM
   EMP
WHERE
   ENAME LIKE 'S%';
```

```
EMP
-----------------------------------
<SMITH CLERK_ID="7369"></SMITH>
<SCOTT ANALYST_ID="7788"></SCOTT>
```

The EVALNAME expression dynamically sets the element name and the attribute name. The expression must return a character value.

XMLCONCAT and XMLFOREST

XMLCONCAT joins multiple xml elements together; XMLFOREST works similarly but accepts number, characters, dates, and XMLTYPE.

```
SELECT
   XMLCONCAT
   (
      XMLELEMENT(EMPNO, EMPNO),
      XMLELEMENT(ENAME, ENAME)
   ),
   XMLFOREST
   (
      EMPNO,
      ENAME
   )
FROM
   EMP
WHERE
   ENAME='SCOTT';
```

```
XMLCONCAT(XMLELEMENT(E   XMLELE XMLFOREST(EMPNO,ENAME)
---------------------    ------------------------------
<EMPNO>7788</EMPNO>       <EMPNO>7788</EMPNO>
<ENAME>SCOTT</ENAME>      <ENAME>SCOTT</ENAME>
```

XPATH

Oracle supports XPATH expressions.

🖫 tablexmltype.sql

```
-- ***************************************************
-- Copyright © 2008 by Rampant TechPress
-- This script is free for non-commercial purposes
-- with no warranties.  Use at your own risk.
--
-- To license this script for a commercial purpose,
-- contact rtp@rampant.cc
-- ***************************************************
-- Id     : $Id: tablexmltype.sql,v 1.2 2008/05/04 19:40:48 Laurent Exp $
-- Author : $Author: Laurent $
-- Date   : $Date: 2008/05/04 19:40:48 $
--
-- Create WORLD XML Table in current schema
--

WHENEVER SQLERROR EXIT

EXEC EXECUTE IMMEDIATE 'DROP TABLE WORLD'; EXCEPTION WHEN OTHERS THEN NULL

-- Create XML Table
CREATE TABLE
   WORLD
OF XMLTYPE;

INSERT INTO
   WORLD
VALUES
(
   XMLTYPE
   ('<COUNTRY ID="CH">
<NAME>Switzerland</NAME>
<CANTON_LIST>
<CANTON ID="ZH">
<NAME>Zurich</NAME>
<DETAILS>
<ENTRY>1351-01-01</ENTRY>
<LANGUAGE>German</LANGUAGE>
</DETAILS>
</CANTON>
<CANTON ID="BE">
<NAME>Bern</NAME>
<DETAILS>
<ENTRY>1353-01-01</ENTRY>
<LANGUAGE_LIST>
<LANGUAGE>German</LANGUAGE>
<LANGUAGE>French</LANGUAGE>
</LANGUAGE_LIST>
</DETAILS>
</CANTON>
```

```
<CANTON ID="LU">
<NAME>Lucerne</NAME>
<DETAILS>
<ENTRY>1332-01-01</ENTRY>
<LANGUAGE>German</LANGUAGE>
</DETAILS>
</CANTON>
<CANTON ID="UR">
<NAME>Uri</NAME>
<DETAILS>
<ENTRY>1291-01-01</ENTRY>
<LANGUAGE>German</LANGUAGE>
</DETAILS>
</CANTON>
<CANTON ID="SZ">
<NAME>Schwyz</NAME>
<DETAILS>
<ENTRY>1291-01-01</ENTRY>
<LANGUAGE>German</LANGUAGE>
</DETAILS>
</CANTON>
<CANTON ID="OW">
<NAME>Obwald</NAME>
<DETAILS>
<ENTRY>1291-01-01</ENTRY>
<LANGUAGE>German</LANGUAGE>
</DETAILS>
</CANTON>
<CANTON ID="NW">
<NAME>Nidwald</NAME>
<DETAILS>
<ENTRY>1291-01-01</ENTRY>
<LANGUAGE>German</LANGUAGE>
</DETAILS>
</CANTON>
<CANTON ID="GL">
<NAME>Glarus</NAME>
<DETAILS>
<ENTRY>1352-01-01</ENTRY>
<LANGUAGE>German</LANGUAGE>
</DETAILS>
</CANTON>
<CANTON ID="ZG">
<NAME>Zug</NAME>
<DETAILS>
<ENTRY>1352-01-01</ENTRY>
<LANGUAGE>German</LANGUAGE>
</DETAILS>
</CANTON>
<CANTON ID="FR">
<NAME>Fribourg</NAME>
<DETAILS>
<ENTRY>1481-01-01</ENTRY>
<LANGUAGE_LIST>
<LANGUAGE>French</LANGUAGE>
<LANGUAGE>German</LANGUAGE>
</LANGUAGE_LIST>
</DETAILS>
```

```
</CANTON>
<CANTON ID="SO">
<NAME>Solothurn</NAME>
<DETAILS>
<ENTRY>1481-01-01</ENTRY>
<LANGUAGE>German</LANGUAGE>
</DETAILS>
</CANTON>
<CANTON ID="BS">
<NAME>Basel-City</NAME>
<DETAILS>
<ENTRY>1501-01-01</ENTRY>
<LANGUAGE>German</LANGUAGE>
</DETAILS>
</CANTON>
<CANTON ID="BL">
<NAME>Basel-Country</NAME>
<DETAILS>
<ENTRY>1501-01-01</ENTRY>
<LANGUAGE>German</LANGUAGE>
</DETAILS>
</CANTON>
<CANTON ID="SH">
<NAME>Schaffhausen</NAME>
<DETAILS>
<ENTRY>1501-01-01</ENTRY>
<LANGUAGE>German</LANGUAGE>
</DETAILS>
</CANTON>
<CANTON ID="AR">
<NAME>AppenzellOuterRhodes</NAME>
<DETAILS>
<ENTRY>1513-01-01</ENTRY>
<LANGUAGE>German</LANGUAGE>
</DETAILS>
</CANTON>
<CANTON ID="AI">
<NAME>AppenzellInnerRhodes</NAME>
<DETAILS>
<ENTRY>1513-01-01</ENTRY>
<LANGUAGE>German</LANGUAGE>
</DETAILS>
</CANTON>
<CANTON ID="SG">
<NAME>St.Gall</NAME>
<DETAILS>
<ENTRY>1803-01-01</ENTRY>
<LANGUAGE>German</LANGUAGE>
</DETAILS>
</CANTON>
<CANTON ID="GR">
<NAME>Graubuenden</NAME>
<DETAILS>
<ENTRY>1803-01-01</ENTRY>
<LANGUAGE_LIST>
<LANGUAGE>German</LANGUAGE>
<LANGUAGE>Romansh</LANGUAGE>
<LANGUAGE>Italian</LANGUAGE>
</LANGUAGE_LIST>
```

```
</DETAILS>
</CANTON>
<CANTON ID="AG">
<NAME>Aargau</NAME>
<DETAILS>
<ENTRY>1803-01-01</ENTRY>
<LANGUAGE>German</LANGUAGE>
</DETAILS>
</CANTON>
<CANTON ID="TG">
<NAME>Thurgau</NAME>
<DETAILS>
<ENTRY>1803-01-01</ENTRY>
<LANGUAGE>German</LANGUAGE>
</DETAILS>
</CANTON>
<CANTON ID="TI">
<NAME>Ticino</NAME>
<DETAILS>
<ENTRY>1803-01-01</ENTRY>
<LANGUAGE_LIST>
<LANGUAGE>Italian</LANGUAGE>
<LANGUAGE>German</LANGUAGE>
</LANGUAGE_LIST>
</DETAILS>
</CANTON>
<CANTON ID="VD">
<NAME>Vaud</NAME>
<DETAILS>
<ENTRY>1803-01-01</ENTRY>
<LANGUAGE>French</LANGUAGE>
</DETAILS>
</CANTON>
<CANTON ID="VS">
<NAME>Valais</NAME>
<DETAILS>
<ENTRY>1815-01-01</ENTRY>
<LANGUAGE_LIST>
<LANGUAGE>French</LANGUAGE>
<LANGUAGE>German</LANGUAGE>
</LANGUAGE_LIST>
</DETAILS>
</CANTON>
<CANTON ID="NE">
<NAME>Neuchatel</NAME>
<DETAILS>
<ENTRY>1815-01-01</ENTRY>
<LANGUAGE>French</LANGUAGE>
</DETAILS>
</CANTON>
<CANTON ID="GE">
<NAME>Geneva</NAME>
<DETAILS>
<ENTRY>1815-01-01</ENTRY>
<LANGUAGE>French</LANGUAGE>
</DETAILS>
</CANTON>
<CANTON ID="JU">
<NAME>Jura</NAME>
```

```
<DETAILS>
<ENTRY>1979-01-01</ENTRY>
<LANGUAGE>French</LANGUAGE>
</DETAILS>
</CANTON>
</CANTON_LIST>
</COUNTRY>')
);

COMMIT;
```

The table WORLD contains one row of XMLTYPE.

The EXTRACT function requires two arguments: an XMLTYPE element and an XPATH string. An optional third parameter specifies the namespace. EXTRACT matches the XPATH expression to the XMLTYPE element and returns an XMLTYPE instance. The XPATH must resolve to a node or node content. The XPATH syntax is defined by the World Wide Web Consortium at http://www.w3.org/TR/xpath.

```
SELECT
    EXTRACT
    (
        OBJECT_VALUE,
        '/COUNTRY/CANTON_LIST/CANTON[@ID="GE" or @ID="GR"]'
    ) CANTON
FROM
    WORLD;
```

```
CANTON
-----------------------------------
<CANTON ID="GR">
   <NAME>Graubuenden</NAME>
   <DETAILS>
      <ENTRY>1803-01-01</ENTRY>
      <LANGUAGE_LIST>
         <LANGUAGE>German</LANGUAGE>
         <LANGUAGE>Romansh</LANGUAGE>
         <LANGUAGE>Italian</LANGUAGE>
      </LANGUAGE_LIST>
   </DETAILS>
</CANTON>
<CANTON ID="GE">
   <NAME>Geneva</NAME>
   <DETAILS>
      <ENTRY>1815-01-01</ENTRY>
      <LANGUAGE>French</LANGUAGE>
   </DETAILS>
</CANTON>
```

OBJECT_VALUE points to the column of the table WORLD. The node of the cantons with the attribute ID equals to GE or GR in the canton list of the country are returned as a well-formed content.

```
SELECT
   EXTRACT
   (
      OBJECT_VALUE,
      '/COUNTRY/NAME/text()'
   ) COUNTRY_NAME
FROM
   WORLD;
```

```
COUNTRY_NAME
------------------
Switzerland
```

The text content of the name of the country is returned. This XMLTYPE is not well-formed.

```
SELECT
   EXTRACT
   (
      OBJECT_VALUE,
      '/COUNTRY/CANTON_LIST/CANTON[NAME="Zurich" or NAME="Zug"]/@ID
   ) CANTON
FROM
   WORLD;
```

```
CANTON
----------

ZHZG
```

The attributes of the cantons named *Zurich* or *Zug* are returned. This XMLTYPE is not well-formed.

The EXTRACTVALUE function returns a scalar.

```
SELECT
   EXTRACTVALUE
   (
      OBJECT_VALUE,
      '/COUNTRY/CANTON_LIST/CANTON[@ID="NE"]//LANGUAGE/text()'
   ) LANGUAGE
FROM
   WORLD
;
```

```
LANGUAGE
----------
French
```

For the canton NE, the language is returned as a VARCHAR2 string. Note the // between the canton and the language. // is typically slower because it implies a search in the node. The LANGUAGE is not necessarily located directly under CANTON.

EXISTSNODE check the existence of an XPATH expression:

```
SELECT
   DECODE
   (
      EXISTSNODE
      (
         OBJECT_VALUE,
         '/COUNTRY/CANTON_LIST/CANTON[NAME="Zurich"]'
      ),
      1, 'TRUE',
      0, 'FALSE'
   ) EXISTSNODE
FROM
   WORLD;
```

```
EXISTSNODE
----------
TRUE
```

The value of 1 reveals that there is at least one canton with a name of Zurich that exists in the document.

XMLSEQUENCE

XMLSEQUENCE returns a collection of XMLTYPEs where each row contains a top element node of the XML content.

```
SELECT
   EXTRACTVALUE(T.COLUMN_VALUE,'/CANTON/NAME') CANTON
FROM
   WORLD,
   TABLE
   (
      XMLSEQUENCE
      (
         EXTRACT
         (
            WORLD.OBJECT_VALUE,
```

```
              '/COUNTRY/CANTON_LIST/CANTON'
          )
      )
   ) T
WHERE
   EXISTSNODE
   (
      T.COLUMN_VALUE,
      '/CANTON/DETAILS//LANGUAGE="French"'
   )=1;
```

```
CANTON
---------
Bern
Fribourg
Vaud
Valais
Neuchatel
Geneva
Jura
```

The cantons are extracted out of the XMLTYPE document. The XMLSEQUENCE function transforms the XMLTYPE content in a collection; TABLE unnests the collection. The column of the table WORLD is referenced in the collection function XMLSEQUENCE.

The NAME values are returned by EXTRACTVALUE and EXISTSNODE restrict the rows to the French speaking cantons.

XMLSEQUENCE also accepts a REF CURSOR as input to transform a defined cursor into a collection of XMLTYPE.

```
SELECT
   ROWNUM,
   COLUMN_VALUE
FROM
   TABLE(XMLSEQUENCE(CURSOR(SELECT * FROM DEPT)));
```

```
ROWNUM COLUMN_VALUE
------ -----------------------------
     1  <ROW>
           <DEPTNO>10</DEPTNO>
           <DNAME>ACCOUNTING</DNAME>
           <LOC>NEW YORK</LOC>
        </ROW>

     2  <ROW>
           <DEPTNO>20</DEPTNO>
           <DNAME>RESEARCH</DNAME>
           <LOC>DALLAS</LOC>
        </ROW>
```

```
3   <ROW>
        <DEPTNO>30</DEPTNO>
        <DNAME>SALES</DNAME>
        <LOC>CHICAGO</LOC>
    </ROW>

4   <ROW>
        <DEPTNO>40</DEPTNO>
        <DNAME>OPERATIONS</DNAME>
        <LOC>BOSTON</LOC>
    </ROW>
```

For the defined cursor, a collection of XMLTYPEs is returned by XMLSEQUENCE, unnested and displayed.

XQuery

In Oracle 10gR2 and later, XQuery extends the XML capabilities. XQuery is defined by the World Wide Web Consortium at http://www.w3.org/TR/xquery.

The function XMLQUERY processes an XQuery program and returns a well-formed content.

```
SELECT
   XMLQUERY
   (
      'let $i := "oracle"
      return <NAME>{$i}</NAME>'
      RETURNING CONTENT
   ) NAME
FROM
   DUAL;
```

```
NAME
--------------------
<NAME>oracle</NAME>
```

The value oracle is assigned to the variable $i and returned as XML content.

XMLTABLE processes an XQuery program and returns rows.

```
SELECT
   XMLELEMENT(N,COLUMN_VALUE) N
FROM
```

```
XMLTABLE
(
    '1 to 10'
);
```

```
N
----------
<N>1</N>
<N>2</N>
<N>3</N>
<N>4</N>
<N>5</N>
<N>6</N>
<N>7</N>
<N>8</N>
<N>9</N>
<N>10</N>
```

The very short XQuery program returns a sequence of numbers from 1
to 10. XMLTABLE returns a row for each value.

XQUERY programs can generate rows like XMLSEQUENCE.

```
SELECT
    NAME
FROM
    WORLD,
    XMLTABLE
    ('
        for $CANTON in $COUNTRY/COUNTRY/CANTON_LIST/CANTON
        where $CANTON//LANGUAGE="Italian"
        order by $CANTON/@ID
        return $CANTON
    '
    PASSING
        OBJECT_VALUE
    AS
        COUNTRY
    COLUMNS
        NAME XMLTYPE PATH '/CANTON/NAME'
    );
```

```
NAME
---------------------------
<NAME>Graubuenden</NAME>
<NAME>Ticino</NAME>
```

XMLTABLE processes the COUNTRY and returns a row for each
canton where the language Italian exists. The rows are sorted by ID and
the column NAME is returned for the name of the canton.

XMLEXISTS (11gR1) is a Boolean function similar to EXISTSNODE with the XQuery syntax.

```
SELECT
    XMLFOREST(EMPNO, ENAME, JOB)
FROM
    EMP
WHERE
    XMLEXISTS
    (
        '/[JOB="ANALYST"]'
        PASSING
        XMLFOREST(EMPNO, ENAME, JOB)
    );
```

```
XMLFOREST(EMPNO,ENAME,JOB)
----------------------------------------
<EMPNO>7788</EMPNO>
<ENAME>SCOTT</ENAME>
<JOB>ANALYST</JOB>

<EMPNO>7902</EMPNO>
<ENAME>FORD</ENAME>
<JOB>ANALYST</JOB>
```

The XPATH expression searches for analysts in the generated content.

Besides selecting literals and column values, XQuery has multiple functions. The function *ora:view* is an Oracle-specific addition to the XQuery language that queries a relational table or view:

```
SELECT
    *
FROM
    XMLTABLE
    (
        '
        for $i in ora:view("EMP"), $j in ora:view("DEPT")
        where $i//JOB="ANALYST" and $i//DEPTNO=$j//DEPTNO
        return (<EMP>{$i//EMPNO}{$i//ENAME}{$j//DNAME}</EMP>)
        '
        COLUMNS
        EMP XMLTYPE PATH '/EMP'
    );
```

```
EMP
-----------------------------------------------------------------------
<EMP><EMPNO>7902</EMPNO><ENAME>FORD</ENAME><DNAME>RESEARCH</DNAME></EMP>
<EMP><EMPNO>7788</EMPNO><ENAME>SCOTT</ENAME><DNAME>RESEARCH</DNAME></EMP>


---------------------------------------------------------------------------
| Id  | Operation          | Name | Rows | Bytes | Cost (%CPU) | Time     |
---------------------------------------------------------------------------
|   0 | SELECT STATEMENT   |      |    1 |    59 |    7   (15) | 00:00:01 |
|*  1 |  HASH JOIN         |      |    1 |    59 |    7   (15) | 00:00:01 |
|*  2 |   TABLE ACCESS FULL| EMP  |    1 |    39 |    3    (0) | 00:00:01 |
|   3 |   TABLE ACCESS FULL| DEPT |    4 |    80 |    3    (0) | 00:00:01 |
---------------------------------------------------------------------------
```

The XML Query selects directly from the EMP and DEPT tables. Note the execution plan: Oracle is doing a hash join of EMP and DEPT, which means the XML Query is analyzed before execution and the optimizer chooses the best possible execution plan. The columns clause defines the name and datatype of the columns that are returned. Without the columns clause, only one column named COLUMN_NAME containing an XMLTYPE is returned. The path string identifies the location of the column within the XML hierarchy.

XML Query can now be an expression.

```
CREATE TABLE
    T
AS
SELECT
    TABLE_NAME
FROM
    USER_TABLES;
SELECT
    TABLE_NAME,
    C
FROM
    T,
    XMLTABLE
    (
        (
        SELECT
            '
            let $j := ora:view("'||T.TABLE_NAME||'")
            return <c>{count($j)}</c>
            '
        FROM
            DUAL
        )
        COLUMNS C NUMBER PATH '/C'
    );
```

```
TABLE_NAME                              C
------------------------------- ----------
SALGRADE                                5
BONUS                                   0
EMP                                    14
DEPT                                    4
```

The query is built dynamically. The table name here is selected from table T, so it could be any expression.

Aggregation

XMLAGG is used to aggregate multiple rows in a single XML document:

```
SELECT
    XMLELEMENT
    (
        EMP,
        XMLAGG
        (
            XMLELEMENT
            (
                DEPT,
                XMLATTRIBUTES(DEPTNO),
                XMLAGG
                (
                    XMLELEMENT
                    (
                        NAME,
                        ENAME
                    )
                    ORDER BY
                        ENAME
                )
            )
            ORDER BY
                DEPTNO
        )
    )
FROM
    EMP
GROUP BY
    DEPTNO;
```

```
EMP
----------------------------
<EMP>
   <DEPT DEPTNO="10">
      <NAME>CLARK</NAME>
      <NAME>KING</NAME>
      <NAME>MILLER</NAME>
   </DEPT>
   <DEPT DEPTNO="20">
      <NAME>ADAMS</NAME>
      <NAME>FORD</NAME>
      <NAME>JONES</NAME>
      <NAME>SCOTT</NAME>
      <NAME>SMITH</NAME>
   </DEPT>
   <DEPT DEPTNO="30">
      <NAME>ALLEN</NAME>
      <NAME>BLAKE</NAME>
      <NAME>JAMES</NAME>
      <NAME>MARTIN</NAME>
      <NAME>TURNER</NAME>
      <NAME>WARD</NAME>
   </DEPT>
</EMP>
```

The inner XMLAGG function aggregates the employees in each department and the outer XMLAGG aggregates the department in the whole table. The result is a well structured document that displays all the employees.

XMLSERIALIZE

XMLSERIALIZE converts an XMLTYPE to a CLOB, a VARCHAR2 or a BLOB. In 11g, the INDENT clause provides indented results for better readability. XMLSERIALIZE accepts both well-formed content and a well-formed document.

```
SELECT
   XMLSERIALIZE
   (
      DOCUMENT
      EXTRACT(OBJECT_VALUE, '//CANTON[@ID="VS"]')
      INDENT SIZE=3
   ) VS
FROM
   WORLD;
```

```
VS
-------------------------------------
<CANTON ID="VS">
    <NAME>Valais</NAME>
    <DETAILS>
        <ENTRY>1815-01-01</ENTRY>
        <LANGUAGE_LIST>
            <LANGUAGE>French</LANGUAGE>
            <LANGUAGE>German</LANGUAGE>
        </LANGUAGE_LIST>
    </DETAILS>
</CANTON>
```

XMLCAST

XMLCAST in 11g casts to various datatypes like NUMBER or DATE.

```
SELECT
    *
FROM
(
    SELECT
        XMLCAST
        (
            EXTRACT
            (
                S.COLUMN_VALUE,
                '/CANTON/@ID'
            )
            AS
            VARCHAR2(2)
        ) ID,
        XMLCAST
        (
            EXTRACT
            (
                S.COLUMN_VALUE,
                '/CANTON/NAME'
            )
            AS
            VARCHAR2(20)
        ) NAME,
        XMLCAST
        (
            EXTRACT
            (
                S.COLUMN_VALUE,
                '/CANTON/DETAILS/ENTRY'
            )
            AS
            DATE
        ) ENTRY
    FROM
        WORLD,
        TABLE(XMLSEQUENCE(EXTRACT(WORLD.OBJECT_VALUE, '//CANTON'))) S
```

```
    ORDER BY
        ENTRY
)
WHERE
    ROWNUM<5;
```

```
ID NAME                    ENTRY
-- --------------------    ----------
UR Uri                     01-JAN-1291
SZ Schwyz                  01-JAN-1291
OW Obwald                  01-JAN-1291
NW Nidwald                 01-JAN-1291
```

ID and NAME are cast to strings and ENTRY is cast to a date.

Document manipulation

Oracle SQL supplies functions to modify the document. Even if the functions are called INSERT or UPDATE or DELETE, they do not change the data in the table, but they modify the columns returned by the query.

UPDATEXML searches for an XPATH expression and updates it.

```
SELECT
    EXTRACT(
        UPDATEXML
        (
            OBJECT_VALUE,
            '//DETAILS[ENTRY="1291-01-01"]/ENTRY',
            XMLELEMENT(ENTRY, TO_DATE('01-08-1291','DD-MM-YYYY'))
        )
        , '//CANTON[NAME="Uri"]'
    ) URI
FROM
    WORLD;
```

```
URI
----------------------------------
<CANTON ID="UR">
   <NAME>Uri</NAME>
   <DETAILS>
      <ENTRY>1291-08-01</ENTRY>
      <LANGUAGE>German</LANGUAGE>
   </DETAILS>
</CANTON>
```

In the WORLD table, each entry of 1291-01-01 is updated by a new date. In the latest versions of Oracle, the XML dates are stored according to the XML convention SYYYY-MM-DD for dates and SYYYY-MM-DD"T"HH24:MI:SSXFF for timestamps. In earlier releases, the date was stored according to the NLS settings.

UPDATEXML can change any element of the document.

```
SELECT
    UPDATEXML
    (
        XMLTYPE
        (
            CURSOR
            (
                SELECT
                    *
                FROM
                    DEPT
            )
        ),
        '//ROW[DEPTNO=10]/LOC',
        XMLTYPE('<CLOSED/>')
    ) DEPT
FROM
    DUAL;
```

```
DEPT
-----------------------------------
<?xml version="1.0"?>
<ROWSET>
    <ROW>
        <DEPTNO>10</DEPTNO>
        <DNAME>ACCOUNTING</DNAME>
        <CLOSED/>
    </ROW>
    <ROW>
        <DEPTNO>20</DEPTNO>
        <DNAME>RESEARCH</DNAME>
        <LOC>DALLAS</LOC>
    </ROW>
    <ROW>
        <DEPTNO>30</DEPTNO>
        <DNAME>SALES</DNAME>
        <LOC>CHICAGO</LOC>
    </ROW>
    <ROW>
        <DEPTNO>40</DEPTNO>
        <DNAME>OPERATIONS</DNAME>
        <LOC>BOSTON</LOC>
    </ROW>
</ROWSET>
```

The location of department 10 is replaced by an empty tag. The underlying table DEPT is not changed, only the result set is modified.

INSERTXMLBEFORE inserts an XML element before the matched XPATH expression.

```
SELECT
   INSERTXMLBEFORE
   (
      XMLTYPE
      (
         CURSOR
         (
            SELECT
               ENAME,
               SAL
            FROM
               EMP
            WHERE
               DEPTNO=10
            ORDER BY
               SAL
         )
      ),
      '//ROW[SAL>=2000]/ENAME',
      XMLTYPE('<HIGH/>')
   ) DEPT10
FROM
   DUAL;
```

```
DEPT10
-------------------------------
<?xml version="1.0"?>
<ROWSET>
   <ROW>
      <ENAME>MILLER</ENAME>
      <SAL>1300</SAL>
   </ROW>
   <ROW>
      <HIGH/>
      <ENAME>CLARK</ENAME>
      <SAL>2450</SAL>
   </ROW>
   <ROW>
      <HIGH/>
      <ENAME>KING</ENAME>
      <SAL>5000</SAL>
   </ROW>
</ROWSET>
```

Each employee with a salary greater than or equal to 2000 gets a HIGH tag before his name.

INSERTCHILDXML (10gR2) appends a tag after the child elements of the XPATH expression.

```
SELECT
   INSERTCHILDXML
   (
      XMLTYPE
      (
         CURSOR
         (
            SELECT
               ENAME,
               SAL
            FROM
               EMP
            WHERE
               DEPTNO=10
            ORDER BY
               SAL
         )
      ),
      '//ROW[SAL>=2000]',
      'HIGH',
      XMLTYPE('<HIGH/>')
   ) INSERTCHILDXML
FROM
   DUAL;
```

```
INSERTCHILDXML
-----------------------------------------
<?xml version="1.0"?>
<ROWSET>
   <ROW>
      <ENAME>MILLER</ENAME>
      <SAL>1300</SAL>
   </ROW>
   <ROW>
      <ENAME>CLARK</ENAME>
      <SAL>2450</SAL>
      <HIGH/>
   </ROW>
   <ROW>
      <ENAME>KING</ENAME>
      <SAL>5000</SAL>
      <HIGH/>
   </ROW>
</ROWSET>
```

INSERTCHILDXML appends a HIGH tag after the child elements of ROW where the salary is greater than or equal to 2000.

When the element is prefixed with a @, it is treated as an attribute.

```
SELECT
   INSERTCHILDXML
   (
```

```
        XMLTYPE
        (
            CURSOR
            (
                SELECT
                    DNAME
                FROM
                    DEPT
                ORDER BY
                    DEPTNO
            )
        ),
        '//ROW[4]',
        '@STATUS',
        'INACTIVE'
    ) DEPT
FROM
    DUAL;
```

```
DEPT
----------------------------------------
<?xml version="1.0"?>
<ROWSET>
    <ROW>
        <DNAME>ACCOUNTING</DNAME>
    </ROW>
    <ROW>
        <DNAME>RESEARCH</DNAME>
    </ROW>
    <ROW>
        <DNAME>SALES</DNAME>
    </ROW>
    <ROW STATUS="INACTIVE">
        <DNAME>OPERATIONS</DNAME>
    </ROW>
</ROWSET>
```

A status is added to the 4th row.

APPENDCHILDXML appends XML content to a node. It works similar to INSERTCHILDXML; additionally, it can add different node types:

```
SELECT
    APPENDCHILDXML
    (
        OBJECT_VALUE,
        '/COUNTRY',
        XMLFOREST(7.5E6 AS POPULATION, '[+]' AS FLAG)
    ) APPENDCHILDXML
FROM
    WORLD;
```

```
APPENDCHILDXML
----------------------------------------------------
<COUNTRY ID="CH">
   <NAME>Switzerland</NAME>
   <CANTON_LIST>
      ...
   </CANTON_LIST>
   <POPULATION>7500000</POPULATION>
   <FLAG>[+]</FLAG>
</COUNTRY>
```

The content generated by the XMLFOREST is appended after the canton list where canton list is the last child of /COUNTRY.

DELETEXML removes elements from the document.

```
SELECT
   DELETEXML
   (
      DELETEXML
      (
         OBJECT_VALUE,
         '//CANTON[DETAILS//LANGUAGE!="French"]'
      ),
      '//DETAILS'
   )
FROM
   WORLD;
```

```
XMLSERIALIZE(DOCUMENTDELETEXML(D
------------------------------
<COUNTRY ID="CH">
   <NAME>Switzerland</NAME>
   <CANTON_LIST>
      <CANTON ID="VD">
         <NAME>Vaud</NAME>
      </CANTON>
      <CANTON ID="NE">
         <NAME>Neuchatel</NAME>
      </CANTON>
      <CANTON ID="GE">
         <NAME>Geneva</NAME>
      </CANTON>
      <CANTON ID="JU">
         <NAME>Jura</NAME>
      </CANTON>
   </CANTON_LIST>
</COUNTRY>
```

The inner DELETEXML removes the cantons with a language different than French and the outer DELETEXML removes every DETAILS instance.

Pivot

The PIVOT operator in 11g aggregates multiple rows as columns. The PIVOT XML aggregates the rows as elements. In addition to the regular PIVOT syntax, PIVOT XML does not require explicit columns listing by allowing the ANY keyword.

```
SELECT
    *
FROM
(
    SELECT
        JOB,
        SAL
    FROM
        EMP
)
PIVOT XML
(
    MIN(SAL) AS "MIN SAL",
    MAX(SAL) AS "MAX SAL",
    COUNT(*) AS "COUNT"
FOR
    (JOB)
IN
    (ANY)
);
```

```
JOB_XML
----------------------------------------------

<PivotSet>
   <item>
      <column name="JOB">ANALYST</column>
      <column name="MIN SAL">3000</column>
      <column name="MAX SAL">3000</column>
      <column name="COUNT">2</column>
   </item>
   <item>
      <column name="JOB">CLERK</column>
      <column name="MIN SAL">800</column>
      <column name="MAX SAL">1300</column>
      <column name="COUNT">4</column>
   </item>
   <item>
      <column name="JOB">MANAGER</column>
      <column name="MIN SAL">2450</column>
      <column name="MAX SAL">2975</column>
      <column name="COUNT">3</column>
   </item>
   <item>
      <column name="JOB">PRESIDENT</column>
      <column name="MIN SAL">5000</column>
      <column name="MAX SAL">5000</column>
      <column name="COUNT">1</column>
   </item>
   <item>
      <column name="JOB">SALESMAN</column>
      <column name="MIN SAL">1250</column>
      <column name="MAX SAL">1600</column>
      <column name="COUNT">4</column>
   </item>
</PivotSet>
```

For each job, the minimum and maximum salary as well as the count of employees is returned.

Conclusion

This chapter is a detailed overview of XML and its various components, including new additions in 11g. Definitions and examples are given for XML Instance, XMLTYPE, XMLELEMENT, XPATH expressions, XQuery and other elements. Examples are also given for well-formed content and documents as well as ones that are not well-formed.

Exercises

1. XMLTYPE

    What are the different arguments accepted by the XMLTYPE constructor?

2. XMLELEMENT

    What is the difference between the two following expressions?

    ```
    SELECT
        XMLELEMENT(DUMMY, DUMMY) EXPR1,
        XMLELEMENT(EVALNAME DUMMY, DUMMY) EXPR2
    FROM
        DUAL;
    ```

3. Concatenation

    What is the difference between the two following queries?

    ```
    SELECT
        XMLFOREST(ENAME, EMPNO) EXPR1
    FROM
        EMP;
    ```

    ```
    SELECT
        XMLCONCAT(ENAME, EMPNO) EXPR2
    FROM
        EMP;
    ```

4. XPATH

    Explain the difference between / and //.

    ```
    SELECT
        EXTRACT(OBJECT_VALUE,'/COUNTRY/NAME') NAME,
        EXTRACT(OBJECT_VALUE,'//CANTON//ENTRY') ENTRY
    FROM
        WORLD;
    ```

5. XMLSEQUENCE

    What is the result of the following query?

    ```
    SELECT
    ```

```
      COUNT(*)
FROM
   WORLD,
   TABLE(XMLSEQUENCE(EXTRACT(OBJECT_VALUE,'/COUNTRY/CANTON_LIST/CANTON')));
```

6. XQUERY

What is the result of the following query?

```
SELECT
   *
FROM
   XMLTABLE
   (
      '
      for $I in 1 to 10
      let $I := $J*$I
      return <I>{$I}</I>
      '
      PASSING 2 AS J
      COLUMNS I NUMBER PATH '/I'
   );
```

7. Aggregation

Compare the following queries:

```
SELECT
   XMLAGG(XMLELEMENT(EVALNAME 'DEPT_'||DEPTNO,SUM(SAL)))
FROM
   EMP
GROUP BY
   DEPTNO;
```

```
SELECT
   DEPTNO_XML
FROM
(
   SELECT
      DEPTNO,
      SAL
   FROM
      EMP
)
PIVOT XML
(
   SUM(SAL)
   FOR
      (DEPTNO)
   IN
      (ANY)
);
```

8. Cast

Compare the two following queries. What are the expected formats for ENTRY?

```
SELECT
    XMLCAST(EXTRACT(OBJECT_VALUE,'//CANTON[@ID="GE"]//ENTRY') AS DATE)
FROM
    WORLD;
```

```
SELECT
    CAST(EXTRACTVALUE(OBJECT_VALUE,'//CANTON[@ID="GE"]//ENTRY') AS DATE)
FROM
    WORLD;
```

9. Document manipulation

In the WORLD table, delete all cantons except Geneva (GE) and delete all details.

Solutions

1. XMLTYPE

   What are the different arguments accepted by the XMLTYPE constructor?

   The XMLTYPE constructor accepts CLOB, BLOB, BFILE, VARCHAR2 and REF Cursor.

2. XMLELEMENT

   What is the difference between the two following expressions?

   ```
   SELECT
      XMLELEMENT(DUMMY, DUMMY) EXPR1,
      XMLELEMENT(EVALNAME DUMMY, DUMMY) EXPR2
   FROM
      DUAL;
   ```

   The first argument is the name of the tag. When prefixed by EVALNAME, the tag name is evaluated dynamically.

   ```
   EXPR1                 EXPR2
   --------------------  --------------------
   <DUMMY>X</DUMMY>      <X>X</X>
   ```

3. Concatenation

   What is the difference between the two following queries?

   ```
   SELECT
      XMLFOREST(ENAME, EMPNO)
   FROM
      EMP;
   ```

   ```
   XMLFOREST(ENAME,EMPNO)
   ----------------------------------------------------------------
   <ENAME>SMITH</ENAME><EMPNO>7369</EMPNO>
   <ENAME>ALLEN</ENAME><EMPNO>7499</EMPNO>
   <ENAME>WARD</ENAME><EMPNO>7521</EMPNO>
   <ENAME>JONES</ENAME><EMPNO>7566</EMPNO>
   <ENAME>MARTIN</ENAME><EMPNO>7654</EMPNO>
   <ENAME>BLAKE</ENAME><EMPNO>7698</EMPNO>
   <ENAME>CLARK</ENAME><EMPNO>7782</EMPNO>
   <ENAME>SCOTT</ENAME><EMPNO>7788</EMPNO>
   <ENAME>KING</ENAME><EMPNO>7839</EMPNO>
   ```

```
<ENAME>TURNER</ENAME><EMPNO>7844</EMPNO>
<ENAME>ADAMS</ENAME><EMPNO>7876</EMPNO>
<ENAME>JAMES</ENAME><EMPNO>7900</EMPNO>
<ENAME>FORD</ENAME><EMPNO>7902</EMPNO>
<ENAME>MILLER</ENAME><EMPNO>7934</EMPNO>
```

XMLFOREST accepts any datatypes as arguments.

```
SELECT
    XMLCONCAT(ENAME, EMPNO)
FROM
    EMP;
ERROR at line 2:
ORA-00932: inconsistent datatypes: expected - got -
```

XMLCONCAT accepts only arguments of XMLTYPE. ENAME is a VARCHAR2 column and EMPNO a number.

4. XPATH

Explain the difference between / and //.

```
SELECT
    EXTRACT(OBJECT_VALUE,'/COUNTRY/NAME') NAME,
    EXTRACT(OBJECT_VALUE,'//CANTON//ENTRY') ENTRY
FROM
    WORLD;
```

```
NAME                          ENTRY
------------------------      --------------------------------------------------
<NAME>Switzerland</NAME>      <ENTRY>1351-01-01</ENTRY><ENTRY>1353-01-01</ENTRY>
                              <ENTRY>1332-01-01</ENTRY><ENTRY>1291-01-01</ENTRY>
                              <ENTRY>1291-01-01</ENTRY><ENTRY>1291-01-01</ENTRY>
                              <ENTRY>1291-01-01</ENTRY><ENTRY>1352-01-01</ENTRY>
                              <ENTRY>1352-01-01</ENTRY><ENTRY>1481-01-01</ENTRY>
                              <ENTRY>1481-01-01</ENTRY><ENTRY>1501-01-01</ENTRY>
                              <ENTRY>1501-01-01</ENTRY><ENTRY>1501-01-01</ENTRY>
                              <ENTRY>1513-01-01</ENTRY><ENTRY>1513-01-01</ENTRY>
                              <ENTRY>1803-01-01</ENTRY><ENTRY>1803-01-01</ENTRY>
                              <ENTRY>1803-01-01</ENTRY><ENTRY>1803-01-01</ENTRY>
                              <ENTRY>1803-01-01</ENTRY><ENTRY>1803-01-01</ENTRY>
                              <ENTRY>1815-01-01</ENTRY><ENTRY>1815-01-01</ENTRY>
                              <ENTRY>1815-01-01</ENTRY><ENTRY>1979-01-01</ENTRY>
```

/ denotes an absolute path where country is the root element and name is a top element directly below country. // is searched in the path, canton is searched in the whole document and entry is searched below the canton in elements and sub-elements.

It is recommended to use / whenever possible because // could imply a higher memory, CPU consumption and response time.

5. XMLSEQUENCE

What is the result of the following query?

```sql
SELECT
    COUNT(*)
FROM
    WORLD,
    TABLE(XMLSEQUENCE(EXTRACT(OBJECT_VALUE,'/COUNTRY/CANTON_LIST/CANTON')));
```

```
  COUNT(*)
----------
        26
```

The XMLTYPE collection of cantons is unnested and the number of cantons is returned.

6. XQUERY

What is the result of the following query?

```sql
SELECT
    *
FROM
    XMLTABLE
    (
        '
        for $I in 1 to 10
        let $I := $J*$I
        return <I>{$I}</I>
        '
        PASSING 2 AS J
        COLUMNS I NUMBER PATH '/I'
    );
```

```
         I
----------
         2
         4
         6
         8
        10
        12
        14
        16
        18
        20
```

The *for* loop generates 10 rows with values of $I from 1 to 10. The value 2 is passed to the variable $J and each value of $I is multiplied by $J, so a list of even numbers is returned.

7. Aggregation

Compare the following queries:

```
SELECT
    XMLAGG(XMLELEMENT(EVALNAME 'DEPT_'||DEPTNO,SUM(SAL)))
FROM
    EMP
GROUP BY
    DEPTNO;
```

```
XMLAGG(XMLELEMENT(EVALNAME
-------------------------
<DEPT_10>8750</DEPT_10>
<DEPT_20>10875</DEPT_20>
<DEPT_30>9400</DEPT_30>
```

```
SELECT
    DEPTNO_XML
FROM
(
    SELECT
        DEPTNO,
        SAL
    FROM
        EMP
)
PIVOT XML
(
    SUM(SAL)
    FOR
        (DEPTNO)
    IN
        (ANY)
);
```

```
DEPTNO_XML
-----------------------------------------------
<PivotSet>
   <item>
      <column name="DEPTNO">10</column>
      <column name="SUM(SAL)">8750</column>
   </item>
   <item>
      <column name="DEPTNO">20</column>
      <column name="SUM(SAL)">10875</column>
   </item>
   <item>
      <column name="DEPTNO">30</column>
      <column name="SUM(SAL)">9400</column>
```

```
    </item>
</PivotSet>
```

The queries are very similar; for each department, the salary is summed and an XML type is returned. Note the first query aggregates the XML elements in an XML content with no root element, whereas PivotSet is a well-formed document.

8. Cast

Compare the two following queries. What are the expected formats for ENTRY?

```
SELECT
    XMLCAST(EXTRACT(OBJECT_VALUE,'//CANTON[@ID="GE"]//ENTRY') AS DATE)
FROM
    WORLD;
```

```
XMLCAST(EXTRACT(OBJECT_VALUE,
---------------------------
Sunday, January 01, 1815
```

The ENTRY date is in the XML format SYYYY-MM-DD.

```
SELECT
    CAST(EXTRACTVALUE(OBJECT_VALUE,'//CANTON[@ID="GE"]//ENTRY') AS DATE)
FROM
    WORLD;
```

```
ERROR at line 2:
ORA-01846: not a valid day of the week
```

The ENTRY is not compatible with the session setting for NLS_DATE_FORMAT. To cast the date with a non-XML function, it is possible to use TO_DATE.

```
SELECT
    TO_DATE
    (
        EXTRACTVALUE(OBJECT_VALUE,'//CANTON[@ID="GE"]//ENTRY'),
        'SYYYY-MM-DD'
    )
FROM
    WORLD;
```

9. Document manipulation

In the WORLD table, delete all cantons except Geneva (GE) and delete all details.

```
SELECT
   DELETEXML
   (
      DELETEXML
      (
         OBJECT_VALUE,'//CANTON[@ID!="GE"]'
      ), '//DETAILS'
   )
FROM
   WORLD;
```

```
DELETEXML(DELETEXML(OBJECT_VALUE
--------------------------------
<COUNTRY ID="CH">
   <NAME>Switzerland</NAME>
   <CANTON_LIST>
      <CANTON ID="GE">
         <NAME>Geneva</NAME>
      </CANTON>
   </CANTON_LIST>
</COUNTRY>
```

The inner DELETEXML deletes all cantons where the attribute ID is not equal to GE. The outer DELETEXML deletes the details. This, however, did not delete anything in the table. To update the node, use UPDATE.

```
UPDATE
   WORLD
SET
   OBJECT_VALUE
   =
   DELETEXML
   (
      DELETEXML
      (
         OBJECT_VALUE,'//CANTON[@ID!="GE"]'
      ), '//DETAILS'
   );
```

Oracle Hierarchies

Hierarchies

Hierarchical Queries

A hierarchy is built upon a parent-child relationship within the same table or view. Hierarchical query is one of the very first features of the Oracle Database and was introduced more than twenty years ago!

In a traditional query, Oracle looks for a good execution plan and retrieves the rows one after the other, in no specific order. In a hierarchy, the rows are organized as a tree:

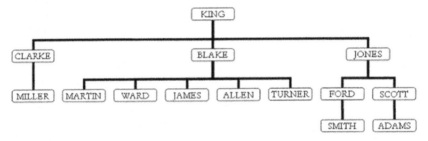

Figure 6.1: *Hierarchy Tree*

In the well known employee (EMP) table, King is the president. Below the president, each manager has his own department. In the accounting department, Clarke has one clerk, Miller. The sales department is under the control of Blake. Blake has four salesmen - Allen, Ward, Martin and Turner - and one clerk, James. Jones leads the research department. The analyst Ford has one clerk named Smith and the analyst Scott also has one clerk, Adams.

Most companies have a very hierarchical structure. The hierarchy can be traversed bottom-up; for example, to retrieve the top hierarchy of an employee, or top-down, to discover all employees under one manager.

One of the most common issues in hierarchies is the cycling. That is, if the top manager is his own boss, Oracle will detect a loop and return an error. This issue is partly fixed in 10g by a new mechanism which sets a flag and stops processing the offending branch.

Until 9i, the fields available were either on the current row or on the parent row. In 10g, the fields at the top of the hierarchy are also accessible, which enables analysis and aggregation over the whole hierarchy. One more addition in 10g is the flag for the bottom of the hierarchy, called the leaf rows.

CONNECT BY, PRIOR and START WITH

There are two mandatory keywords to build a hierarchy, CONNECT BY and PRIOR. A hierarchy is built when one row is the parent of another row. START WITH defines the first ancestor.

```
SELECT
    ENAME
FROM
    EMP
CONNECT BY
    PRIOR EMPNO = MGR
START WITH
    ENAME = 'JONES';
```

```
ENAME
----------
JONES
SCOTT
ADAMS
FORD
SMITH
```

Jones and his employees are returned. Adams is an employee of Scott and Scott is an employee of Jones so Adams is also returned.

LEVEL

The pseudo-column level returns the depth of the hierarchy. The first level is the root:

```
SELECT
    ENAME
FROM
    EMP
WHERE
    LEVEL=2
CONNECT BY
    PRIOR EMPNO = MGR
START WITH
    ENAME = 'JONES';
```

```
ENAME
--------
SCOTT
FORD
```

Only the direct employees of Jones are returned. Jones is the first ancestor and has a level of 1. Adams and Smith are one level below the direct employees and belong to the third level started by Jones.

The tree is displayed with the children indented under their parents by using padding with a number of spaces proportional to LEVEL.

```
SELECT
    CONCAT
    (
        LPAD
        (
            ' ',
            LEVEL*3-3
        ),
        ENAME
    ) ENAME
FROM
    EMP
CONNECT BY
    PRIOR EMPNO = MGR
START WITH
    MGR IS NULL;
```

```
ENAME
------------------
KING
   JONES
      SCOTT
         ADAMS
      FORD
         SMITH
   BLAKE
      ALLEN
      WARD
      MARTIN
      TURNER
      JAMES
   CLARK
      MILLER
```

Starting with the top manager, the names of the employees are padded with white spaces according to their level.

ORDER SIBLINGS BY

The rows in a hierarchical query are returned as a tree, the children following the parent. ORDER SIBLINGS BY preserves the hierarchy and orders the children of each parent.

```
SELECT
   CONCAT
   (
      LPAD
      (
         ' ',
         LEVEL*3-3
      ),
      ENAME
   ) ENAME
FROM
   EMP
CONNECT BY
   PRIOR EMPNO = MGR
START WITH
   MGR IS NULL
ORDER SIBLINGS BY
   EMP.ENAME;
```

```
ENAME
----------------
KING
    BLAKE
        ALLEN
        JAMES
        MARTIN
        TURNER
        WARD
    CLARK
        MILLER
    JONES
        FORD
            SMITH
        SCOTT
            ADAMS
```

Clark comes after Blake and before Jones; they are under King and ordered by their name. Their children are sorted and the hierarchical appearance is preserved.

ORDER BY without SIBLINGS destroys the hierarchy:

```
SELECT
    CONCAT
    (
        LPAD
        (
            ' ',
            LEVEL*3-3
        ),
        ENAME
    ) ENAME
FROM
    EMP
CONNECT BY
    PRIOR EMPNO = MGR
START WITH
    MGR IS NULL
ORDER BY
    EMP.ENAME;
```

```
ENAME
--------------
        ADAMS
     ALLEN
  BLAKE
  CLARK
       FORD
       JAMES
  JONES
KING
       MARTIN
       MILLER
       SCOTT
         SMITH
       TURNER
       WARD
```

The names are sorted.

PRIOR

The PRIOR keyword in the CONNECT BY clause defines the relationship between the parent and the child. PRIOR identifies the column of the child row where the value matches another column of the parent row.

PRIOR is also useful to select some child and some parent values simultaneously.

```
SELECT
   EMPNO,
   ENAME,
   PRIOR EMPNO MGR_EMPNO,
   PRIOR ENAME MGR_ENAME
FROM
   EMP
WHERE
   LEVEL=2
CONNECT BY
   MGR=PRIOR EMPNO
ORDER BY
   ENAME;
```

```
     EMPNO ENAME      MGR_EMPNO MGR_ENAME
---------- ---------- ---------- ----------
      7876 ADAMS           7788 SCOTT
      7499 ALLEN           7698 BLAKE
      7698 BLAKE           7839 KING
      7782 CLARK           7839 KING
      7902 FORD            7566 JONES
      7900 JAMES           7698 BLAKE
```

```
7566 JONES          7839 KING
7654 MARTIN         7698 BLAKE
7934 MILLER         7782 CLARK
7788 SCOTT          7566 JONES
7369 SMITH          7902 FORD
7844 TURNER         7698 BLAKE
7521 WARD           7698 BLAKE
```

```
-------------------------------------------------
| Id  | Operation                      | Name |
-------------------------------------------------
|   0 | SELECT STATEMENT               |      |
|   1 |  SORT ORDER BY                 |      |
| * 2 |   FILTER                       |      |
| * 3 |    CONNECT BY WITHOUT FILTERING|      |
|   4 |     TABLE ACCESS FULL          | EMP  |
-------------------------------------------------
```

Each employee is selected with his manager. The execution plan reveals that the table is selected only once.

SYS_CONNECT_BY_PATH

The function SYS_CONNECT_BY_PATH returns the hierarchy from the first ancestor to the current row. Each name is separated by a specific character.

```
SELECT
    SYS_CONNECT_BY_PATH(ENAME, '/')
FROM
    EMP
START WITH
    MGR IS NULL
CONNECT BY
    PRIOR EMPNO=MGR;
```

```
SYS_CONNECT_BY_PATH(ENAME,'/')
--------------------------------
/KING
/KING/JONES
/KING/JONES/SCOTT
/KING/JONES/SCOTT/ADAMS
/KING/JONES/FORD
/KING/JONES/FORD/SMITH
/KING/BLAKE
/KING/BLAKE/ALLEN
/KING/BLAKE/WARD
/KING/BLAKE/MARTIN
/KING/BLAKE/TURNER
/KING/BLAKE/JAMES
/KING/CLARK
/KING/CLARK/MILLER
```

The ancestors are concatenated into a slash separated string. The second argument of SYS_CONNECT_BY_PATH must be a single character literal.

CONNECT_BY_ROOT

The function CONNECT_BY_ROOT returns the first ancestor:

```
SELECT
    CONNECT_BY_ROOT ENAME as ANCESTOR,
    ENAME
FROM
    EMP
WHERE
    LEVEL>1
CONNECT BY
    PRIOR EMPNO=MGR;
```

```
ANCESTOR    ENAME
----------  ---------
SCOTT       ADAMS
FORD        SMITH
JONES       SCOTT
JONES       ADAMS
JONES       FORD
JONES       SMITH
BLAKE       ALLEN
BLAKE       WARD
BLAKE       MARTIN
BLAKE       TURNER
BLAKE       JAMES
CLARK       MILLER
KING        JONES
KING        SCOTT
KING        ADAMS
KING        FORD
KING        SMITH
KING        BLAKE
KING        ALLEN
KING        WARD
KING        MARTIN
KING        TURNER
KING        JAMES
KING        CLARK
KING        MILLER
```

Each parent-child relation is defined. For each employee, a list of all his subordinates is returned. Root rows are discarded since they represent the ancestor himself. This revolutionary new capability has been introduced in 10g.

Hierarchies

In Oracle 9i, the CONNECT_BY_ROOT is simulated by using
SUBSTR and SYS_CONNECT_BY_PATH:

```
SELECT
   SUBSTR
   (
      SYS_CONNECT_BY_PATH(ENAME,'/'),
      2,
      INSTR
      (
         SYS_CONNECT_BY_PATH(ENAME,'/'),
         '/',
         2
      )-2
   ) ANCESTOR,
   ENAME
FROM
   EMP
WHERE
   LEVEL>1
CONNECT BY
   PRIOR EMPNO=MGR;
```

```
ANCESTOR   ENAME
---------- ---------
SCOTT      ADAMS
FORD       SMITH
JONES      SCOTT
JONES      ADAMS
JONES      FORD
JONES      SMITH
BLAKE      ALLEN
BLAKE      WARD
BLAKE      MARTIN
BLAKE      TURNER
BLAKE      JAMES
CLARK      MILLER
KING       JONES
KING       SCOTT
KING       ADAMS
KING       FORD
KING       SMITH
KING       BLAKE
KING       ALLEN
KING       WARD
KING       MARTIN
KING       TURNER
KING       JAMES
KING       CLARK
KING       MILLER
```

In each path, the first ancestor is selected by using SUBSTR + INSTR.

CONNECT_BY_ROOT allows subtrees to be aggregated and analyzed.

```
SELECT
    ANCESTOR,
    COUNT(NULLIF(ENAME,ANCESTOR)) COUNT,
    XMLAGG(DECODE(ENAME,ANCESTOR,NULL,XMLELEMENT(ENAME,ENAME))) EMPLOYEES
FROM
(
    SELECT
        CONNECT_BY_ROOT ENAME as ANCESTOR,
        ENAME
    FROM
        EMP
    CONNECT BY
        PRIOR EMPNO=MGR
)
GROUP BY
    ANCESTOR
ORDER BY
    ANCESTOR;
```

```
ANCESTOR    COUNT EMPLOYEES
---------- ----- ------------------------------------------------------------
--
ADAMS          0
ALLEN          0
BLAKE          5
<ENAME>ALLEN</ENAME><ENAME>JAMES</ENAME><ENAME>MARTIN</ENAME>
                 <ENAME>TURNER</ENAME><ENAME>WARD</ENAME>

CLARK          1 <ENAME>MILLER</ENAME>
FORD           1 <ENAME>SMITH</ENAME>
JAMES          0
JONES          4 <ENAME>ADAMS</ENAME><ENAME>FORD</ENAME><ENAME>SCOTT</ENAME>
                 <ENAME>SMITH</ENAME>

KING          13
<ENAME>ADAMS</ENAME><ENAME>ALLEN</ENAME><ENAME>BLAKE</ENAME>
                 <ENAME>CLARK</ENAME><ENAME>FORD</ENAME><ENAME>JAMES</ENAME>

<ENAME>JONES</ENAME><ENAME>MARTIN</ENAME><ENAME>MILLER</ENAME>

<ENAME>SCOTT</ENAME><ENAME>SMITH</ENAME><ENAME>TURNER</ENAME>
                 <ENAME>WARD</ENAME>

MARTIN         0
MILLER         0
SCOTT          1 <ENAME>ADAMS</ENAME>
SMITH          0
TURNER         0
WARD           0
```

For each employee, the count of his employees and an XML instance
containing the name of the employees is returned.

CONNECT BY LOOP

A loop in user data generates an "ORA-01436: CONNECT BY loop in user data" error. A loop is defined in the Oracle Database SQL Language Reference (11.1) documentation as:

"A loop occurs if one row is both the parent (or grandparent or direct ancestor) and a child (or a grandchild or a direct descendent) of another row":

```
WITH
    T
AS
(
    SELECT
        'JOHN' EMPLOYEE,
        'JACK' MANAGER
    FROM
        DUAL
    UNION ALL
    SELECT
        'JACK' EMPLOYEE,
        'JOHN' MANAGER
    FROM
        DUAL
)
SELECT
    EMPLOYEE,
    MANAGER
FROM
    T
CONNECT BY
    PRIOR EMPLOYEE = MANAGER;
```

```
ERROR:
ORA-01436: CONNECT BY loop in user data
```

There is a loop in the user data because John is both the manager and the employee of Jack.

CONNECT BY NOCYCLE and CONNECT_BY_ISCYCLE

With the 10g keyword NOCYCLE, hierarchical queries detect loops and do not generate errors. CONNECT_BY_ISCYCLE pseudo-column is a flag that can be used to detect which row is cycling.

```
WITH
    T
AS
(
    SELECT
        'JOHN' EMPLOYEE,
        'JACK' MANAGER
    FROM
        DUAL
    UNION ALL
    SELECT
        'JACK' EMPLOYEE,
        'JOHN' MANAGER
    FROM
        DUAL
)
SELECT
    SYS_CONNECT_BY_PATH (EMPLOYEE,'/') as EMPLOYEE,
    MANAGER,
    CONNECT_BY_ISCYCLE
FROM
    T
CONNECT BY
NOCYCLE
    PRIOR EMPLOYEE = MANAGER;
```

```
EMPLOYEE         MANAGER CONNECT_BY_ISCYCLE
--------------   ------- ------------------
/JOHN            JACK                     0
/JOHN/JACK       JOHN                     1
/JACK            JOHN                     0
/JACK/JOHN       JACK                     1
```

Sub-employee Jack is cycling because he is the child and parent of John. John is also cycling, because he is the child and parent of Jack.

CONNECT BY without PRIOR

A very popular usage of hierarchical query, documented by Vadim Tropashko in his book *SQL Design Patterns*, is to generate rows.

```
SELECT
    SYS_CONNECT_BY_PATH(DUMMY, '/')
FROM
    DUAL
CONNECT BY
    LEVEL<4;
```

```
SYS_CONNECT_BY_PATH(DUMMY,'/')
--------------------------------
/X
/X/X
/X/X/X
```

According to the official documentation, PRIOR is mandatory.
Oracle Database SQL Language Reference (11.1)
"In a hierarchical query, one expression in the CONNECT BY condition must be qualified by the PRIOR operator".

The single row of dual is both the parent and the child of itself but no loop is generated. It is a very efficient way to generate rows.

CONNECT_BY_IS_LEAF

The 10g pseudo-column CONNECT_BY_IS_LEAF identifies rows that do not have descendants.

```
SELECT
    SYS_CONNECT_BY_PATH(ENAME, '/')
FROM
    EMP
WHERE
    CONNECT_BY_IS_LEAF=1
START WITH
    MGR IS NULL
CONNECT BY
    PRIOR EMPNO=MGR;
```

```
SYS_CONNECT_BY_PATH(ENAME,'/')
-----------------------------------
/KING/JONES/SCOTT/ADAMS
/KING/JONES/FORD/SMITH
/KING/BLAKE/ALLEN
/KING/BLAKE/WARD
/KING/BLAKE/MARTIN
/KING/BLAKE/TURNER
/KING/BLAKE/JAMES
/KING/CLARK/MILLER
```

Only complete paths from the ancestor where MGR is null to the last descendants are displayed.

WHERE and JOIN

Oracle detects in the where clause if the condition is a join condition or a not-join condition. There is a big difference between a join and a not-join condition in that the former is performed before the building of the hierarchy and the later is performed after the hierarchy.

```
SELECT
    SYS_CONNECT_BY_PATH(EMP.ENAME, '/') P
FROM
    EMP,
    TABLE
    (
        SYS.ODCINUMBERLIST(20, 30)
    ) T
WHERE
    EMP.DEPTNO=T.COLUMN_VALUE
CONNECT BY
    PRIOR EMP.EMPNO=EMP.MGR
START WITH
    MGR IS NULL;
no rows selected
```

Oracle detects the join and selects the matching rows.

Only rows from the departments 20 and 30 are used to build the hierarchy. No row in the departments 20 and 30 satisfies the condition MGR IS NULL.

```
SELECT
    SYS_CONNECT_BY_PATH(EMP.ENAME, '/') P
FROM
    EMP
WHERE
    EMP.DEPTNO IN (20, 30)
CONNECT BY
    PRIOR EMPNO=MGR
START WITH
    MGR IS NULL;
```

```
P
---------------------------
/KING/JONES
/KING/JONES/SCOTT
/KING/JONES/SCOTT/ADAMS
/KING/JONES/FORD
/KING/JONES/FORD/SMITH
/KING/BLAKE
/KING/BLAKE/ALLEN
/KING/BLAKE/WARD
/KING/BLAKE/MARTIN
/KING/BLAKE/TURNER
/KING/BLAKE/JAMES
```

The condition is not a join; therefore, the hierarchy is built with all rows. Later, the condition is applied to the children.

```
SELECT
    P
FROM
    (
        SELECT
            SYS_CONNECT_BY_PATH(EMP.ENAME, '/') P,
            DEPTNO
        FROM
            EMP
        CONNECT BY
            PRIOR EMPNO=MGR
        START WITH
            MGR IS NULL
    )
WHERE
    DEPTNO IN (20, 30);
```

```
P
--------------------------
/KING/JONES
/KING/JONES/SCOTT
/KING/JONES/SCOTT/ADAMS
/KING/JONES/FORD
/KING/JONES/FORD/SMITH
/KING/BLAKE
/KING/BLAKE/ALLEN
/KING/BLAKE/WARD
/KING/BLAKE/MARTIN
/KING/BLAKE/TURNER
/KING/BLAKE/JAMES
```

The same query again appears with a subquery. This time, the hierarchy is built with all rows in the subquery and the condition applies to the main query.

The JOIN syntax allows more flexibility to define what should be processed before the hierarchy and what should be processed after.

```
SELECT
    SYS_CONNECT_BY_PATH(ENAME, '/') P
FROM
    EMP
JOIN
    DUAL
ON
(
    HIREDATE > DATE '1981-06-01'
)
```

```
WHERE
   JOB='CLERK'
CONNECT BY
   PRIOR EMPNO=MGR
START WITH
   MGR IS NULL;


P
--------------------
/KING/CLARK/MILLER
```

The DUAL table is joined to EMP. The ON clause is defined before computing the hierarchy, so the whole tree will contain only employees hired after June 1, 1981. The WHERE clause returns only the clerks. The path from the president to the clerks exclusively contains new employees.

Aggregation

It is possible to use aggregation, hierarchies and analytics within the same query:

```
SELECT
   DEPTNO,
   DECODE
   (
      CONNECT_BY_IS_LEAF,
      0, 'LEADER',
      1, 'EMPLOYEE',
      'TOTAL'
   ) LEADFUNC,
   COUNT(*),
   SUM
   (
      COUNT(*)
   )
   OVER
   (
      PARTITION BY DEPTNO
   ) TOTAL_DEPT
FROM
   EMP
CONNECT BY
   PRIOR EMPNO=MGR
START WITH
   MGR IS NULL
GROUP BY
   DEPTNO,
   CONNECT_BY_IS_LEAF
ORDER BY
   DEPTNO,
```

```
CONNECT_BY_IS_LEAF;
```

```
    DEPTNO LEADFUNC    COUNT(*) TOTAL_DEPT
---------- --------  ---------- ----------
        10 LEADER             2          3
        10 EMPLOYEE           1          3
        20 LEADER             3          5
        20 EMPLOYEE           2          5
        30 LEADER             1          6
        30 EMPLOYEE           5          6
```

For each department, the leaves, or employees with no subordinate, and the leaders are aggregated. A global count over the whole department is returned.

Aggregation within a hierarchy is done using the first ancestor operator CONNECT_BY_ROOT (10g).

```
SELECT
   R_ENAME MANAGER,
   MAX(ENAME) KEEP
      (
         DENSE_RANK FIRST
         ORDER BY SAL DESC
      ) BEST_PAID_EMPLOYEE,
   MAX(SAL) SALARY,
   ROUND(AVG(SAL)) AVERAGE_SAL_EMPLOYEES
FROM
   (
      SELECT
         CONNECT_BY_ROOT ENAME R_ENAME,
         ENAME,
         SAL
      FROM
         EMP
      WHERE
         CONNECT_BY_IS_LEAF=1
         AND
         LEVEL>1
      CONNECT BY
         PRIOR EMPNO=MGR
   )
GROUP BY
   R_ENAME;
```

```
MANAGER BEST_PAID_    SALARY AVERAGE_SAL_EMPLOYEES
------- ----------  ---------- ---------------------
BLAKE   ALLEN             1600                  1310
CLARK   MILLER            1300                  1300
FORD    SMITH              800                   800
JONES   ADAMS             1100                   950
KING    ALLEN             1600                  1219
SCOTT   ADAMS             1100                  1100
```

The subquery selects bosses with their employees. CONNECT_BY_ROOT (10g) saves the ancestor when traversing the hierarchy. CONNECT_BY_IS_LEAF returns the subordinates with no leading function. LEVEL>1 prevents returning the employee as his own ancestor.

The main query then groups by the root name and returns the best paid employee with his name and his salary. Additionally, the average salary is returned.

A common application of hierarchy is finding the shortest path between two nodes.

🖫 tablepath.sql

```
-- ************************************************
-- Copyright © 2008 by Rampant TechPress
-- This script is free for non-commercial purposes
-- with no warranties.  Use at your own risk.
--
-- To license this script for a commercial purpose,
-- contact rtp@rampant.cc
-- ************************************************
-- Id      : $Id: tablepath.sql,v 1.1 2008/05/23 13:45:23 Laurent Exp $
-- Author : $Author: Laurent $
-- Date    : $Date: 2008/05/23 13:45:23 $
--
-- Create PATH Table in current schema
--

WHENEVER SQLERROR EXIT

EXEC EXECUTE IMMEDIATE 'DROP TABLE PATH'; EXCEPTION WHEN OTHERS THEN NULL

-- Create Table
CREATE TABLE
    PATH
(
    SRC VARCHAR2(3),
    DST VARCHAR2(3),
    DISTANCE NUMBER
);

INSERT INTO
    PATH(SRC,DST,DISTANCE)
VALUES
    ( 'A', 'A', 0);
INSERT INTO
    PATH(SRC,DST,DISTANCE)
VALUES
```

```
   ( 'A', 'B', 8);
INSERT INTO
   PATH(SRC,DST,DISTANCE)
VALUES
   ( 'A', 'C', null);
INSERT INTO
   PATH(SRC,DST,DISTANCE)
VALUES
   ( 'A', 'D', 40);
INSERT INTO
   PATH(SRC,DST,DISTANCE)
VALUES
   ( 'B', 'A', 8);
INSERT INTO
   PATH(SRC,DST,DISTANCE)
VALUES
   ( 'B', 'B', 0);
INSERT INTO
   PATH(SRC,DST,DISTANCE)
VALUES
   ( 'B', 'C', 15);
INSERT INTO
   PATH(SRC,DST,DISTANCE)
VALUES
   ( 'B', 'D', 50);
INSERT INTO
   PATH(SRC,DST,DISTANCE)
VALUES
   ( 'C', 'A', null);
INSERT INTO
   PATH(SRC,DST,DISTANCE)
VALUES
   ( 'C', 'B', 15);
INSERT INTO
   PATH(SRC,DST,DISTANCE)
VALUES
   ( 'C', 'C', 0);
INSERT INTO
   PATH(SRC,DST,DISTANCE)
VALUES
   ( 'C', 'D', 1);
INSERT INTO
   PATH(SRC,DST,DISTANCE)
VALUES
   ( 'D', 'A', 40);
INSERT INTO
   PATH(SRC,DST,DISTANCE)
VALUES
   ( 'D', 'B', 50);
INSERT INTO
   PATH(SRC,DST,DISTANCE)
VALUES
   ( 'D', 'C', 1);
INSERT INTO
   PATH(SRC,DST,DISTANCE)
VALUES
   ( 'D', 'D', 0);
```

```
COMMIT;
```

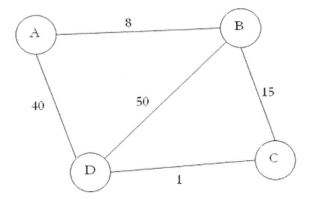

Figure 6.2: *Distances Between Nodes*

```
CREATE FUNCTION EVAL(EXPR VARCHAR2) RETURN NUMBER IS
   RC NUMBER;
BEGIN
   EXECUTE IMMEDIATE 'BEGIN :1 := '||EXPR||'; END;' USING OUT RC;
   RETURN RC;
END;
/
```

```
SELECT
   ROOTSRC,
   DST,
   MIN(N)
FROM
(
   SELECT
      CONNECT_BY_ROOT SRC ROOTSRC,
      DST,
      EVAL(SYS_CONNECT_BY_PATH(NVL(TO_CHAR(DISTANCE),'NULL'),'+')) N
   FROM
      PATH
   CONNECT BY
   NOCYCLE
      PRIOR DST=SRC
   )
GROUP BY
   ROOTSRC,
   DST
ORDER BY
   ROOTSRC,
   DST;
```

```
R D     MIN(N)
- - ----------
A A          0
A B          8
A C         23
A D         24
B A          8
B B          0
B C         15
B D         16
C A         23
C B         15
C C          0
C D          1
D A         24
D B         16
D C          1
D D          0
```

There are multiple ways to go from B to D, but the shortest is via C for a cost of 15+1=16. To evaluate the cost of the path, the SYS_CONNECT_BY_PATH returns a plus-separated string. This string is evaluated in the function EVAL that uses dynamic SQL.

Conclusion

Hierarchical queries, which are where a hierarchy is built upon a parent-child relationship within the same table or view, have been a part of Oracle databases for more than 20 years. The main keywords in building a hierarchy are STAND BY, PRIOR and START WITH. From there, several different functions can be used to acquire different results such as SYS_CONNECT_BY_PATH, CONNECT_BY_ROOT, and CONNECT_BY_IS_LEAF. These keywords and functions are just some of the elements of hierarchies that covered in this chapter.

Exercises

1. CONNECT BY, PRIOR and START WITH

   Retrieve the top hierarchy of Adams. Use LPAD to format output.

2. LEVEL

   Starting with KING, retrieve all level-4 employees.

3. PRIOR

   For each employee, retrieve the ratio of his salary to the salary of his manager. Return the rows in descending order of the ratio.

4. SYS_CONNECT_BY_PATH

   Using SYS_CONNECT_BY_PATH and aggregation, return an aggregated list of employees grouped by department.

5. CONNECT_BY_ROOT

   For each employee, retrieve the sum of his salary and the salary of all his employees.

6. Cycle

   Retrieve the three employees that make the query fail.

```
SELECT
    SYS_CONNECT_BY_PATH(ENAME,'/')
FROM
    EMP
CONNECT BY
    PRIOR NVL(MGR,7788)=EMPNO
START WITH
    ENAME='ADAMS';
```
```
ERROR:
ORA-01436: CONNECT BY loop in user data

no rows selected
```

7. Reverse the hierarchy:

```
CREATE TABLE
    HEMP
AS SELECT
    ROWNUM R,
    LEVEL L,
```

```
    ENAME,
    EMPNO
FROM
    EMP
CONNECT BY
    MGR=PRIOR EMPNO
START WITH
    MGR IS NULL;
```

The table HEMP contains the rows of employees in hierarchical order with the level:

```
         R          L ENAME          EMPNO
---------- ---------- ---------- ----------
         1          1 KING            7839
         2          2 JONES           7566
         3          3 SCOTT           7788
         4          4 ADAMS           7876
         5          3 FORD            7902
         6          4 SMITH           7369
         7          2 BLAKE           7698
         8          3 ALLEN           7499
         9          3 WARD            7521
        10          3 MARTIN          7654
        11          3 TURNER          7844
        12          3 JAMES           7900
        13          2 CLARK           7782
        14          3 MILLER          7934
```

Using an analytic function, retrieve the manager of each employee in the table HEMP.

Solutions

1. CONNECT BY, PRIOR and START WITH

   Retrieve the top hierarchy of Adams. Use LPAD to format output:

   ```
   SELECT
       LPAD(' ',3*LEVEL-3)||ENAME
   FROM
       EMP
   CONNECT BY
       PRIOR MGR=EMPNO
   START WITH
       ENAME='ADAMS';
   ```
   ```
   LPAD('',3*LEVEL-3)||ENAME
   -------------------------
   ADAMS
      SCOTT
         JONES
            KING
   ```

   Starting with Adams, the bottom-up hierarchy is retrieved.

2. LEVEL

   Starting with KING, retrieve all level-4 employees.

   ```
   SELECT
       ENAME
   FROM
       EMP
   WHERE
       LEVEL=4
   CONNECT BY
       MGR=PRIOR EMPNO
   START WITH
       ENAME='KING';
   ```
   ```
   ENAME
   ----------
   ADAMS
   SMITH
   ```

3. PRIOR

   For each employee, retrieve the ratio of his salary to the salary of his manager. Return the rows in descending order of the ratio.

   ```
   SELECT
       ENAME,
   ```

```
   SAL,
   PRIOR ENAME MGRNAME,
   PRIOR SAL MGRSAL,
   TO_CHAR(100*SAL/PRIOR SAL,'990.00L','NLS_CURRENCY=%') RATIO
FROM
   EMP
CONNECT BY
   MGR=PRIOR EMPNO
START WITH
   MGR IS NULL
ORDER BY
   SAL/PRIOR SAL DESC NULLS FIRST;
```

ENAME	SAL	MGRNAME	MGRSAL	RATIO
KING	5000			
SCOTT	3000	JONES	2975	100.84%
FORD	3000	JONES	2975	100.84%
JONES	2975	KING	5000	59.50%
BLAKE	2850	KING	5000	57.00%
ALLEN	1600	BLAKE	2850	56.14%
MILLER	1300	CLARK	2450	53.06%
TURNER	1500	BLAKE	2850	52.63%
CLARK	2450	KING	5000	49.00%
WARD	1250	BLAKE	2850	43.86%
MARTIN	1250	BLAKE	2850	43.86%
ADAMS	1100	SCOTT	3000	36.67%
JAMES	950	BLAKE	2850	33.33%
SMITH	800	FORD	3000	26.67%

PRIOR is used in the SELECT and in the ORDER BY clauses to retrieve the salary of the manager.

4. SYS_CONNECT_BY_PATH

Using SYS_CONNECT_BY_PATH and aggregation, return an aggregated list of employees grouped by department.

```
SELECT
   DEPTNO,
   SUBSTR(MAX(SYS_CONNECT_BY_PATH(ENAME,';')),2) ENAME
FROM
   EMP
CONNECT BY
   ENAME<PRIOR ENAME
   AND
   DEPTNO=PRIOR DEPTNO
GROUP BY
   DEPTNO;
```

DEPTNO	ENAME
30	WARD;TURNER;MARTIN;JAMES;BLAKE;ALLEN
20	SMITH;SCOTT;JONES;FORD;ADAMS
10	MILLER;KING;CLARK

The hierarchy is defined within a department with the condition that the name of the parent must be bigger, alphabetically, than the child. As a result, the names within the aggregated string are alphabetically sorted in descending order.

5. CONNECT_BY_ROOT

For each employee, retrieve the sum of his salary and the salary of all his employees.

```
WITH
    T
AS
(
    SELECT
        CONNECT_BY_ROOT ENAME ENAME,
        SAL
    FROM
        EMP
    CONNECT BY
        MGR=PRIOR EMPNO
)
SELECT
    ENAME,
    SUM(SAL)
FROM
    T
GROUP BY
    ENAME;
```

ENAME	SUM(SAL)
ALLEN	1600
JONES	10875
FORD	3800
MILLER	1300
CLARK	3750
WARD	1250
SMITH	800
SCOTT	4100
MARTIN	1250
TURNER	1500
ADAMS	1100
JAMES	950
BLAKE	9400
KING	29025

For each employee, a hierarchy is built in the subquery T and aggregated in the main query

6. Cycle

Retrieve the three employees that make the query fail.

```
SELECT
    SYS_CONNECT_BY_PATH(ENAME,'/')
FROM
    EMP
CONNECT BY
    PRIOR NVL(MGR,7788)=EMPNO
START WITH
    ENAME='ADAMS';
```

```
ERROR:
ORA-01436: CONNECT BY loop in user data

no rows selected
```

```
SELECT
    DISTINCT ENAME MGR, PRIOR ENAME EMP
FROM
    EMP
WHERE
    CONNECT_BY_ISCYCLE=1
CONNECT BY
NOCYCLE
    PRIOR NVL(MGR,7788)=EMPNO;
```

```
MGR         EMP
----------  ----------
KING        JONES
JONES       SCOTT
SCOTT       KING
```

In this query, Scott (7788) is the manager of the top manager King; King is the manager of Jones, who is the manager of Scott. CONNECT_BY_ISCYCLE returns 1 for cycling rows.

7. Reverse the hierarchy:

```
         R           L ENAME           EMPNO
---------- ---------- ---------- ----------
         1           1 KING             7839
         2           2 JONES            7566
         3           3 SCOTT            7788
         4           4 ADAMS            7876
         5           3 FORD             7902
         6           4 SMITH            7369
         7           2 BLAKE            7698
         8           3 ALLEN            7499
         9           3 WARD             7521
        10           3 MARTIN           7654
        11           3 TURNER           7844
        12           3 JAMES            7900
        13           2 CLARK            7782
        14           3 MILLER           7934
```

Using an analytic function, retrieve the manager of each employee in the table HEMP.

```
SELECT
   EMPNO,
   ENAME,
   LAST_VALUE(EMPNO)
   OVER
   (
      ORDER BY L*1E12+R
      RANGE BETWEEN UNBOUNDED PRECEDING AND 1E12 PRECEDING
   ) MGR
FROM
   HEMP;
```

```
    EMPNO ENAME            MGR
---------- ---------- ----------
      7839 KING
      7566 JONES           7839
      7698 BLAKE           7839
      7782 CLARK           7839
      7788 SCOTT           7566
      7902 FORD            7566
      7499 ALLEN           7698
      7521 WARD            7698
      7654 MARTIN          7698
      7844 TURNER          7698
      7900 JAMES           7698
      7934 MILLER          7782
      7876 ADAMS           7788
      7369 SMITH           7902
```

The manager is the last value that has a level higher than the current row.

SQL For Modeling

SQL for Modeling

A model is a multidimensional array created with existing and new data. The MODEL clause was originally named SQL Spreadsheet and designed to provide an SQL model directly in the database instead of the traditional approach of loading data in a tool like Microsoft Excel and performing calculations in a worksheet. MODEL is part of the core database engine and is usable at no extra cost.

The model designer describes the partitions, dimensions and measures and writes the model code. Without the model clause, the rows are selected from a table or view, but there are no calculations after the rows are returned. Each row is accessed using the dimension, which could be initialized by a column or a scalar.

Most worksheet calculations require computing results from multiple cells; similarly, SQL MODEL provides inter-rows calculation and row generation.

Another feature missing in SQL is iteration. Processing the rows more than once to evaluate complex calculation is traditionally done with a programming language like PL/SQL or Java. Model enhances SQL capabilities by providing for loops and iteration.

Partitions, dimensions and measures

The model query has partitions, dimensions and measures.

Department 10

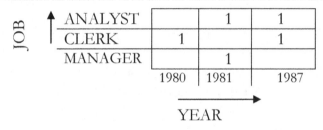

	MANAGER	1	
JOB ↑	PRESIDENT	1	
	CLERK		1
		1981	1982

YEAR →

Department 20

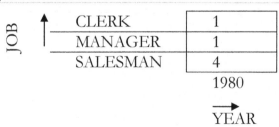

	ANALYST		1	1
JOB ↑	CLERK	1		1
	MANAGER		1	
		1980	1981	1987

YEAR →

Department 30

	CLERK	1
JOB ↑	MANAGER	1
	SALESMAN	4
		1980

YEAR →

```
SELECT
    *
FROM
    EMP
GROUP BY
    DEPTNO,
    JOB,
    TRUNC(HIREDATE,'Y')
MODEL
PARTITION BY
(
    DEPTNO
)
DIMENSION BY
(
    JOB,
    TRUNC(HIREDATE,'Y') YEAR
)
MEASURES
(
    COUNT(*) C
)
();
```

The PARTITION clause splits the result set into different datasets. Each partition is isolated. The DIMENSION clause determines the indexes of the array. The MEASURES clause defines the calculated cells that will be returned by the MODEL query.

Partition is optional; both dimension and measure clauses are required. The partition can be neither changed nor inserted. Dimensions cannot be changed, but new values can be inserted.

```
SELECT
    *
FROM
    EMP
WHERE
    DEPTNO=10
MODEL
DIMENSION BY
    (EMPNO)
MEASURES
    (ENAME, SAL)
();
```

```
    EMPNO ENAME            SAL
---------- ---------- ----------
      7782 CLARK           2450
      7839 KING            5000
      7934 MILLER          1300
```

```
---------------------------------------------------------------------
| Id  | Operation             | Name | Rows | Bytes | Cost (%CPU)| Time     |
---------------------------------------------------------------------
|   0 | SELECT STATEMENT      |      |    3 |    51 |    3   (0)| 00:00:01 |
|   1 |  SQL MODEL ORDERED FAST|     |    3 |    51 |           |          |
|*  2 |   TABLE ACCESS FULL   | EMP  |    3 |    51 |    3   (0)| 00:00:01 |
---------------------------------------------------------------------

Predicate Information (identified by operation id):
---------------------------------------------------

   2 - filter("DEPTNO"=10)
```

The employees in department 10 are used as data input for the model calculation. The employee number is the dimension of the array and the name and the salary are the measures.

The optimizer has multiple access operations for MODEL. One of them is SQL MODEL ORDERED FAST. Note that the cost and time columns are not filled.

```
SELECT
    *
FROM
    EMP
GROUP BY
    DEPTNO,
    JOB
MODEL
PARTITION BY
    (DEPTNO)
DIMENSION BY
    (JOB)
MEASURES
    (SUM(SAL) SAL)
()
ORDER BY
    DEPTNO,
    SAL DESC;
```

```
DEPTNO JOB              SAL
---------- --------- ----------
        10 PRESIDENT      5000
        10 MANAGER        2450
        10 CLERK          1300
        20 ANALYST        6000
        20 MANAGER        2975
        20 CLERK          1900
        30 SALESMAN       5600
        30 MANAGER        2850
        30 CLERK           950
```

The result set of the query is partitioned by department number. In each partition, the dimension is the job and the sum of salaries is the measure.

Update

Each measure can be updated with an UPDATE statement within the model code block. Only the result is updated, so the table itself does not change.

```
SELECT
    *
FROM
    DEPT
JOIN
    EMP
USING
(
    DEPTNO
)
MODEL
RETURN UPDATED ROWS
DIMENSION BY
(
    EMP.ENAME
)
MEASURES
(
    DEPT.DNAME,
    EMP.SAL
)
(
    UPDATE DNAME['SCOTT']='FINANCE',
    UPDATE SAL['JONES']=SAL['SCOTT']
);
```

```
ENAME      DNAME            SAL
---------- --------------- ----------
JONES      RESEARCH         3000
SCOTT      FINANCE          3000
```

The model is instructed to return only the updated rows. In the MODEL code, there are two rules: The department of Scott is set to FINANCE and the salary of Jones is set to the salary of Scott. Each individual measure can be retrieved and updated.

Upsert

Not only can MODEL update the existing values of the measures, but it can also generate new values for the dimensions.

```
SELECT
    *
FROM
    EMP
MODEL
RETURN UPDATED ROWS
DIMENSION BY
(
    ENAME,
    DEPTNO
)
MEASURES
(
    SAL
)
(
    UPSERT SAL['SCOTT', 20]=4000,
    UPSERT SAL['FRED', 40]=2900
);
```

```
ENAME          DEPTNO          SAL
----------  ----------  ----------
SCOTT              20         4000
FRED               40         2900
```

The dimensions ENAME and DEPTNO uniquely identify the model. The UPSERT (UPDATE + INSERT) statement updates the salary of Scott to 2900 and inserts a salary of 2900 for the new employee Fred in the department 40. A SELECT statement never inserts a row in the table; instead, it adds a new row in the result set.

There is no INSERT statement in model. If the row exists, it will be updated. The default is UPSERT.

```
SELECT
    *
```

```
FROM
   DEPT
MODEL
DIMENSION BY
(
   DEPTNO
)
MEASURES
(
   DNAME
)
(
   DNAME[50]='FINANCE'
);
```

```
    DEPTNO DNAME
---------- --------------
        10 ACCOUNTING
        20 RESEARCH
        30 SALES
        40 OPERATIONS
        50 FINANCE
```

The department 50 is created.

Used with partition, UPSERT creates a new dimension in each partition:

```
SELECT
   *
FROM
   EMP
WHERE
   JOB='MANAGER'
MODEL
PARTITION BY
(
   DEPTNO
)
DIMENSION BY
(
   JOB
)
MEASURES
(
   ENAME,
   0 BONUS
)
(
   BONUS['MANAGER']=100,
   BONUS['ASSOCIATE']=250
);
```

```
DEPTNO JOB          ENAME          BONUS
------ ----------   ----------     ----------
    30 MANAGER      BLAKE             100
    30 ASSOCIATE                      250
    20 MANAGER      JONES             100
    20 ASSOCIATE                      250
    10 MANAGER      CLARK             100
    10 ASSOCIATE                      250
```

CV

The function CV returns the current value of a dimension or a partition.

```
SELECT
    *
FROM
    EMP
MODEL
UNIQUE SINGLE REFERENCE
PARTITION BY
(
    DEPTNO
)
DIMENSION BY
(
    JOB
)
MEASURES
(
    ENAME,
    CAST(NULL AS VARCHAR2(30)) DESCRIPTION
)
RULES UPDATE
(
    DESCRIPTION['MANAGER']=CV(JOB)||' OF DEPARTMENT '||CV(DEPTNO),
    DESCRIPTION['SALESMAN']=CV(JOB),
    DESCRIPTION['PRESIDENT']=CV(JOB)||' '||ENAME[CV()]
)
ORDER BY
    DEPTNO;
```

```
DEPTNO JOB        ENAME      DESCRIPTION
-------- --------- ---------- --------------------------
    10 MANAGER   CLARK      MANAGER OF DEPARTMENT 10
    10 CLERK     MILLER
    10 PRESIDENT KING       PRESIDENT KING
    20 MANAGER   JONES      MANAGER OF DEPARTMENT 20
    20 ANALYST   FORD
    20 CLERK     SMITH
    20 CLERK     ADAMS
    20 ANALYST   SCOTT
    30 SALESMAN  TURNER     SALESMAN
    30 MANAGER   BLAKE      MANAGER OF DEPARTMENT 30
    30 SALESMAN  MARTIN     SALESMAN
    30 SALESMAN  WARD       SALESMAN
    30 CLERK     JAMES
    30 SALESMAN  ALLEN      SALESMAN
```

UNIQUE SINGLE REFERENCE has to be used when the dimension is not unique within a partition. In EMP, for instance, there is more than one clerk in department 20. The default UNIQUE DIMENSION returns an error if the dimension is not unique. When using SINGLE REFERENCE, duplicate values for a single reference cannot be accessed individually.

RULES UPDATES change the default behavior from upsert to update in the model code. The description is a column initialized with the null string of type VARCHAR2(30). The model query fails if the measure datatype is too small to contain the assigned values. The description is assigned if the job is CLERK, SALESMAN or PRESIDENT.

When used as a dimension in ENAME[CV()], it is not mandatory to specify the argument to the CV function.

Conditions

Logical tests are applied on the dimensions to update more than one row at the same time:

```
SELECT
    *
FROM
    EMP
MODEL
RETURN UPDATED ROWS
DIMENSION BY
```

```
(
    EMPNO
)
MEASURES
(
    SAL
)
(
    SAL[EMPNO BETWEEN 7000 AND 7500]=1000
);
```

```
       EMPNO         SAL
---------- ----------
      7369         1000
      7499         1000
```

```
---------------------------------------------------------------------------
| Id  | Operation                    | Name  | Rows | Bytes | Cost (%CPU)| Time     |
---------------------------------------------------------------------------
|   0 | SELECT STATEMENT             |       |    4 |    32 |    2   (0)| 00:00:01 |
|   1 |  SQL MODEL ORDERED           |       |    4 |    32 |           |          |
|   2 |   TABLE ACCESS BY INDEX ROWID| EMP   |    4 |    32 |    2   (0)| 00:00:01 |
|*  3 |    INDEX RANGE SCAN          | PK_EMP|    4 |       |    1   (0)| 00:00:01 |
---------------------------------------------------------------------------

Predicate Information (identified by operation id):
---------------------------------------------------
   3 - access("EMPNO">=7000 AND "EMPNO"<=7500)
```

MODEL updates the salaries of the employees between 7000 and 7500.
It is interesting to note that the optimizer chooses an index range scan to
access those two rows. That is, the model code is analyzed before the
execution and the predicates are pushed to the main query.

In addition to the standard SQL conditions, the dimension IS ANY is a
condition that always returns true:

```
SELECT
    *
FROM
    EMP
MODEL
DIMENSION BY
(
    DEPTNO,
    EMPNO
)
MEASURES
(
    COMM
)
(
    COMM[DEPTNO IN (10,20), EMPNO IS ANY]=1000,
    COMM[30,ANY]=2000
)
ORDER BY
```

```
DEPTNO;

    DEPTNO      EMPNO       COMM
---------- ---------- ----------
        10       7782       1000
        10       7839       1000
        10       7934       1000
        20       7566       1000
        20       7369       1000
        20       7876       1000
        20       7788       1000
        20       7902       1000
        30       7499       2000
        30       7654       2000
        30       7900       2000
        30       7844       2000
        30       7521       2000
        30       7698       2000
```

In departments 10 and 20, each employee receives a 1000 commission. In department 30, the commission is 2000. Both syntaxes are equivalent.

Another syntax specific to model is the cell IS PRESENT condition. The IS PRESENT condition checks if the cell is present in the base query.

```
SELECT
    *
FROM
    DEPT
MODEL
DIMENSION BY
(
    DEPTNO
)
MEASURES
(
    DNAME
)
(
    DNAME[50]='FINANCE',
    DNAME[ANY]=
        CASE
            WHEN DNAME[CV()] IS PRESENT
            THEN LOWER(DNAME[CV()])
            ELSE UPPER(DNAME[CV()])
        END
);
```

```
    DEPTNO DNAME
---------- --------------
        10 accounting
        20 research
        30 sales
        40 operations
        50 FINANCE
```

The departments 10 to 40 are present in the base query. They are converted to lower case. The department 50 is not present in DEPT; it is uppercased.

FOR loops

FOR loops are used to upsert more than one row at the same time.

The first syntax uses an expressions list.

```
SELECT
    *
FROM
    EMP
MODEL
RETURN UPDATED ROWS
DIMENSION BY
(
    EMPNO,
    ENAME
)
MEASURES
(
    'N' NOMINATED
)
(
    NOMINATED[FOR (EMPNO,ENAME) IN ((7788,'SCOTT'),(7777,'LEO'))]='Y'
);
```

```
     EMPNO ENAME      N
---------- ---------- -
      7788 SCOTT      Y
      7777 LEO        Y
```

Employees Scott and Leo got a nomination. Employee Leo does not exist in table EMP; therefore, a new row is created.

The second syntax uses a subquery:

```
SELECT
```

```
    *
FROM
    DEPT
MODEL
DIMENSION BY
(
    DEPTNO
)
MEASURES
(
    DNAME,



    'Y' EMPTY
)
(
    EMPTY[FOR DEPTNO IN (SELECT DEPTNO FROM EMP)]='N'
);
```

```
    DEPTNO DNAME           E
---------- --------------- -
        10 ACCOUNTING      N
        20 RESEARCH        N
        30 SALES           N
        40 OPERATIONS      Y
```

For each department in EMP, the measure EMPTY is updated to N.

The third syntax uses a sequence. The sequence contains lower and upper bounds and an increment or a decrement followed by a positive number or interval.

```
SELECT
    A
FROM
    DUAL
MODEL
RETURN UPDATED ROWS
DIMENSION BY
(
    0 A
)
MEASURES
(
    0 X
)
(
    X[FOR A FROM 101 TO 103 INCREMENT 1]=0
);
```

```
         A
----------
       101
       102
       103
```

For the dimension A from 101 to 103, a row is upserted.

The bounds could also be dates. In this case, the increment or decrement is either a numeric (in days) or an interval.

```
SELECT
    TO_CHAR(B, 'FMMonth YYYY') B
FROM
    DUAL
MODEL
RETURN UPDATED ROWS
DIMENSION BY
(
    SYSDATE B
)
MEASURES
(
    0 X
)
(
    X
    [
        FOR
            B
        FROM
            DATE '2000-01-01'
        TO
            DATE '2000-03-01'
        INCREMENT
            INTERVAL '1' MONTH
    ]=0
);
```

```
B
--------------
January 2000
February 2000
March 2000
```

The dimension is a date and a sequence of months from January to March 2000 is generated.

In a multidimensional model, if there is a condition on one dimension and a sequence on the other dimension, the default is to update the rows. UPSERT ALL clause instructs to upsert all rows.

```
SELECT
    *
FROM
    DEPT
MODEL
RETURN UPDATED ROWS
DIMENSION BY
(
    DEPTNO,
    'XXXXXXXX' C
)
MEASURES
(
    0 X
)
(
    X[DEPTNO<25,FOR C LIKE 'REC%' FROM 99 TO 97 DECREMENT 1]=0
);
no rows selected

SELECT
    *
FROM
    DEPT
MODEL
RETURN UPDATED ROWS
DIMENSION BY
(
    DEPTNO,
    'XXXXXXXX' C
)
MEASURES
(
    0 X
)
(
    UPSERT ALL X[DEPTNO<25,FOR C LIKE 'REC%' FROM 99 TO 97 DECREMENT 1]=0
);
```

```
    DEPTNO C                 X
---------- -------- ----------
        10 REC99            0
        10 REC98            0
        10 REC97            0
        20 REC99            0
        20 REC98            0
        20 REC97            0
```

The sequence generates numbers from 99 to 97 descending; the LIKE clause is used for character dimensions to add a prefix. In the first query, a condition is applied to the DEPTNO column and no rows are updated. In the second query, the addition of UPSERT ALL creates rows for each department with DEPTNO smaller than 25.

Iterations

The model rules are executed once by default. Model uses ITERATE to process the code more than once.

```
SELECT
    N
FROM
    DUAL
MODEL
DIMENSION BY
(
    0 X
)
MEASURES
(
    1 N
)
RULES ITERATE (10)
(
    N[0]=N[0]*(ITERATION_NUMBER+1)
);
```

```
         N
----------
   3628800
```

The function ITERATION_NUMBER returns the current iteration where 0 is the first iteration. The measure N is initialized to 1 and multiplied by one, two, three, ... up to ten. This means the returned value is 10 factorial.

The iteration also ends when the UNTIL clause is reached.

```
SELECT
    ENAME,
    SAL,
    RATE YEARLY_RATE,
    TO_CHAR(SAVING,'99999$') SAVING,
    YEAR
FROM
    EMP
MODEL
```

```
PARTITION BY
(
    ENAME
)
DIMENSION BY
(
    0 X
)
MEASURES
(
    SAL,
    SAL*12/10 RATE,
    .03 INTEREST,
    0 SAVING,
    0 YEAR
)
RULES ITERATE (20) UNTIL (SAVING[0]>=50000)
(
    SAVING[0]=SAVING[0]*(1+INTEREST[0]),
    SAVING[0]=SAVING[0]+RATE[0],
    YEAR[0]=ITERATION_NUMBER+1
);
```

ENAME	SAL	YEARLY_RATE	SAVING	YEAR
ALLEN	1600	1920	$51591	20
JONES	2975	3570	$50666	12
FORD	3000	3600	$51091	12
CLARK	2450	2940	$50234	14
MILLER	1300	1560	$41918	20
SMITH	800	960	$25796	20
WARD	1250	1500	$40306	20
MARTIN	1250	1500	$40306	20
SCOTT	3000	3600	$51091	12
TURNER	1500	1800	$48367	20
ADAMS	1100	1320	$35469	20
BLAKE	2850	3420	$53413	13
KING	5000	6000	$53354	8
JAMES	950	1140	$30632	20

Each employee starts a savings plan and deposits 10% of his salary each year on a special account that has 3% interest. The calculation ends after 20 iterations or if the savings reaches $50000.

Reference Model

A reference model is a read-only model that is used in the main model.

```
SELECT
    *
FROM
    EMP
MODEL
```

```
REFERENCE
    D
    ON
    (
        SELECT
            *
        FROM
            DEPT
    )
    DIMENSION BY
    (
        DEPTNO
    )
    MEASURES
    (
        DNAME
    )
MAIN
    E
PARTITION BY
(
    DEPTNO
)
DIMENSION BY
(
    EMPNO
)
MEASURES
(
    ENAME,
    CAST(NULL AS VARCHAR2(14)) DNAME
)
(
    E.DNAME[ANY]=D.DNAME[CV(DEPTNO)]
);
```

```
DEPTNO     EMPNO ENAME        DNAME
---------- ---------- ---------- --------------
        30      7499 ALLEN        SALES
        30      7521 WARD         SALES
        30      7654 MARTIN       SALES
        30      7698 BLAKE        SALES
        30      7844 TURNER       SALES
        30      7900 JAMES        SALES
        20      7369 SMITH        RESEARCH
        20      7566 JONES        RESEARCH
        20      7788 SCOTT        RESEARCH
        20      7876 ADAMS        RESEARCH
        20      7902 FORD         RESEARCH
        10      7782 CLARK        ACCOUNTING
        10      7839 KING         ACCOUNTING
        10      7934 MILLER       ACCOUNTING
```

```
--------------------------------------------------------------------
| Id | Operation         | Name | Rows | Bytes | Cost (%CPU)| Time     |
--------------------------------------------------------------------
|  0 | SELECT STATEMENT  |      |   14 |   182 |    3   (0)| 00:00:01 |
|  1 |  SQL MODEL ORDERED|      |   14 |   182 |           |          |
|  2 |   REFERENCE MODEL | D    |    4 |    80 |    3   (0)| 00:00:01 |
|  3 |    TABLE ACCESS FULL| DEPT |    4 |    80 |    3   (0)| 00:00:01 |
|  4 |    TABLE ACCESS FULL| EMP  |   14 |   182 |    3   (0)| 00:00:01 |
--------------------------------------------------------------------
```

The main model E contains the employees, partitioned by department. The dimension is the employee name. The measure is initialized to null cast to VARCHAR2(14).

A reference model D is defined on the DEPT table with a dimension DEPTNO and a measure DNAME. The reference model can be neither upserted nor updated.

The execution plan shows the REFERENCE MODEL operation. A reference model is comparable as an external worksheet in Excel.

The REFERENCE MEASURES can be used as assignment for the MAIN MODEL but cannot be selected outside of the model clause.

```
SELECT
    *
FROM
    DEPT
MODEL
REFERENCE
    EMP
ON
    (
        SELECT
```

```
            EMPNO,
            SAL
        FROM
            EMP
    )
    DIMENSION BY
    (
        EMPNO
    )
    MEASURES
    (
        SAL
    )
MAIN
    DEPT
DIMENSION BY
(
    DEPTNO
)
MEASURES
(
    DNAME,
    0 BONUS
)
(
    BONUS[10]=SAL[7782]*10+SAL[7839],
    BONUS[20]=SAL[7788]+SAL[7839],
    BONUS[30]=SAL[7844]/2
);
```

```
    DEPTNO DNAME              BONUS
---------- --------------- ----------
        40 OPERATIONS             0
        10 ACCOUNTING         29500
        20 RESEARCH            8000
        30 SALES                750
```

```
---------------------------------------------------------------------
| Id | Operation             | Name | Rows | Bytes | Cost (%CPU)| Time     |
---------------------------------------------------------------------
|  0 | SELECT STATEMENT      |      |    4 |    52 |    3   (0)| 00:00:01 |
|  1 |  SQL MODEL ORDERED FAST|     |    4 |    52 |           |          |
|  2 |   REFERENCE MODEL     | EMP  |   14 |   112 |    3   (0)| 00:00:01 |
|  3 |    TABLE ACCESS FULL  | EMP  |   14 |   112 |    3   (0)| 00:00:01 |
|  4 |    TABLE ACCESS FULL  | DEPT |    4 |    52 |    3   (0)| 00:00:01 |
---------------------------------------------------------------------
```

There is no relation between DEPT and EMP here. A random access to the EMP worksheet retrieves the salaries of Clark, King, Scott and Turner and assigns them to the bonus column of the main worksheet.

The execution plan shows a TABLE ACCESS FULL of EMP. The optimizer did not recognize the access by primary key in this example.

Aggregation

Used in rules, the aggregate function is evaluated on a measure expression and the dimension limits the scope of the aggregation.

```
SELECT
    DESCRIPTION,
    TOTAL
FROM
    EMP
MODEL
UNIQUE SINGLE REFERENCE
RETURN UPDATED ROWS
DIMENSION BY
(
    JOB,
    DEPTNO,
    CAST(NULL AS VARCHAR2(30)) DESCRIPTION
)
MEASURES
(
    0 TOTAL,
    SAL
)
(
    TOTAL[NULL,NULL,'Manager']=SUM(SAL)['MANAGER',ANY,NULL],
    TOTAL[NULL,NULL,'Sales']=SUM(SAL)[ANY,30,NULL],
    TOTAL[NULL,NULL,'Research analyst/clerk']=
        SUM(SAL)[JOB IN ('CLERK','ANALYST'),20,NULL]
);
```

```
DESCRIPTION                        TOTAL
------------------------------- ----------
Research analyst/clerk              7900
Sales                               9400
Manager                             8275
```

The total for manager is computed by summing all salaries where the job is manager, the department is ANY and the description is NULL. The total for sales is the sum of salaries where the job is ANY, the department is 30 and the description is NULL. The total for research analyst/clerk is the sum of salaries where the job is either clerk or analyst, the department is 20 and the description is NULL.

There are three dimensions: The job and the department, which are set to NULL in the subtotal; the description, which is initialized to NULL and set to a text literal for the subtotals; and the SUM function in the

MODEL rules has a special syntax and does not require a GROUP BY clause in the base query.

When the base query is using a GROUP BY clause, any group by expression or aggregate function can be used in partition, dimension or measure expressions.

```
SELECT
    *
FROM
    EMP
GROUP BY
    ROLLUP(DEPTNO),JOB
MODEL
PARTITION BY
(
    DEPTNO
)
DIMENSION BY
(
    JOB
)
MEASURES
(
    SUM(SAL) SAL
)
RULES SEQUENTIAL ORDER
(
    SAL[JOB='PRESIDENT']=SAL['PRESIDENT']*10,
    SAL[JOB='CLERK']=SAL['CLERK']*1.1,
    SAL[NULL]=SUM(SAL)[ANY]
)
ORDER BY
    DEPTNO,
    JOB;
```

```
DEPTNO JOB              SAL
---------- --------- ----------
        10 CLERK           1430
        10 MANAGER         2450
        10 PRESIDENT      50000
        10                53880
        20 ANALYST         6000
        20 CLERK           2090
        20 MANAGER         2975
        20                11065
        30 CLERK           1045
        30 MANAGER         2850
        30 SALESMAN        5600
        30                 9495
           ANALYST         6000
           CLERK           4565
           MANAGER         8275
           PRESIDENT      50000
           SALESMAN        5600
                          74440
```

The base query is using a GROUP BY clause. The department partition and job dimension are GROUP BY expressions. The salary measure is an expression that uses the aggregate function SUM. The aggregated salary of the president is multiplied by 10 while the clerks get a 10% raise only. The subtotal per job and the grand total are evaluated in the rules. Sequential order is the default; first, the president gets +900%; then the clerks get +10%; and finally, the subtotals per department and grand total are upserted.

Analytics

Oracle analytic functions are applied to a selected portion of model.

```
SELECT
    *
FROM
    EMP
MODEL
PARTITION BY
(
    DEPTNO
)
DIMENSION BY
(
    ENAME,
    JOB
)
MEASURES
(
```

```
    SAL,
    CAST(NULL AS NUMBER) CUMSAL
)
(
    CUMSAL[ANY,JOB NOT IN ('PRESIDENT','MANAGER')]=
        SUM(SAL) OVER (ORDER BY ENAME)
)
ORDER BY
    DEPTNO,
    ENAME;
```

```
    DEPTNO ENAME      JOB              SAL     CUMSAL
---------- ---------- ---------- ---------- ----------
        10 CLARK      MANAGER          2450
        10 KING       PRESIDENT        5000
        10 MILLER     CLERK            1300       1300
        20 ADAMS      CLERK            1100       1100
        20 FORD       ANALYST          3000       4100
        20 JONES      MANAGER          2975
        20 SCOTT      ANALYST          3000       7100
        20 SMITH      CLERK             800       7900
        30 ALLEN      SALESMAN         1600       1600
        30 BLAKE      MANAGER          2850
        30 JAMES      CLERK             950       2550
        30 MARTIN     SALESMAN         1250       3800
        30 TURNER     SALESMAN         1500       5300
        30 WARD       SALESMAN         1250       6550
```

The cumulative salary within each department is evaluated only for employees that are neither manager nor president. The excluded rows are not used in the calculations.

Ordered Rows

In MODEL, the results of the calculation may depend on the order in which rules are evaluated. The default is to process the code statements sequentially.

```
SELECT
    *
FROM
    EMP
WHERE
    DEPTNO=10
MODEL
DIMENSION BY
(
    ENAME
)
MEASURES
(
```

```
   SAL
)
RULES SEQUENTIAL ORDER
(
   SAL['CLARK']=SAL['KING'],
   SAL['KING']=6000
);
```

```
ENAME           SAL
----------  ----------
MILLER          1300
CLARK           5000
KING            6000
```

Clark gets the salary of King and King gets a salary of 6000.

When using automatic order, dependencies between rules are resolved.

```
SELECT
   *
FROM
   EMP
WHERE
   DEPTNO=10
MODEL
DIMENSION BY
(
   ENAME
)
MEASURES
(
   SAL
)
RULES AUTOMATIC ORDER
(
   SAL['CLARK']=SAL['KING'],
   SAL['KING']=6000
);
```

```
ENAME           SAL
----------  ----------
MILLER          1300
CLARK           6000
KING            6000
```

The salary of Clark depends on the salary of King. The salary of King is evaluated first.
An ORDER BY clause on the left operand is required when multiple rows are accessed and depend on each other.

```
SELECT
```

```
        *
FROM
    EMP
WHERE
    DEPTNO=10
MODEL
DIMENSION BY
(
    ENAME
)
MEASURES
(
    SAL
)
(
    SAL[ANY] ORDER BY SAL=SAL[CV()]+MAX(SAL)[ANY]/10
);
```

```
ENAME               SAL
---------- ----------
MILLER             1800
CLARK              2950
KING               5500
```

Each employee's salary is uplifted by 10% of the maximum salary. The salary of Miller is updated first, than the salary of Clark and finally, the salary of King.

Conclusion

Modeling allows functionality similar to what can be achieved with a spreadsheet. The MODEL clause was originally named SQL Spreadsheet. The model designer describes the partitions, dimensions and measures and writes the model code. Without the model clause, the rows are selected from a table or view, but there are no calculations after the rows are returned. Most worksheet calculations require computing results from multiple cells; similarly, SQL MODEL provides inter-rows calculation and row generation.

The model query has partitions, dimensions and measures and can be updated and upserted. Other parts of modeling include FOR loops, iterations, and reference models as well as aggregate and analytic functions.

Exercises

1. Partition

   The partition is the department number, the dimension is the employee name and the measure is the salary. Is it possible to assign the salary of analyst Scott to salesman Ward?

2. Upsert

   Return one row with the first day of the current month and one row with the last day of the current month.

3. Aggregation

   A deprecated syntax in Microsoft SQL Server is GROUP BY ALL.

   ```
   SELECT DEPTNO,SUM(SAL) FROM EMP WHERE DEPTNO=20 GROUP BY ALL DEPTNO;
       DEPTNO    SUM(SAL)
   ---------- ----------
           10
           20      10875
           30
   ```

   Use model to compute the sum of salaries in department 20 and return the other departments with NULL.

4. Analytic

   Return the list of employees with their salaries. For the managers only, return their respective salary ranking.

5. Analytic II

   NTILE(4) OVER (ORDER BY DBMS_RANDOM.VALUE) forms four groups of employees. In each group, return the employee name and the salary with the name and salary of the best paid employee who has a salary at least 100 below the current employee.

   Here is a sample output:

   ```
           N     EMPNO ENAME1          SAL1 ENAME2          SAL2
   --------- --------- ---------- --------- ---------- ---------
           1      7934 MILLER          1300
   ```

```
1       7844 TURNER        1500 MILLER          1300
1       7566 JONES         2975 TURNER          1500
1       7788 SCOTT         3000 TURNER          1500
2       7369 SMITH          800
2       7900 JAMES          950 SMITH            800
2       7654 MARTIN        1250 JAMES            950
2       7782 CLARK         2450 MARTIN          1250
3       7876 ADAMS         1100
3       7521 WARD          1250 ADAMS           1100
3       7839 KING          5000 WARD            1250
4       7499 ALLEN         1600
4       7698 BLAKE         2850 ALLEN           1600
4       7902 FORD          3000 BLAKE           2850
```

In group 1, the best paid employee who has a salary 100 lower than Scott is Turner.

6. Iteration

The undocumented WM_CONCAT function returns a comma-separated list of values.

```
SELECT DEPTNO, WM_CONCAT(ENAME) FROM EMP GROUP BY DEPTNO;
    DEPTNO WM_CONCAT(ENAME)
---------- ------------------------------------------
        10 CLARK,KING,MILLER
        20 SMITH,FORD,ADAMS,SCOTT,JONES
        30 ALLEN,BLAKE,MARTIN,TURNER,JAMES,WARD
```

Using model, provide the same output, but sorted alphabetically.

7. Keep

Return the name of the oldest employee and the number of employees with a higher salary.

8. Reference and loop

Using a reference model, loop from the first year to the last year of hire dates and return the count of employees. Also include results for years with no hires.

9. Ordered rows

In EMP, order the employees by hire date, then by name in case of duplicate hire dates. For each employee, set the salary to the salary of the previous employee and set the commission to the commission of the next employee.

Ex: Turner gets the salary of Clark (2850) and the commission of Martin (1400).

Solutions

1. Partition

   A partition completely isolates the rows; therefore, it is not possible to assign to an analyst the salary of a salesman.

2. Upsert

```
SELECT
    *
FROM
    DUAL
MODEL
DIMENSION BY
(
    1 R
)
MEASURES
(
    SYSDATE D
)
(
    D[1]=TRUNC(D[1],'MM'),
    D[2]=LAST_DAY(D[1])
);
```

```
         R D
---------- ---------
         1 01-JUN-08
         2 30-JUN-08
```

The first row is updated to contain the first day of the month. A second row is created with the last day.

3. Aggregation

```
SELECT
    DEPTNO,
    SAL
FROM
    EMP
MODEL
RETURN UPDATED ROWS
DIMENSION BY
(
    DEPTNO,
    EMPNO
)
MEASURES
(
    SAL
```

```
)
(
    UPSERT ALL SAL[ANY,NULL]=NULL,
    SAL[20,NULL]=SUM(SAL)[20,ANY]
);
```

```
    DEPTNO        SAL
---------- ----------
        10
        20      10875
        30
```

The total is arbitrarily identified by a NULL employee number. A
row with a null salary is upserted in all departments. In department
20, the sum of salaries is aggregated.

4. Analytic

```
SELECT
    *
FROM
    EMP
MODEL
DIMENSION BY
(
    JOB,
    ENAME
)
MEASURES
(
    SAL,
    CAST(NULL AS NUMBER) RANK
)
(
    RANK['MANAGER',ANY]=RANK() OVER (ORDER BY SAL DESC)
);
```

```
JOB        ENAME             SAL       RANK
---------  ----------  ----------  ----------
CLERK      SMITH              800
SALESMAN   ALLEN             1600
SALESMAN   WARD              1250
SALESMAN   MARTIN            1250
ANALYST    SCOTT             3000
PRESIDENT  KING              5000
SALESMAN   TURNER            1500
CLERK      ADAMS             1100
CLERK      JAMES              950
ANALYST    FORD              3000
CLERK      MILLER            1300
MANAGER    JONES             2975           1
MANAGER    BLAKE             2850           2
MANAGER    CLARK             2450           3
```

The RANK analytic function is applied only to the managers.

5. Analytic II

```
SELECT
    *
FROM
    EMP
MODEL
PARTITION BY
(
    NTILE(4) OVER (ORDER BY DBMS_RANDOM.VALUE) N
)
DIMENSION BY
(
    EMPNO
)
MEASURES
(
    ENAME ENAME1,
    SAL SAL1,
    ENAME ENAME2,
    SAL SAL2
)
(
    ENAME2[ANY] =
        LAST_VALUE(ENAME1)OVER
            (ORDER BY SAL1 RANGE BETWEEN UNBOUNDED PRECEDING AND 100
PRECEDING),
    SAL2[ANY] =
        LAST_VALUE(SAL1)OVER
            (ORDER BY SAL1 RANGE BETWEEN UNBOUNDED PRECEDING AND 100
PRECEDING)
);
```

N	EMPNO	ENAME1	SAL1	ENAME2	SAL2
1	7782	CLARK	2450		
1	7566	JONES	2975	CLARK	2450
1	7902	FORD	3000	CLARK	2450
1	7839	KING	5000	FORD	3000
2	7369	SMITH	800		
2	7900	JAMES	950	SMITH	800
2	7521	WARD	1250	JAMES	950
2	7934	MILLER	1300	JAMES	950
3	7654	MARTIN	1250		
3	7499	ALLEN	1600	MARTIN	1250
3	7788	SCOTT	3000	ALLEN	1600
4	7876	ADAMS	1100		
4	7844	TURNER	1500	ADAMS	1100
4	7698	BLAKE	2850	TURNER	1500

The table is partitioned in four random groups. The employee number is chosen as the dimension. For each employee, the best paid employee 100 below his salary is selected using the LAST_VALUE function.

The function NTILE is used to initialize the partition. The functions LAST_VALUE are used in the model rules to assign values to the measures SAL1 and SAL2.

6. Iteration

```
SELECT
    DEPTNO,
    ENAME
FROM EMP
MODEL
RETURN UPDATED ROWS
PARTITION BY
(
    DEPTNO
)
DIMENSION BY
(
    ROW_NUMBER() OVER (PARTITION BY DEPTNO ORDER BY ENAME) R
)
MEASURES
(
    CAST(ENAME AS VARCHAR2(4000)) ENAME
)
RULES ITERATE (4000) UNTIL (ENAME[ITERATION_NUMBER+2] IS NULL)
(
    ENAME[NULL] =
        ENAME[NULL] ||
        ENAME[ITERATION_NUMBER+1] ||
        DECODE(ENAME[ITERATION_NUMBER+2],NULL,NULL,',')
);
```

```
    DEPTNO ENAME
---------- ------------------------------------------
        10 CLARK,KING,MILLER
        20 ADAMS,FORD,JONES,SCOTT,SMITH
        30 ALLEN,BLAKE,JAMES,MARTIN,TURNER,WARD
```

7. Keep

Return the name of the oldest employee and the number of employees better paid than him.

```
SELECT
    ENAME,
    COUNT
FROM
    EMP
MODEL
RETURN UPDATED ROWS
```

```
DIMENSION BY
(
   ENAME ID,
   SAL S
)
MEASURES
(
   SAL,
   HIREDATE,
   ENAME,
   0 COUNT
)
(
   ENAME[NULL,NULL]=
      MAX(ENAME)KEEP(DENSE_RANK FIRST ORDER BY HIREDATE)[ANY,ANY],
   SAL[NULL,NULL]=
      MAX(SAL)[ENAME[NULL,NULL],ANY],
   COUNT[NULL,NULL]=
      COUNT(*)[ANY,S>SAL[NULL,NULL]]
);
```

```
ENAME                    COUNT
---------- ----------------
SMITH                       13
```

Smith is in the company since 1980 and his salary of 800 is the lowest.

8. Reference

A reference cell can be used as a boundary in loops.

```
SELECT
   *
FROM
   EMP
GROUP BY
   EXTRACT(YEAR FROM HIREDATE)
MODEL
IGNORE NAV
   REFERENCE REFERENCEMODEL
   ON
   (
      SELECT
         0 ID,
         MIN(EXTRACT(YEAR FROM HIREDATE)) MINYEAR,
         MAX(EXTRACT(YEAR FROM HIREDATE)) MAXYEAR
      FROM
         EMP
   )
   DIMENSION BY
   (
      ID
   )
   MEASURES
```

```
    (
        MINYEAR,
        MAXYEAR
    )
MAIN MAINMODEL
DIMENSION BY
(
    EXTRACT(YEAR FROM HIREDATE) YEAR
)
MEASURES
(
    COUNT(*) COUNT
)
(
    COUNT[FOR YEAR FROM MINYEAR[0] TO MAXYEAR[0] INCREMENT 1]=COUNT[CV()]
)
ORDER BY
    YEAR;
```

```
    YEAR      COUNT
---------- ----------
    1980          1
    1981         10
    1982          1
    1983          0
    1984          0
    1985          0
    1986          0
    1987          2
```

The employees are counted by hire year. The reference model evaluates the first and the last year. For each year from the earliest to the latest hire date, a row is upserted with its own value. IGNORE NAV instructs the model to use 0 for non-existent numeric cell references. This could be done with the NVL function.

9. Ordered rows

```
SELECT
    *check
FROM
(
    SELECT
        *
    FROM
        EMP
    ORDER BY
        HIREDATE,
        ENAME
)
MODEL
DIMENSION BY
(
    ROWNUM R
```

```
)
MEASURES
(
    HIREDATE,
    ENAME,
    SAL,
    COMM
)
(
    SAL[ANY] ORDER BY R DESC=SAL[CV()-1],
    COMM[ANY] ORDER BY R=COMM[CV()+1]
);
```

```
         R HIREDATE  ENAME               SAL       COMM
--------- --------- ----------- ---------- ----------
         1 17-DEC-80 SMITH                         300
         2 20-FEB-81 ALLEN              800        500
         3 22-FEB-81 WARD              1600
         4 02-APR-81 JONES             1250
         5 01-MAY-81 BLAKE             2975
         6 09-JUN-81 CLARK             2850          0
         7 08-SEP-81 TURNER            2450       1400
         8 28-SEP-81 MARTIN            1500
         9 17-NOV-81 KING              1250
        10 03-DEC-81 FORD              5000
        11 03-DEC-81 JAMES             3000
        12 23-JAN-82 MILLER             950
        13 19-APR-87 SCOTT             1300
        14 23-MAY-87 ADAMS             3000
```

The rows are ordered by hire date and employee name in a subquery. ROWNUM is used as a dimension where the hire date, name, salary and commission are the measures. From the latest to the earliest, the employee gets the salary of the previous employee. From the earliest to the latest, the employee gets the commission of the next employee. This exercise demonstrates the use of ORDER BY in the left operand in the RULES clause. Another solution would consist of storing the updated salary and commission in a separate column.

Appendix: SQL*Plus

SQL*Plus is a powerful tool for running scripts and generating text reports.

Starting SQL*Plus

SQL*Plus is started from the command line and requires the ORACLE_HOME environment variable, or, under Windows, a registry entry. The option –s[ilent] runs SQL*Plus in silent mode. Neither the SQL*Plus prompt nor the banner is displayed in silent mode. The option –l[ogon] exits after the first unsuccessful login.

The first argument specifies the login credential. When connecting to the local machine, the ORACLE_SID entry is retrieved from the registry or the environment. /NOLOG starts SQL*Plus without establishing a connection.

The next argument is the name of a file containing an SQL script, prefixed by @; the script filename may be followed by some script arguments. EXIT and QUIT exit the SQL*Plus utility.

Windows

```
reg query hklm\software\oracle /s
HKEY_LOCAL_MACHINE\software\oracle\KEY_OraDb10g_home1
    ORACLE_HOME    REG_SZ    C:\app\oracle\product\10.2.0\db_1
HKEY_LOCAL_MACHINE\software\oracle\KEY_OraDb11g_home1
    ORACLE_HOME    REG_SZ    C:\app\oracle\product\11.1.0\db_1
reg query hklm\software\oracle\key_oradb11g_home1 /v ORACLE_SID
HKEY_LOCAL_MACHINE\software\oracle\key_oradb11g_home1
    ORACLE_SID    REG_SZ    lsc01
C:\app\oracle\product\11.1.0\db_1\bin\sqlplus scott/tiger
SQL*Plus: Release 11.1.0.6.0 - Production on Fri Aug 1 11:54:09 2008
Copyright (c) 1982, 2007, Oracle.  All rights reserved.
```

Advanced Oracle SQL Programming

```
Connected to:
Oracle Database 11g Enterprise Edition Release 11.1.0.6.0 - Production
With the Partitioning, OLAP, Data Mining and Real Application Testing
options
quit
Disconnected from Oracle Database 11g Enterprise Edition Release 11.1.0.6.0
- Production
With the Partitioning, OLAP, Data Mining and Real Application Testing
options
```

In a Windows environment with multiple ORACLE_HOMEs, the registry's entries are selected according to the PATH of SQL*Plus.

Unix/Linux

```
echo $ORACLE_HOME
/app/oracle/product/11.1/db_1
echo $ORACLE_SID
LSC01
$ORACLE_HOME/bin/sqlplus scott/tiger
SQL*Plus: Release 11.1.0.6.0 - Production on Fri Aug 1 12:02:04 2008
Copyright (c) 1982, 2007, Oracle.  All rights reserved.
Connected to:
Oracle Database 11g Enterprise Edition Release 11.1.0.6.0 - Production
With the Partitioning, OLAP, Data Mining and Real Application Testing
options
quit
Disconnected from Oracle Database 11g Enterprise Edition Release 11.1.0.6.0
- Production
With the Partitioning, OLAP, Data Mining and Real Application Testing
options
```

Under UNIX, the ORACLE_HOME and ORACLE_SID have to be exported in the current shell.

SQL*Plus Statements

SQL*Plus can run SQL statements:

```
CREATE TABLE T(X NUMBER);
Table created.
```

The table T is created and the output resulting from the SQL statement is displayed.

SQL*Plus can also run PL/SQL statements:

```
BEGIN NULL; END;
/
PL/SQL procedure successfully completed.
```

The anonymous block is run.

```
SET SERVEROUT ON
EXEC dbms_output.put_line('Hello!')
Hello!
PL/SQL procedure successfully completed.
```

The procedure PUT_LINE of the package DBMS_OUTPUT is executed and the output is printed on the screen.

SQL*Plus can run XQUERY statements and has done so since 10gR2.

```
XQUERY 1 to 10
/

Result Sequence
---------------
1
2
3
4
5
6
7
8
9
10

10 item(s) selected.
```

The XQUERY program is run and the result is displayed.

SQL*Plus can run server manager commands.

```
CONNECT / AS SYSDBA
Connected.
SHUTDOWN IMMEDIATE
Database closed.
Database dismounted.
ORACLE instance shut down.
STARTUP QUIET
ORACLE instance started.
Database mounted.
```

```
Database opened.
ARCHIVE LOG LIST
Database log mode              No Archive Mode
Automatic archival             Disabled
Archive destination            C:\app\oracle\product\11.1.0\db_1\RDBMS
Oldest online log sequence     121
Current log sequence           123
DISCONNECT
Disconnected from Oracle Database 11g Enterprise Edition Release 11.1.0.6.0
- Production
With the Partitioning, OLAP, Data Mining and Real Application Testing
options
```

A SYSDBA connection to the database server is instanced. Then the database is immediately shut down. The database is started without displaying SGA details and the ARCHIVELOG settings are displayed. Finally, the session is disconnected.

Various SQL*Plus statements allow editing in command line mode, thereby controlling the output and interacting with the operating system.

SQL*Plus provides a help system. When help is installed, it loads all the help information into the table HELP of the SYSTEM schema.

```
CONNECT system/manager
Connected.
@@?\sqlplus\admin\help\hlpbld helpus
...
?
```

```
HELP
----
Accesses this command line help system. Enter HELP INDEX or ? INDEX
for a list of topics.
You can view SQL*Plus resources at
    http://www.oracle.com/technology/tech/sql_plus/
and the Oracle Database Library at
    http://www.oracle.com/technology/documentation/

HELP|? [topic]
```

This shows that the HELP system is installed into the database in the SYSTEM schema.

```
? index
```

```
Enter Help [topic] for help.

@               COPY          PAUSE                    SHUTDOWN
@@              DEFINE        PRINT                    SPOOL
/               DEL           PROMPT                   SQLPLUS
ACCEPT          DESCRIBE      QUIT                     START
APPEND          DISCONNECT    RECOVER                  STARTUP
ARCHIVE LOG     EDIT          REMARK                   STORE
ATTRIBUTE       EXECUTE       REPFOOTER                TIMING
BREAK           EXIT          REPHEADER                TTITLE
BTITLE          GET           RESERVED WORDS (SQL)     UNDEFINE
CHANGE          HELP          RESERVED WORDS (PL/SQL)  VARIABLE
CLEAR           HOST          RUN                      WHENEVER OSERROR
COLUMN          INPUT         SAVE                     WHENEVER SQLERROR
COMPUTE         LIST          SET                      XQUERY
CONNECT         PASSWORD      SHOW
```

The list of SQL*Plus statements is displayed.

Formatting

SQL*Plus contains dozens of settings which may be modified using the SET statement. Most settings can be abbreviated.

SQL*Plus can print a report on multiple pages. The default PAGES[IZE] setting is 14 lines and the LIN[ESIZE] setting is 80 characters.

```
SELECT * FROM EMP;
```

```
    EMPNO ENAME      JOB             MGR HIREDATE         SAL       COMM
---------- ---------- ---------- ----------- --------- ---------- ----------
    DEPTNO
----------
     7369 SMITH      CLERK          7902 17-DEC-80       800
       20

     7499 ALLEN      SALESMAN       7698 20-FEB-81      1600        300
       30

     7521 WARD       SALESMAN       7698 22-FEB-81      1250        500
       30

    EMPNO ENAME      JOB             MGR HIREDATE         SAL       COMM
---------- ---------- ---------- ----------- --------- ---------- ----------
    DEPTNO
----------
     7566 JONES      MANAGER        7839 02-APR-81      2975
       20

     7654 MARTIN     SALESMAN       7698 28-SEP-81      1250       1400
       30

     7698 BLAKE      MANAGER        7839 01-MAY-81      2850
       30

    EMPNO ENAME      JOB             MGR HIREDATE         SAL       COMM
---------- ---------- ---------- ----------- --------- ---------- ----------
    DEPTNO
----------
     7782 CLARK      MANAGER        7839 09-JUN-81      2450
       10

     7788 SCOTT      ANALYST        7566 19-APR-87      3000
       20

     7839 KING       PRESIDENT           17-NOV-81      5000
       10

    EMPNO ENAME      JOB             MGR HIREDATE         SAL       COMM
---------- ---------- ---------- ----------- --------- ---------- ----------
    DEPTNO
----------
     7844 TURNER     SALESMAN       7698 08-SEP-81      1500          0
       30

     7876 ADAMS      CLERK          7788 23-MAY-87      1100
       20

     7900 JAMES      CLERK          7698 03-DEC-81       950
       30

    EMPNO ENAME      JOB             MGR HIREDATE         SAL       COMM
---------- ---------- ---------- ----------- --------- ---------- ----------
    DEPTNO
----------
     7902 FORD       ANALYST        7566 03-DEC-81      3000
       20

     7934 MILLER     CLERK          7782 23-JAN-82      1300
       10

14 rows selected.
```

The headers are printed on each page. The HEA[DING] is ON. The number of rows selected is printed as FEED[BACK] when it exceeds 6 rows.

```
SET HEA OFF FEED OFF
SELECT * FROM DEPT;
```

```
            10 ACCOUNTING     NEW YORK
            20 RESEARCH       DALLAS
            30 SALES          CHICAGO
            40 OPERATIONS     BOSTON
```

To keep the header but remove the separator, UND[ERLINE] is turned OFF.

```
SET HEA ON UND OFF
SELECT * FROM DEPT;
```

```
    DEPTNO DNAME           LOC
            10 ACCOUNTING     NEW YORK
            20 RESEARCH       DALLAS
            30 SALES          CHICAGO
            40 OPERATIONS     BOSTON
```

To disable the paging mechanism, it is possible to set the PAGESIZE to 0. To allow the headers to be printed even without paging, the EMB[EDDED] setting is turned to ON. Setting NEWP[AGE] to NONE disables the new page special character (^L).

By default, the blanks at the end of each line are not displayed on the terminal. To change this, set TRIM[OUT] to OFF. TRIMS[POOL] does the same to spooled output.

The default width for numeric columns NUM[WIDTH] is 10 characters.

```
SET PAGES 0 EMB ON NEWP NONE LIN 32000 TRIM ON TRIMS ON HEA ON UND ON NUM 4
SELECT * FROM EMP;
```

```
EMPNO ENAME       JOB        MGR HIREDATE   SAL COMM DEPTNO
----- ---------- --------- ---- --------- ---- ---- ------
 7369 SMITH       CLERK      7902 17-DEC-80  800         20
 7499 ALLEN       SALESMAN   7698 20-FEB-81 1600  300    30
 7521 WARD        SALESMAN   7698 22-FEB-81 1250  500    30
 7566 JONES       MANAGER    7839 02-APR-81 2975         20
 7654 MARTIN      SALESMAN   7698 28-SEP-81 1250 1400    30
```

```
7698 BLAKE      MANAGER    7839 01-MAY-81 2850          30
7782 CLARK      MANAGER    7839 09-JUN-81 2450          10
7788 SCOTT      ANALYST    7566 19-APR-87 3000          20
7839 KING       PRESIDENT       17-NOV-81 5000          10
7844 TURNER     SALESMAN   7698 08-SEP-81 1500     0    30
7876 ADAMS      CLERK      7788 23-MAY-87 1100          20
7900 JAMES      CLERK      7698 03-DEC-81  950          30
7902 FORD       ANALYST    7566 03-DEC-81 3000          20
7934 MILLER     CLERK      7782 23-JAN-82 1300          10
```

The headers of numeric columns are justified right and the width is the width of the header or the NUM[WIDTH] setting, whichever is greater.

The headers of non-numeric columns are truncated to the size of the column. SQL*Plus evaluates the size of the column prior to execution.

```
SELECT DUMMY, LPAD('X',2+2), TO_CHAR(SYSDATE,'DL') FROM DUAL;

D LPAD TO_CHAR(SYSDATE,'DL')
- ---- -----------------------------
X    X Tuesday, July 15, 2008
```

According to the dictionary, the column DUMMY is one character long, the LPAD returns a string of four characters, and the DL format returns a string with a maximum of 29 characters like "Wednesday, September 10, 2008".

COL[UMN] FOR[MAT] specifies the formatting of one column. For any non-numeric column, the available formatting is the width of the column, expressed as A*n*, where *n* is the width of the column. To truncate to a maximum width, the option TRU[NCATE] is used.

```
COL DNAME FOR A3 TRU
SELECT * FROM DEPT;

    DEPTNO DNA LOC
---------- --- -------------
        10 ACC NEW YORK
        20 RES DALLAS
        30 SAL CHICAGO
        40 OPE BOSTON
```

The department name is truncated to three characters.

A column is hidden by the NOPRI[NT] option.

```
COL LOC NOPRI
SELECT * FROM DEPT;
```

```
    DEPTNO DNAME
---------- --------------
        10 ACCOUNTING
        20 RESEARCH
        30 SALES
        40 OPERATIONS
```

The location is not printed.

Numeric columns support the format model elements of the TO_CHAR(number) function.

```
COL SAL FOR 9,990.00$
COL COMM LIKE SAL
SELECT ENAME, SAL, COMM FROM EMP;
```

```
ENAME             SAL        COMM
---------- ---------- ----------
SMITH          $800.00
ALLEN        $1,600.00     $300.00
WARD         $1,250.00     $500.00
JONES        $2,975.00
MARTIN       $1,250.00   $1,400.00
BLAKE        $2,850.00
CLARK        $2,450.00
SCOTT        $3,000.00
KING         $5,000.00
TURNER       $1,500.00       $0.00
ADAMS        $1,100.00
JAMES          $950.00
FORD         $3,000.00
MILLER       $1,300.00
```

The format uses the dollar sign as currency, the comma as thousands separator and the dot as decimal point. The commission uses the same options as the salary.

To define the default width of numeric columns, the SET option NUM[WIDTH] is used.

```
SET NUM 4
SELECT EMPNO "no", ENAME "name", SAL "sal" FROM EMP;
```

```
  no name           sal
  ---- ----------   ----
  7369 SMITH          800
  7499 ALLEN         1600
  7521 WARD          1250
  7566 JONES         2975
  7654 MARTIN        1250
  7698 BLAKE         2850
  7782 CLARK         2450
  7788 SCOTT         3000
  7839 KING          5000
  7844 TURNER        1500
  7876 ADAMS         1100
  7900 JAMES          950
  7902 FORD          3000
  7934 MILLER        1300
```

The size of numeric columns is four. It could contain numbers like .001 or 9999 or -999. Any number smaller than -1000 or greater than 10000 is displayed as ####. Fractions will be rounded to fit the column width.

The header of a numeric column is never truncated. The header can be changed with the HEADING option for a specific column. A specific format is defined with the FORMAT directive.

```
COL COMM HEA "Commission" FOR 999
COL ENAME HEA "Name"
SELECT ENAME, COMM FROM EMP WHERE DEPTNO=30;
```

```
Name       Commission
---------- ----------
ALLEN             300
WARD              500
MARTIN           ####
BLAKE
TURNER              0
JAMES
```

The commission of Martin is 1400 and cannot be displayed with the given format.

The alignment of the HEA[DING] of the column is changed to [L]EFT, [C]ENTER or [R]IGHT with the JUS[TIFY] setting. COLSEP sets the separator between the columns and by default, it is a space " ".

The null values are not displayed by default; the NULL global setting and the NULL per column setting define a string to display for nulls.

```
SET NUM 4 COLSEP |
COL EMPNO HEA NO JUS L
COL ENAME FOR A6 TRU HEA NAME
COL JOB FOR A9 TRU
COL MGR JUS L
COL SAL JUS L
COL DEPTNO HEA DEPT JUS L
COL COMM JUS L NUL "    0"
SET NULL null
SELECT * FROM EMP;
```

```
NO   |NAME  |JOB      |MGR |HIREDATE |SAL |COMM|DEPT
---- |------|---------|----|---------|----|----|----
7369 |SMITH |CLERK    |7902|17-DEC-80| 800|   0| 20
7499 |ALLEN |SALESMAN |7698|20-FEB-81|1600| 300| 30
7521 |WARD  |SALESMAN |7698|22-FEB-81|1250| 500| 30
7566 |JONES |MANAGER  |7839|02-APR-81|2975|   0| 20
7654 |MARTIN|SALESMAN |7698|28-SEP-81|1250|1400| 30
7698 |BLAKE |MANAGER  |7839|01-MAY-81|2850|   0| 30
7782 |CLARK |MANAGER  |7839|09-JUN-81|2450|   0| 10
7788 |SCOTT |ANALYST  |7566|19-APR-87|3000|   0| 20
7839 |KING  |PRESIDENT|null|17-NOV-81|5000|   0| 10
7844 |TURNER|SALESMAN |7698|08-SEP-81|1500|   0| 30
7876 |ADAMS |CLERK    |7788|23-MAY-87|1100|   0| 20
7900 |JAMES |CLERK    |7698|03-DEC-81| 950|   0| 30
7902 |FORD  |ANALYST  |7566|03-DEC-81|3000|   0| 20
7934 |MILLER|CLERK    |7782|23-JAN-82|1300|   0| 10
```

Date formatting is not done in SQL*Plus but in SQL. However, SQL*Plus initializes the NLS session parameters according to the NLS environment variables like NLS_LANG, NLS_DATE_FORMAT, and such.

Large objects use the settings LONG and LONGC[HUNKSIZE] to define the amount of information to display. The default of 80 truncates any lob longer than 80. When the LONGCHUKSIZE is smaller than the LONG, the long text is split into multiple lines.

```
SET LONG 60 LONGC 20
SELECT XMLQUERY('1 to 100' RETURNING CONTENT).GETCLOBVAL() FROM DUAL;
```

```
XMLQUERY('1TO100'RET
--------------------
1 2 3 4 5 6 7 8 9 10
 11 12 13 14 15 16 1
7 18 19 20 21 22 23
```

The first 60 characters are displayed in three lines of 20 characters.

Not only can the long columns be split, but any non-numeric column is split if its size exceeds the width set in the COL[UMN] FOR[MAT] option. The WRA[PPED] option is the default, and WOR[D_WRAPPED] avoids, if possible, to split in the middle of a word.

```
COL DNAME FOR A4 WRA
COL LOC FOR A7 WOR
SELECT * FROM DEPT;

    DEPTNO DNAM LOC
---------- ---- -------
        10 ACCO NEW
           UNTI YORK
           NG

        20 RESE DALLAS
           ARCH

        30 SALE CHICAGO
           S

        40 OPER BOSTON
           ATIO
           NS
```

The setting of a COL[UMN] can be CLE[AR].

```
COL DNAME FOR A4 WRA
COL DNAME
COLUMN    DNAME ON
FORMAT    A4
wrap
COL DNAME CLE
COL DNAME
SP2-0046: COLUMN 'DNAME' not defined
```

The setting for the DNAME column is clear.

It is also possible to CL[EAR] all COL[UMNS].

```
CL COL
columns cleared
COL
SP2-0045: * no COLUMN defined
```

The setting for all columns is cleared.

Calling a Script

An SQL script is called with the @ or @@ command. The difference between @ and @@ is that, when nested, the @@ search for scripts in the working directory of the super script.

Per default, the commands of the script are not echoed and the output is displayed in the current terminal. The behavior can be changed with the ECHO and TERMOUT settings.

Spooling

PRO[MPT] displays a simple text and SPO[OL] saves the output in a text file.

```
SPO helloworld.txt
PRO Hello World!
SPO OFF
```

The message Hello World is saved in a file called helloworld.txt.

Substitution Variables

Besides bind variables that are specific to PL/SQL, SQL*Plus offers substitution variables. By default, substitution variables are prefixed by & and optionally suffixed by dot.

When using substitution variables in an SQL command, SQL*Plus displays the old and new values of the variable. This default can be turned OFF with the VER[IFY] setting.

Optionally, the DEF[INE] character can be escaped by the ESC[APE] setting.

The DEF[INE] command defines the variable and the UNDEF[INE] command undefines it. When used without an assignment, the define command will show the current value of the variable and will not change it.

Before setting DEF[INE] and ESC[APE], it is necessary to turn off escaping and variable substitutions, otherwise the SET command itself will be misinterpreted by SQL*Plus.

```
SET ESC OFF DEF OFF
SET DEF & VER OFF ESC \ CON .
DEF NO=7788
SELECT '&NO._'||ENAME "EMPNO \& ENAME" FROM EMP WHERE EMPNO=&NO;
```

```
EMPNO & ENAME
---------------
7788_SCOTT
```

NO is defined to 7788 and used in the SELECT query. The dot after the NO prevents SQL*Plus from using "NO_" as the variable name and the backslash before the ampersand escapes the character.

Some variables are predefined by SQL*Plus.

```
DEF _DATE
DEFINE _DATE           = "16-JUL-08" (CHAR)
```

The _DATE variable is defined in 10g SQL*Plus and is dynamic. It contains the exact time and is formatted according to the NLS formats.

```
ALTER SESSION SET NLS_DATE_FORMAT='HH24:MI:SS';
DEF _DATE
DEFINE _DATE           = "12:08:46" (CHAR)
DEF _DATE
DEFINE _DATE           = "12:08:48" (CHAR)
```

The time is not set when the user is first logged on, but it is always the current time.

Variables are set by the user in the interactive mode with the ACC[EPT] command.

```
ACC d DATE FOR YYYY-MM-DD DEF 2000-01-01 PROMPT "Enter hire date:" HIDE
Enter hire date:**********
DEF D
DEFINE D               = "2008-07-25" (CHAR)
```

The ACC[EPT] command reads a user input and validates the date FOR[MAT]. The PROMPT message is displayed. It is possible to HIDE the user input. If the user enters no date, January 1, 2000 is used as a DEF[AULT].

When an undefined variable is used in a query, SQL*Plus prompts the user for an input. When using &, the variable is prompted each time and remains undefined. With &&, the variable is prompted once and remains defined at the end of the query.

```
SET VER ON
SELECT DNAME DEPT_&&DEPTNO FROM DEPT WHERE DEPTNO=&&DEPTNO;
Enter value for deptno: 30
old   1: SELECT DNAME DEPT_&&DEPTNO FROM DEPT WHERE DEPTNO=&&DEPTNO
new   1: SELECT DNAME DEPT_30 FROM DEPT WHERE DEPTNO=30
```

```
DEPT_30
--------------
SALES
```

The department number is asked for only once.

The COL[UMN] NEW_V[ALUE] option stores the latest value of a query in a variable.

```
COL ENAME NEW_V ENAME
SELECT ENAME FROM EMP ORDER BY SAL;
```

```
ENAME
----------
SMITH
JAMES
ADAMS
WARD
MARTIN
MILLER
TURNER
ALLEN
CLARK
BLAKE
JONES
SCOTT
FORD
KING
```

```
DEF ENAME
DEFINE ENAME           = "KING" (CHAR)
```

The variable ENAME is defined.

If a query returns no row, the variable is defined but remains unchanged. This is a useful workaround to default a variable to NULL.

```
DEF X
SP2-0135: symbol x is UNDEFINED
SQL> DEF Y
DEFINE Y               = "1" (CHAR)
SQL> SELECT 0 X, 0 Y FROM DUAL WHERE 1=0;
no rows selected
SQL> DEF X
DEFINE X               = "" (CHAR)
SQL> DEF Y
DEFINE Y               = "1" (CHAR)
```

X is defined and Y remains unchanged.

The variables &1, &2 and following represent the first, second and following arguments of a script.

🖫 emp-ename.sql

```
-- **************************************************
-- Copyright © 2008 by Rampant TechPress
-- This script is free for non-commercial purposes
-- with no warranties.  Use at your own risk.
--
-- To license this script for a commercial purpose,
-- contact rtp@rampant.cc
-- **************************************************
-- Id       : $Id: emp-ename.sql,v 1.3 2008/08/01 10:13:27 Laurent Exp $
-- Author : $Author: Laurent $
-- Date     : $Date: 2008/08/01 10:13:27 $
--
-- SELECT Employee number and name
--
-- An optional argument &1 limit the output to a single employee

WHENEVER SQLERROR EXIT FAILURE
WHENEVER OSERROR CONTINUE

COL 1 NEW_V 1
SET FEED OFF VER OFF HEA OFF TERM ON
SPO emp.txt
SELECT 1 FROM DUAL WHERE NULL IS NOT NULL;
SELECT EMPNO, ENAME FROM EMP WHERE ENAME='&1' OR '&1' IS NULL;
SPO OFF
QUIT SUCCESS
```

The file is called with the @ sign or with the sta[rt] SQL*Plus command.

```
@emp-ename
```

The result is saved in a file called emp.txt.

Due to TERMOUT ON, the output is displayed (default). With TERMOUT OFF, the output is not displayed, but it is saved in the file.

WHENEVER SQLERROR specifies to EXIT with a FAILURE return code after any ORA error. WHENEVER OSERROR specifies to CONTINUE after a filesytem error on emp.txt.

The return code can be checked in the OS.

Windows

```
sqlplus -s -L scott/tiger @emp-ename SCOTT
     7788 SCOTT
echo %ERRORLEVEL%
0
```

UNIX/Linux

```
sqlplus -s -L scott/tiger @emp-ename SCOTT
     7788 SCOTT
echo $?
0
```

In batch mode, it is possible to pass the SQL*Plus commands and SQL statements through a pipe.

Windows/UNIX/Linux

```
(
   echo conn scott/tiger
   echo SET FEED OFF HEA OFF PAGES 0
   echo SELECT ENAME FROM EMP
   echo ORDER BY 1
   echo /
   echo quit
) | sqlplus -s -L  /nolog
```

```
ADAMS
ALLEN
BLAKE
CLARK
FORD
JAMES
JONES
KING
MARTIN
MILLER
SCOTT
SMITH
TURNER
WARD
```

The commands between the parentheses are processed and the output is passed to the SQL*Plus command. The output is printed. The output could be redirected to a file with >file.txt or processed further in a loop.

Windows

```
echo off
for /F "tokens=1,2,* delims==- " %A IN (
   'sqlplus -s -L scott/tiger @emp-ename'
) DO (
   if %A == ORA (
      echo error... %A-%B %C
   ) else if %A == "" (
      echo.
   ) else if %A == SP2 (
      echo error... %A-%B %C
   ) else (
      echo Processing %A/%B ...
      rem save / mail / ftp / alert / print ...
   )
)
```

```
Processing 7369/SMITH ...
Processing 7499/ALLEN ...
Processing 7521/WARD ...
Processing 7566/JONES ...
Processing 7654/MARTIN ...
Processing 7698/BLAKE ...
Processing 7782/CLARK ...
Processing 7788/SCOTT ...
Processing 7839/KING ...
Processing 7844/TURNER ...
Processing 7876/ADAMS ...
Processing 7900/JAMES ...
Processing 7902/FORD ...
Processing 7934/MILLER ...
echo on
```

UNIX/Linux

```
sqlplus -s -L scott/tiger @emp-ename|
   while read empno ename
   do
      if [ "$empno" = ORA ]
      then
         echo error... $empno-$ename
      elif [ "$empno" = "" ]
      then
         echo
      elif [ "$empno" = "SP2" ]
      then
         echo error... $empno-$ename
      else
         echo Processing $empno/$ename ...
         # save / mail / ftp / alert / print ...
      fi
   done
```

```
Processing 7369/SMITH ...
Processing 7499/ALLEN ...
Processing 7521/WARD ...
Processing 7566/JONES ...
Processing 7654/MARTIN ...
Processing 7698/BLAKE ...
Processing 7782/CLARK ...
Processing 7788/SCOTT ...
Processing 7839/KING ...
Processing 7844/TURNER ...
Processing 7876/ADAMS ...
Processing 7900/JAMES ...
Processing 7902/FORD ...
Processing 7934/MILLER ...
```

Each line of output is processed, for instance, by another batch file. Note that in windows batch mode, the %A, %B and %C must be replaced by %%A, %%B and %%C.

HTML

Both interactive and non-interactive modes allow HTML output.

Windows/UNIX/Linux

```
(
   echo SET FEED OFF PAGES 50000 HEA ON
   echo select deptno,empno,ename,job,sal from emp order by deptno
   echo /
)|sqlplus -s -L -M  "HTML on HEAD <TITLE>employees</TITLE>"
scott/tiger>emp.htm
```

DEPTNO	EMPNO	ENAME	JOB	SAL
10	7782	CLARK	MANAGER	2450
10	7839	KING	PRESIDENT	5000
10	7934	MILLER	CLERK	1300
20	7566	JONES	MANAGER	2975
20	7902	FORD	ANALYST	3000
20	7876	ADAMS	CLERK	1100
20	7369	SMITH	CLERK	800
20	7788	SCOTT	ANALYST	3000
30	7521	WARD	SALESMAN	1250
30	7844	TURNER	SALESMAN	1500
30	7499	ALLEN	SALESMAN	1600
30	7900	JAMES	CLERK	950
30	7698	BLAKE	MANAGER	2850
30	7654	MARTIN	SALESMAN	1250

An HTML document is generated and redirected to emp.htm. The file contains an HTML table with the output of the query and the HEADERS are repeated every 50000 rows (maximum) and bold. The – M options allow customizing of the header, body and table.

In an SQL script, the HTML output is started by SET MARKUP HTML ON and ended by SET MARKUP HTML OFF.

Index

[

[[:alpha:]] 80

A

ABS 69
ALL 22
AND 22
antijoin 24
ANY 22
APPENDCHILDXML 183
ASC 19
ASCIISTR 96
AUTOTRACE 7
AVG 49, 108

B

BEGINTIME 150
BETWEEN 139
BFILE 160
BFILENAME 160
BIN_TO_NUM 68
BINARY_DOUBLE 48, 67, 91
BINARY_FLOAT 48, 67, 91
BITAND 68
BLOB 160, 177

C

CASE 98
CAST 94
CC 71
CEIL 69
CHAR 50
CHR 84, 96
CLOB 177
COALESCE 100
CONCAT 51

CONNECT BY 20, 197, 201
CONNECT_BY_IS_LEAF 208, 213
CONNECT_BY_ISCYCLE 206
CONNECT_BY_ROOT .203, 204, 212, 213
correlated subquery 27
COUNT 132
COUNT DISTINCT 109
COUNT(*) 108
CROSS JOIN 35
CUBE 114, 117, 143
CURRENT ROW 138
CV 231

D

D 71, 72
DATE 48, 70, 178
DAY 87
dbms_rowid 58
DD 71
DECODE 97
DELETEXML 184
DENSE_RANK 135
DESC 19
DIMENSION 226
DISTINCT 16, 20, 109, 110, 150
DUAL 15, 211

E

ENAME 83
ENDTIME 150
equijoin 28
EVALNAME 163
EXCLUDE NULLS 123
execution plan7, 107, 175, 196, 202, 242, 243
EXISTS 22
EXISTSNODE 170, 171, 174

EXTRACT..............................85, 86, 168
EXTRACTVALUE....................169, 171

F

FAST DUAL..16
FF...89
FIRST_VALUE...................................145
FLOOR...69
FM...88, 91
FOLLOWING.....................................139
FOR loops..235
FROM..6, 20
full outer join.................................32, 33
function-based indexes.........................72

G

GREATEST...97
greedy expression................................82
GROUP BY..........20, 114, 116, 132, 142
GROUP_ID...119
GROUPING...143
GROUPING SETS............114, 117, 143

H

hash join..175
HASH JOIN FULL OUTER..............33
HAVING..119
HEXTORAW..84
HH...71, 88
HH24..88
HOUR...87

I

IGNORE NULLS..............................146
IN...22
INCLUDE NULLS..............................124
INITCAP...78
inline view...................................21, 122
INSERTCHILDXML..............181, 182
INSERTXMLBEFORE.....................181

INSTR...75, 96
INSTR2..96
INSTR4..96
INSTRB..96
INSTRC..96
INTERSECT...44
IS ANY...233
IS PRESENT.....................................234
ITERATE..239
ITERATION_NUMBER..................239
IW...71, 72

J

J...89
join...28
JOIN..29, 210

K

KEEP.....................................111, 112, 132

L

LAG...134
LAST_VALUE...................................145
LEAD...134
LEAST...97
LENGTH......................................76, 96
LENGTH2..96
LENGTH4..96
LENGTHB..96
LENGTHC..96
LEVEL.......................................198, 213
LNNVL..100
LOWER...78
LPAD...76
LTRIM...76

M

materialized views.......................37, 72
MAX..114, 117
MEASURES......................................226

MI 71
MINUS 43
MINUTE 87
MM 71
MOD 74
MODEL 20, 224, 226, 233
modulo 67, 74
MONTH 87

N

NATURAL JOIN 29
NCHR 96
nested subquery 24, 111
NLS_CHARSET_ID 160
NLS_DATE_TERRITORY 92
NLS_INITCAP 94
NLS_LOWER 94
NLS_SORT 94
NLS_TERRITORY 93
NLS_UPPER 94
NOCYCLE 206
non-greedy expression 82
NOT EXISTS 22
NOT IN 22, 24
NOT NULL 24
NULL 52, 99
NULLIF 100
NUMBER 48, 67, 178
NUMTODSINTERVAL 87
NUMTOYMINTERVAL 87
NVL 100
NVL2 100

O

OBJECT_VALUE 169
OCCURRENCE 81
ON 30, 211
ora:view 174
Oracle Calendar 89
Oracle Locale Builder 94
ORDER BY ... 18, 19, 107, 134, 138, 200
ORDER SIBLINGS BY 199

outer join 31
OVER 132

P

PARTITION 226
PARTITION BY 133
partition key 36
partition views 38
partitioned outer join 36
PERIODBEGIN 150
PIVOT 120, 185
PIVOT XML 185
POSIX 80
PRECEDING 139
PRIOR 197, 201
pseudo column 54

Q

Q 71

R

RANGE 139, 140, 141
RANGE BETWEEN 141
RANGE CURRENT ROW 141
RANK 135
RATIO_TO_REPORT 143
RAW 85
RAWTOHEX 85
REF CURSOR 171
REGEXP_COUNT 79
REGEXP_INSTR 79
REGEXP_LIKE 79
REGEXP_REPLACE 79, 81
REGEXP_SUBSTR 79, 83
REMAINDER 74
REPLACE 78, 81
RM 89, 91
ROLLUP 114, 115, 116, 117, 143
ROUND 69, 70
ROW_NUMBER 134, 143
ROWNUM 54

ROWS............................. 139, 141
ROWS BETWEEN 137
ROWS CURRENT ROW..................141
RPAD 76
RR..90
RTRIM..76
RULES UPDATES............................232

S

scalar subquery 26, 27, 63
SECOND....................................87
SELECT......................................6
semijoin.....................................26
session-independent views 72
SIBLINGS 200
SIGN..69
SINGLE REFERENCE....................232
single-row subquery................................27
SOME..22
SORT GROUP BY 107
SORT UNIQUE...............................43
SP 88
SQL Spreadsheet............................224
SSSSS..89
START WITH...............................197
STATS_MODE 108
STOPKEY 57
subquery factoring 22
SUBSTR 75, 96, 204
SUBSTR2...................................96
SUBSTR4...................................96
SUBSTRB....................................96
SUBSTRC 96
SUM 49, 111
SYS_CONNECT_BY_PATH . 202, 204
SYS_GUID....................................85

T

TERMOUT OFF 276
TERMOUT ON 276
TH...88
TIMESTAMP......................................70

TO_BINARY_DOUBLE..............91, 92
TO_BINARY_FLOAT.................91, 92
TO_BLOB...................................93
TO_CHAR 72, 88, 90, 92, 96
TO_CLOB....................................93
TO_DATE..............................89, 92
TO_DSINTERVAL 87
TO_NCHAR 96
TO_NCLOB 96
TO_NUMBER...................72, 85, 91, 92
TO_TIMESTAMP.........................89, 92
TO_TIMESTAMP_TZ.................89, 92
TO_YMINTERVAL 87
TRANSLATE 78
TRIM 76
TRUNC............................... 69, 70, 72

U

UNBOUNDED FOLLOWING......138
UNBOUNDED PRECEDING.......138
UNION 43
UNION ALL 33, 37, 43
UNION-ALL PARTITION...............41
UNIQUE 16
UNIQUE DIMENSION..................232
UNIQUE SINGLE REFERENCE.232
UNISTR 96
UNPIVOT......................120, 123, 124
UNTIL..239
UPDATE......................................228
UPDATEXML................................179
UPPER 78
UPSERT......................................229
UPSERT ALL 238
USING 30

V

V 91
VARCHAR2................................ 50, 177
VSIZE..85

W

W 71, 72
WHERE 17
WITH.. 21
WW 71, 72

X

XMLAGG.. 176
XMLCAST... 178
XMLCONCAT.................................... 163
XMLELEMENT 161
XMLEXISTS....................................... 174

XMLFOREST............................ 163, 184
XMLQUERY 172
XMLSEQUENCE 170
XMLSERIALIZE................................ 177
XMLTYPE 159
XPATH 168, 174, 179
XQuery 172
XQUERY... 262

Y

Y 71
YEAR.. 87
YY 90

About Laurent Schneider

Laurent Schneider is one of the most respected authors in Oracle technology, with many years of experience as a Systems Engineer and Database Engineer.

Laurent achieved the highest level of DBA certification in 2004, being the first Oracle Certified Master in Switzerland and recipient of the prestigious Oracle Technology Network ACE trophy.

Laurent has over a decade of expertise in development - specializing in data warehousing and database modeling as well as database administration. He currently works for a successful Swiss bank as application architect/developer.

In his spare time, Laurent enjoys studying Chinese Chess strategy and has won the Swiss Championship. He lives on the sunny side of the Uetliberg with his wife Bertille, his daughter Dora and his son Loïc.

About Chen Shapira

Chen Shapira was born in Jerusalem, Israel, and studied Computer Science and Statistics at the Tel-Aviv University. While studying, she worked as a Linux system administrator. After graduating, she started working as a web applications developer for Mercury Interactive, where she was first introduced to the wonderful world of SQL programming and became fascinated by database systems.

Chen is an Oracle Certified Professional (OCP) and is currently working as a production Oracle DBA for Hewlett-Packard's Software-as-a-Service department. She specializes in scalability and high-availability solutions such as RAC and Streams.

When she is not helping HP customers achieve better availability and performance, Chen can be found giving advice on many Oracle related forums. She enjoys sharing tips and anecdotes from over 10 years of IT experience in her blog – http://prodlife.wordpress.com.

Chen lives in Cupertino, California, where she enjoys mountain biking, painting and studying math.

About Tom Routen

Tom Routen plies his trade in Switzerland, lives in Germany and is English, which demonstrates his flexibility, his love of variety and indeed, of Europe itself.

As an impressionable youth, he eagerly studied philosophy. Later he rather futilely tried to whip the artificial intelligence donkey for a while, but then pragmatically and decisively jumped on the lunatic speed bullet train of web software development and is still trying to catch his breath.

He set up his own software company in 2000. It is now famous in its own back yard for an interesting Enterprise 2.0 server (called the GA Server), version 4 of which is nearly finished and will be 100% perfect. Yes, it can be used with Oracle.

Made in the USA
Middletown, DE
06 May 2019